Tax and Robotics

Nijhoff Law Specials

VOLUME 108

The titles published in this series are listed at *brill.com/nlsp*

Tax and Robotics

By

Álvaro Falcón Pulido

Translated from Spanish by

Deirdre B. Jerry

BRILL | NIJHOFF

LEIDEN | BOSTON

Originally published as Fiscalidad y robótica, Tirant lo Blanch, Valencia, 2022. © Álvaro Falcón Pulido and Tirant lo Blanch.

Research conducted within the framework of the European Project INBOTS "Inclusive Robotics for a better Society" (at UCM and WP2), Horizon 2020, Robotics and Artificial Intelligence Unit (780073) http://inbots.eu.

Library of Congress Cataloging-in-Publication Data

Names: Falcón Pulido, Álvaro, author.
Title: Tax and robotics / Álvaro Falcón Pulido ; translated from Spanish by Deirdre B. Jerry.
Other titles: Fiscalidad y robótica. English
Description: Leiden ; Boston : Brill/Nijhoff, 2023. | Series: Nijhoff law specials, 0924-4549 ; volume 108 | Includes bibliographical references and index. |
Identifiers: LCCN 2023026741 (print) | LCCN 2023026742 (ebook) | ISBN 9789004538504 (paperback) | ISBN 9789004538511 (ebook)
Subjects: LCSH: Robots–Taxation–Law and legislation. | Robots–Taxation–Law and legislation–Spain. | Artificial intelligence–Taxation–Law and legislation. | Artificial intelligence–Taxation–Law and legislation–Spain. | Taxing power–Spain. | Taxation–Law and legislation–Spain.
Classification: LCC K4487.C65 F3513 2023 (print) | LCC K4487.C65 (ebook) | DDC 343.05/585629892–dc23/eng/20230614
LC record available at https://lccn.loc.gov/2023026741
LC ebook record available at https://lccn.loc.gov/2023026742

Typeface for the Latin, Greek, and Cyrillic scripts: "Brill". See and download: brill.com/brill-typeface.

ISSN 0924-4549
ISBN 978-90-04-53850-4 (paperback)
ISBN 978-90-04-53851-1 (e-book)

This book is printed on acid-free paper and produced in a sustainable manner.

For my mother and my father

Well-designed robots should, at the very least, be programmed to be tax compliant. Unless one day they decide to refuse to pay taxes ... without representation.

XAVIER OBERSON

Contents

Foreword

The first reaction of most people to a title like *Tax and Robotics* is probably bewilderment. Are there even enough robot-specific regulations to fill a book? The easy answer is no – quite the opposite. And yet no one can remain indifferent to the subject discussed here. In fact, recent years have witnessed repeated expressions of society's concern about this issue. It therefore needs to be addressed in order to discover and confirm fundamental principles that will ensure the development of a legal framework consistent with the rule of law in our state.

It is quite significant that the interdisciplinary research which inspired this book shares the priorities set by the European Commission and the Spanish Ministry of Science, Innovation and Universities on two competitive projects: INBOTS CSA, G.A. No. 780073 (http://inbots.eu/), as part of the Horizon 2020 program; and AudIT-S, PID2019-105959RB-I00 (https://www.ucm.es/proyecto-audit-s/) in the "social challenges" category of the National R&D + i Plan.

This book by Álvaro Falcón Pulido grew out of the PhD dissertation he successfully defended in the Department of Commercial, Financial, and Tax Law at the Law School of the Complutense University of Madrid, which received the highest possible score and on which I had the pleasure of acting as doctoral advisor. His fiscal construction has the dual merit of diligently adding to and enriching the contributions of those branches of law which first addressed the potential risks and opportunities of robotization and, at the same time, judiciously engaging in the lively debates that have originated in different non-legal disciplines (particularly ethics and economics). I derived true intellectual pleasure and great satisfaction from supervising this dissertation and discovering the valuable insights of its author, whom I wholeheartedly encourage to continue in this direction and imagine new ways of achieving what is right and necessary in our increasingly divided and polarized society.

This critical approach, grounded in common law, methodically surveys certain existing categories in financial and tax law and, in some cases, proposes amendments or improvements. The seasoned researcher skillfully applies useful concepts, even drawing on Roman and civil law, to his vision of an improved tax and social security system. His remarkable study opens up new horizons while simultaneously blazing new trails which he invites us to explore. He has approached this task in a thought-provoking way, offering clear explanations of a patently complex phenomenon, and the result is an eminently readable book written in plain, easily comprehensible language.

Working from premises firmly established by case law, Dr. Falcón Pulido dares to sketch the tentative legal contours of potentially useful taxation tools in today's uncertain context. The author explains the reasoning behind his ideas, in the midst of the inevitable controversy inherent to these changing times. His efforts to systematize and adapt reasonable proposals to our existing legal system are the product of serious, rigorous scholarship. At the same time, thanks to his experience as a practicing lawyer, pragmatism always permeates his discussions of particularly sensitive issues. In this way, he upholds his family's fine academic and professional traditions.

We are now entering an age when taxation affects the decision to roll out robotics, artificial intelligence, and related technology, and these in turn overtly influence the development of taxation itself. Naturally, this has caught the attention of experts in the fields of tax and labor law in the context of national and international organizations. For proof we need look no further than the collective work *Interactive Robotics: Legal, Ethical, Social and Economic Aspects*, published by Springer in 2021, to which Álvaro Falcón contributed a chapter, or an article of his that previously appeared in *Revista Técnica Tributaria* of the Asociación Española de Asesores Fiscales.

This volume comes at a particularly opportune moment, when different fields and industries are eager to find better uses for robotic tools, as it points out various strategies that are directly or indirectly related to smart automation (such as taxing transactions involving data). At times boldly and at others more discreetly, Dr. Falcón Pulido gives his informed opinion, refined in the forges of time and experience. Thanks to his perseverance and dedication to his chosen subject, he has managed to identify the principal problems and propose interesting solutions. The solidity of his legal arguments is a welcome contrast to certain fickle political initiatives on the international stage.

By offering a vision that ranges from the origins of the technological and legislative phenomenon to its foreseeable future developments, the author sensibly identifies points of overlap between conflicting interests, given the legal uncertainty generated by differences in the pace at which technological advances are implemented (as is the case of the responsible use of tax incentives to promote innovation in robotics). In short, thanks to the solid editorial commitment of Tirant lo Blanch, readers now have before them an illuminating text that clearly lays out the different legislative and regulatory options in this field, one destined to become an invaluable source in light of the intensity and scope of the incipient robotization processes now underway in Spain, the European Union, and the rest of the world.

María Amparo Grau Ruiz
Professor of Financial and Tax Law
Universidad Complutense de Madrid

Acknowledgement

With immense gratitude to Professor María Amparo Grau Ruiz, advisor on the PhD dissertation on which this book is based, for her ever generous help and invaluable guidance.

PART 1

Robots and their Impact

CHAPTER 1

Concept and Types

A Legal Concept of a Robot

The European Parliament has warned that humankind stands on the threshold of the robotic era, and technological advances in robotics bring with them a host of new legal and financial problems.[1] No one can deny the enormous impact and consequences of what is poised to be a fourth industrial revolution, and the law must adapt to this new reality.[2] The issues are not as simple as the loss of public revenue or jobs. Bringing smart robots into labor, contractual, and economic settings raises brand-new questions from a legal perspective.

One of the greatest fears is that, in the fourth industrial revolution, fewer jobs will mean less revenue generated by employment-related taxes.[3] With more and more robots in the workplace – and not just in industrial settings – the destruction of jobs by AI is an increasingly pertinent and heated debate.[4] In any case, the medium and long-term consequences of the mass introduction of robots in the job market are not yet clear.

The most pressing question is how that change will happen, and what benefits and costs it will have. The principal benefit of automation will be increased productivity and competitiveness. Robotization replaces human workers and eliminates jobs, but it also creates new skilled job positions that did not exist

1 European Parliament, *Report with recommendations to the Commission on Civil Law Rules on Robotics (2015/2103(INL))*, session document A8-005/2017, January 27, 2017, Letter B of the Introduction to the Motion for a European Parliament *Resolution*.

2 María Amparo Grau Ruiz, "El Derecho artificial y la artificiosidad de los derechos," in María José Falcón y Tella and Juan Antonio Martínez Muñoz (dirs.), *Estudios Jurídicos Multidisciplinares. José Iturmendi Morales, Maestro Complutense. Homenaje*, Tirant lo Blanch, Valencia, 2020, pp. 839–857. English versión: María José Falcón y Tella and Juan Antonio Martínez Muñoz (eds.), *Challenges to Legal Theory: Essays in Honour of Professor José Iturmendi Morales*, Brill Nijhoff, Leiden-Boston, 2021, pp. 227–242.

3 People as famous as Bill Gates have predicted that, by the year 2030, robots will have taken a large part of all existing jobs and should therefore be taxed in order to generate income for the state. Kevin J. Delanay, "The robot that takes your job should pay taxes, says Bill Gates," *Quartz* (qz.com), February 17, 2017.

4 The INBOTS project, part of the EU's Horizon 2020 program, discussed this topic at length in INBOTS: D.2.2. *White Paper on Interactive Robotics: Legal, Ethical & Socioeconomic Aspects*, 2021.

 | DOI:10.1163/9789004538511_002

before. So, the real question is this: In the long term, will AI create more jobs than it destroys?

Another advantage of robotization is reduced environmental impact, as robots will be able to perform certain tasks that humans cannot and do other jobs more efficiently.[5]

All these changes come with a slew of legal problems that will require regulation. One is the question of taxing robots or their owners: Should robots pay taxes? Can they? Do they have the financial capacity to pay? Or the responsibility? Can they be considered entrepreneurs for VAT purposes? Creating a specific legal personality or considering the tax capacity of robots, and possibly changing the current system of social security contributions, are factors that must be kept in mind and carefully weighed when creating a legal framework to face the challenges posed by the robotization process inherent in this fourth revolution.

1 *What Is a Robot?*

In order to discuss robot regulation, we must first define the concept of "robot."[6] Even in non-legal fields that deal with robots, there is no clear consensus on the definition of the term.[7] In fact, so far experts have only been able to agree

---

5 More on this topic at https://ifr.org/.

6 On this subject, see: N. Nevejans, "Les robots: tentative de definition," in Besaumon, *Les robots, objets scientifiques, objets de droit,* Collection de Presses Universitaires de Sceaux, 2016. Carmen Tirado Robles, "What is a robot? Comparative legal analysis of the Japanese and European proposals," in Mirai, *Estudios japoneses*, vol. 4, 2020: *Monográfico: Japón en un mundo global: iniciativas y posicionamientos*, Ediciones Complutenses, 2020, pp. 35–48. Antonio Barrientos, *Fundamentos de robótica*, McGraw-Hill, Interamericana de España, Madrid, 2007. Carlos Rogel Vide (dir.), *Los robots y el Derecho*, Reus, Madrid, 2018. With articles such as: "Robots y personas," by Carlos Rogel Vide; "Potencialidades de los robots y capacidades de las personas," by Miguel L. Lacruz Mantecón; "La revolución tecnológica y sus retos: medios de control, fallos de los sistemas y ciberdelincuencia," by Antonio Mozo Seoane; and "Robots y respondabilidad civil," by Silvia Díaz Alabart. M. Ryan Calo and Michael A. Froomkin (eds.), *Robot Law*, Edward Elgar, Cheltenham, UK – Northampton, MA, USA, 2016. Moisés Barrio Andrés (dir.), Michael Froomkin, Ana María Aransay Alejandre, *Derecho de los robots*, La Ley, Wolters Kluwer, Madrid, 2019. Jan de Bruyne and Cedric Vanleenhove (eds.), *Artificial intelligence and the law*, Intersentia Ltd., Cambridge, 2021. Laura Caballero Trenado, Review of Moises Barrio Andrés (dir.), *Derecho de los robots,* in *Revista de Derecho Privado*, 37, 2019, pp. 367–371. Silvia Barona Vilar, *Algoritmización del Derecho y de la justicia: de la Inteligencia Artificial a la Smart Justice*, Tirant lo Blanch, Valencia, 2021. Enrique Fernández-Macías, David Klenert and José Ignacio Antón, "Not so disruptive yet? Characteristics, distribution and determinants of robots in Europe," in *Structural Change and Dynamics*, 58, 2021, pp. 76–89. A. Bensoussan and J. Bensoussan, *Droit des robots*, Larcier, 2015.

7 Juan García-Prieto Cuesta, "¿Qué es un Robot?", in Moisés Barrio Andrés, (dir.), *Derecho de los Robots,* La Ley, Wolter Kluwer, 2018, p. 37.

on "the considerable difficulty of arriving at a definition of robot which accurately conveys the multiple existing forms of robotic implementation."[8] Yet determining what does or does not constitute a robot is the "perennial, albeit negative, point of departure for any discussion of the topic."[9] There are even those who believe that we will never have a universally accepted definition of robot.[10]

This problem, though not exclusive to tax law, clearly affects the definition of robots' potential tax liability. Without a fairly concrete definition of what a robot is, we cannot levy taxes on its use, its ownership, or the income it generates.

a Appearance of the "Robot" Concept

The Merriam-Webster Dictionary defines a robot as "a device that automatically performs complicated, often repetitive tasks," or as "a machine that resembles a living creature in being capable of moving independently [...] and performing complex actions."

The English word "robot" comes from the Czech *robota*, meaning "forced labor." It was first used in the modern sense in a 1920 play called *R.U.R.* (*Rossum's Universal Robots*)[11] by Czech writer Karel Čapek. The robots in *R.U.R.* are living creatures with no feelings whose sole purpose is to serve human beings. This would not be their last literary appearance, of course; Isaac Asimov famously set out the Three Laws of Robotics in his science-fiction novels and stories.[12] Today robots are part of our lives, even though many people's idea of a robot still differs significantly from reality.

---

8 Moisés Barrio Andrés, "Hacia una personalidad electrónica para los robots," *Revista de Derecho Privado*, 102, 3, (March-April) 2018, pp. 93–94. *Id.*, *Robótica, inteligencia artificial y Derecho*, ARI, Análisis del Real Instituto Elcano, 103, 2018. *Id.*, "Del Derecho de Internet al Derecho de los Robots," in *Derecho de los robots*, *op. cit.*, pp. 61–86. *Id.*, "El Derecho de los robots, una disciplina jurídica naciente," in *Estudios de Derecho Público en Homenaje a Luciano Parejo Alfonso*, Vol. 1, Tirant lo Blanch, Valencia, 2018, pp. 1119–1143.

9 Erica Palmerini, "Robótica y Derecho: sugerencias, confluencias, evoluciones en el marco de una investigación europea," *Revista de Derecho Privado*, 32, January-June 2017, p. 64.

10 Bernard Roth, "Introducción," in Bruno Siciliano and Oussuma Khatib (eds.), *Springer Handbook of robotics*, viii, Berlin, 2008.

11 Karel Čapek, *R.U.R. Rossum's Universal Robots*, Penguin Random House, Penguin Classics, London, 2004.

12 A classic of robot literature from the 1950s is Isaac Asimov, *Robot*, Gnome Press, New York, 1950. See also H. Jonas, *The Imperative of Responsibility: In Search of an Ethics for the Technological Age*, Chicago University Press, Chicago, 1984.

b Historical Evolution

Robots are not new. History shows us that people have been trying to create artificial life for hundreds of years. Examples of mechanical inventions and machines include Hero of Alexandria's automata (85 CE), the iron man of Albertus Magnus (1204–1282), Roger Bacon's talking head (1214–1294), the mechanical lion created by Leonardo da Vinci (1452), and Juanelo Turriano's stick man (1500–1588).[13]

The first "programmable automata," which used punched tape or cards, appeared during the Industrial Revolution.[14] Jacques de Vaucanson (1709–1782) invented several machines "that could excite public curiosity," including one for spinning silk thread.[15] These inventions were the forerunners of today's industrial robots.

However, the first true robots did not appear until the mid-twentieth century. In the 1950s, Alan Turing, considered the father of artificial intelligence (hereafter AI)[16] and

---

13 Juan García-Prieto Cuesta, "¿Qué es un Robot?," in Moisés Barrio Andrés (dir.), *Derecho de los Robots, op. cit.*, p. 29.

14 *Ibid.*, p. 30.

15 John Jordan, *Robots*, MIT Press, Cambridge, Massachusetts, 2016, p. 29.

16 On the challenges posed by artificial intelligence, see the recent study by María Yolanda Sánchez-Urán Azaña and María Amparo Grau Ruiz (dirs.); Bruno César Lorencini and José Carlos Francisco (coords.), *Nuevas tecnologías y Derecho. Retos y oportunidades planteados por la Inteligencia Artificial y la Robótica*, Juruá, Porto, 2019. With the following articles, among others: "Robótica y Derecho: primera aproximación," by Carlos Rogel Vide, pp. 13–30; "Internet de las Cosas: desafíos jurídicos en un mundo de la conectividad total," by Moisés Barrio Andrés, pp. 31–47; "Internet das coisas e os aspectos economicos de cibersegurança ante a criaçao no Brasil de criaçao da autoridade nacional de proteçao de dados," by Thiago Lopes Matsushita, pp. 49–69; "Herramientas fiscales innovadoras y tributación de los robots," by César García Novoa, pp. 73–88; "Una Seguridad Social para el futuro, con un apunte sobre automatización, robots y Seguridad Social," by Alberto Llorente Álvarez, pp. 127–147; and "Epílogo – Nuevas Tecnologías y Derecho. Retos y oportunidades planteados por la Inteligencia Artificial y la Robótica: Balance y prospectiva," by María Yolanda Sánchez-Urán Azaña and María Amparo Grau Ruiz, pp. 263–274. On the same topic, see also Agustí Cerrillo i Martínez and Miguel Peguera Poch (coords.), *Retos jurídicos de la inteligencia artificial*, Thomson Reuters – Aranzadi, Cizur Menor, Navarra, 2020, with the following articles, among others: "Cómo la inteligencia artificial está impactando en las sociedades," by Lorena Jaume-Palasí, pp. 27–39; "En búsqueda de un marco normativo para la inteligencia artificial," by Miguel Peguera Poch, pp. 41–56; "Retos de la inteligencia artificial y adaptabilidad del Derecho de daños," by Antoni Rubí Puig, pp. 57–71; "El impacto de la inteligencia artificial en las Administraciones Públicas: estado de la cuestión y una agenda," by Agustí Cerrillo i Martínez, pp. 75–92; "Automatización, inteligencia artificial y empleados públicos," by Ramón Galindo Caldés, pp. 93–109; "Automatización y obsolescencia humana," by Ignasi Beltrán de Heredia Ruiz, pp. 113–124; "La inteligencia artificial, su uso en la gestión de recursos humanos y los riesgos para los

computing,[17] developed what is now known as the "Turing test."[18] According to this test, if a person asks another person and a machine a series of questions and, based on their answers, is unable to tell the machine from the human, the machine is AI. In the 1980s, John Searle published his "Chinese room" argument,[19] a similar experiment that attempts to illustrate the difference between human and simulated intelligence.

Automated assembly line manufacturing and production entered a new era when the first industrial robot was installed in 1961.[20] By 2014 there were already over one million robots in operation, according to the International Federation of Robotics.[21]

In recent decades, "supercomputers" using AI have gradually surpassed human beings at games and activities once considered to be the exclusive domain of human intelligence. In 1996 and 1997, the IBM computer Deep Blue beat Garry Kasparov at chess. In 2011 its successor, the IBM Watson, won the television game show *Jeopardy!* In 2016, Google's AlphaGo program won at Go, a highly challenging game, against South Korean Lee Sedol, one of the best Go players in the world.

Robots have since made forays into the fields of medicine (the Da Vinci surgical system) and law (the robot lawyer Ross). Robots have even been awarded citizenship: on October 25, 2017, "Sophia"[22] was made a citizen of Saudi Arabia.

---

trabajadores," by Antonio Fernández García, pp. 125–141; "Luces y sombras del uso de la inteligencia artificial en el sistema de justicia penal," by Marc Balcells, pp. 145–159; and "Inteligencia artificial y acceso a la justicia: retos y prospectiva," by Aura Esther Vilalta Nicuesa, pp. 161–178. Also S. J. Russell and P. Norvig, *Artificial Intelligence: A Modern Approach*, Pearson Prentice Hall, 2nd ed., 2003.

17 Xavier Oberson, *Taxing Robots*, Edward Elgar, Cheltenham, UK, 2019, p. 6. *Id.*, "Taxer les robots? L'émergence d'une capacité contributive électronique," *Aktuelle Juristische Praxis* (*AJP*)/*Pratique Juridique Actuelle* (*PJA*), 2, 2017. *Id.*, "Taxing robots? From the emergence of an electronic ability to pay to a tax on robots or the use of robots?," *World Tax Journal*, 2017.

18 Alan Mathison Turing, "Computing Machinery and Intelligence," *Mind*, 49, 1950, pp. 433–460.

19 John Searle, *Minds, Brains and Science*, Harvard University Press, Cambridge, Massachusetts,1984, pp. 28ff.

20 The robot was the Unimate 2000 made by Unimation. Later, in the mid-1960s, the same company created the PUMA (Programmable Universal Machine for Assembly): in Elena García Armada, *Robots*, Catarata, Madrid, 2015, p. 10.

21 John Jordan, *Robots*, *op. cit.*, pp. 73–74.

22 On this robot, see the press article: "¿Cómo funciona Sofía?, la primera robot ciudadana del mundo," *El País*, October 27, 2017.

i *Industry Definition of "Robot"*

Various organizations and associations in Spain and abroad have given different definitions of the term "robot." All have been proposed by the robotics industry for self-regulatory purposes. The *International Organization for Standardization*, in ISO 8373:2012, defines a robot as an "actuated mechanism programmable in two or more axes with a degree of autonomy, moving within its environment, to perform intended tasks." An industrial robot, on the other hand, is an "automatically controlled, reprogrammable, multipurpose manipulator, programmable in three or more axes, which can be either fixed in place or mobile for use in industrial automation applications."

According to the *Robotic Industries Association* (RIA), an industrial robot is a "reprogrammable, multifunctional manipulator designed to move material, parts, tools or specialized devices through variable programmed motions for the performance of a variety of tasks."[23]

For the *Association Française de Normalisation* (AFNOR), a robot is an "automated, reprogrammable, multipurpose, servo-controlled manipulator capable of positioning and arranging pieces, tools, or specialized devices, following variable reprogrammable paths, to carry out a variety of tasks."[24]

And, finally, the *International Federation of Robotics* (IFR) defines an industrial robot as an "automatically controlled, reprogrammable multipurpose manipulator programmable in three or more axes, which can be either fixed in place or mobile, designed to move material, parts, tools, or specialized devices in order to perform various tasks in different industrial production stages."[25]

These definitions all have points in common, but they are overly technical and too focused on the mechanical aspects of industrial robots, overlooking the countless types of non-industrial robots that exist. Therefore, these definitions are insufficient if we want to consider all robots and legally regulate their activity.

ii *Published Academic Definition of "Robot"*

Most of the scholarly literature agrees that a robot must have certain characteristics but does not share one precise, definitive definition of the term.

The three elemental characteristics are "sense-think-act"[26] These traits of perception, decision, and action, which most scholars consider basic and

---

23 Juan García-Prieto Cuesta, "¿Qué es un Robot?," in Moisés Barrio Andrés (dir.), *Derecho de los Robots*, *op. cit.*, p. 38.

24 *Ibid.*, p. 38.

25 *Ibid.*, p. 38.

26 Expression coined by Professors Pfeifer and Scheier, in Rolf Pfeifer and Christian Scheier, *Understanding Intelligence*, MIT Press, Cambridge, Massachusetts, 1999, p. 37.

distinctive,[27] correspond to the following mechanical components: sensors, processors, and actuators.[28]

In general, all definitions primarily view the robot as a machine, mechanism, or manipulator. This implies that a robot is an object or thing, devoid of biological life. And as a physical or embodied thing, it has a material form.

According to Calo,[29] robotics has three "exclusive properties,"[30] which are corporeality, unpredictability, and social impact. Yet not all scholars consider physical presence an essential trait. Balkin[31] warns that there are many AI systems which, without being corporeal, can have an impact on the physical world and even do harm.

Santos González defines a smart robot as "a physical machine which, by means of intelligent sensors and programs, can autonomously make decisions based on logic and artificial intelligence, predicting the needs of humans and of the situations in which they find themselves, acting, alternating, and interacting with the physical world, all under the constant control of humans."[32]

2 *The Need for a Legal Definition of Robot*

The European Parliament resolution of February 16, 2017, with recommendations to the Commission on Civil Law Rules on Robotics, underscored the "need to create a generally accepted definition of robot and AI that is flexible

---

27 See, for instance, Paul Singer, *Wired for War: The Robotics Revolution and Conflict in the 21st Century*, Penguin Press, New York, 2009; Ryan Calo, "Robots and privacy," in Patrick Lin (ed.), *Robot Ethics: The Ethical and Social Implications of Robotics*, MIT Press, Cambridge, Massachusetts, 2012, p. 187; Elena García Armada, *Robots, op. cit.*, p. 12; and Erica Palmerini, "Liability and risk management in robotics," *Digital Revolution: Challenges for Contract Law in Practice Nomos*, Vol. 1, Issue 1, 2016.

28 Moisés Barrio Andrés, "Hacia una personalidad electrónica para los robots," *cit.*, p. 94.

29 Ryan Calo, "Robots as legal metaphors," *Harvard Journal of Law and Technology*, Vol. 30, Issue 1, 2016, pp. 209–237. *Id.*, "Robots in American Law," *University of Washington School of Law Research Paper*, 4, 2016.

30 Moisés Barrio Andrés, "Hacia una personalidad electrónica para los robots," *cit.*, p. 96.

31 Jack Balkin, "The path of robotics law," *California Law Review Circuit*, 6, 2015, pp. 45–60.

32 María José Santos González, "Regulación Legal de la Robótica y la Inteligencia Artificial: Retos de Futuro," *Revista Jurídica de la Universidad de León*, 4, 2017, p. 32. Similarly, García Armada defines a robot as "a machine designed to perform a specific task, endowed with a sensor system for receiving information on the robot's state and surroundings, a program that tells it how to act in each state and situation, and an action system for carrying out the designated task," in Elena García Armada, *Robots, op. cit.*, p. 13. Additionally, García-Prieto Cuesta defines a robot as "a machine with a certain degree of complexity in its components, design, and behavior, which processes information about its environment in order to interact with it," in Juan García-Prieto Cuesta, "¿Qué es un Robot?", in Moisés Barrio Andrés (dir.), *Derecho de los Robots, op. cit.*, p. 38.

and is not hindering innovation." This is one of the prerequisites of any attempt to regulate robots, for if we do not know what a robot is, we will not even be able to determine to what or whom the law applies.

This question is particularly relevant in tax law, as Article 14 of Spain's General Tax Act "establishes that the law is required to specify at least the basic facts which give rise to tax liability and benefits [...] In this respect, a principle of legislative specificity applies, albeit less intensely than for penalties,"[33] as extensive interpretation (though not analogy) is allowed. This means that, in order to levy taxes on robots, we must first define what a robot is, as a taxable entity, and determine which characteristics of robots – or of their owners or users – allow a particular tax treatment.

In my opinion, the legal definition of a robot should be the basis for all future legislation in any field of law. That common definition should guide legislators as they consider, on a case-by-case basis, the particularities of each new matter requiring regulation. Therefore, "the definition of robots should be broad enough in order to correspond with the rapid evolution of AI and its impact on the possibilities of robots."[34] However, lawmakers should ideally be able to work from a common ground when legislating robots and their impact on society, especially within the European Union. As each state will regulate the impact of robotics independently, having a shared definition would at least ensure that their laws are more coordinated and even synchronized in some respects.

a Absence of a Legal Definition of Robot

At present, there is no legal definition of robot in Spanish or EU law. However, the aforementioned European Parliament resolution of February 16, 2017, derived from Maddy Delvaux's report, lists the following characteristics of a smart robot:

- the acquisition of autonomy through sensors and/or by exchanging data with its environment (inter-connectivity) and the trading and analysing of those data;
- self-learning from experience and by interaction (optional criterion);
- at least a minor physical support;
- the adaptation of its behaviour and actions to the environment;
- absence of life in the biological sense.

33 Ramón Falcón y Tella, *Derecho Financiero y Tributario (Parte General)*, Servicio de Publicaciones, Facultad de Derecho, Universidad Complutense de Madrid, 8th ed., 2019, pp. 179–180.

34 Xavier Oberson, *Taxing Robots*, *op. cit.*, p. 16.

Robots are mere products, although they are very close to being something more than just an object.

Yet other countries have come up with a legal definition of robot. For example, according to South Korean legislation, "the term 'intelligent robot' means a mechanical device (including software required for operating the mechanical device) that perceives the external environment for itself, discerns circumstances, and moves voluntarily."[35] This definition is given in the Intelligent Robots Development and Distribution Promotion Act, a law passed by the South Korean government for the "enhancement of the quality of life of citizens and the national economy by establishing and promoting a policy for the sustainable development of the intelligent robot industry to facilitate the development and distribution of intelligent robots and lay down the foundation therefor."[36]

As we can see, this definition has the same characteristics – with the exception of self-learning – as those outlined by the European Parliament.

b Possibility of a Legal-Tax Definition of Robot

An interesting question is whether tax law ought to come up with its own definition, without waiting for other legal branches, and if that definition can differ from theirs (in civil law, say, for the purposes of liability).

"As has often been said, the law is always slower than society, for the technological or social change comes first, and later it is the law's job to regulate the new situation."[37] Yet tax law has historically been one of the first to regulate new sources of potential revenue. In this case, as taxation is essential to maintaining a welfare state, tax law will probably pave the way in regulating robotics for the purpose of levying taxes.

Tax law is a field that has legislative freedom in Spain, as established by the Constitutional Court in STC 45/1989 of February 20 (TOL80.256),[38] which states that legislators are not limited by the marital/civil statuses that define the family unit, and STC 37/2017 of March 1 (TOL6.026.505),[39] which says that

---

35 Article 2.1. of the South Korean Intelligent Robots Development and Distribution Promotion Act.

36 As stated in Article 1 of said act.

37 Silvia Díaz Alabart, *Robots y responsabilidad civil*, Reus, Madrid, 2018, p. 28.

38 In this ruling, the court analyzed the obligation of spouses to file a single, joint tax return and declared it unconstitutional. Specifically, the court ruled that "tax legislators are, in principle, free to independently come up with their own terms and descriptions and are certainly not bound by the existing marital/civil categories of legal relations and institutions."

39 In this ruling, the Constitutional Court analyzed and declared unconstitutional certain precepts of the capital gains tax on property transfers of developed land in the historical

legislators are free to determine the existence of financial capacity with regard to the IIVTNNU property tax.

These rulings confirm that "tax legislators have full autonomy when it comes to describing and signifying concepts, giving them a license that means they are not strictly limited by categorizations or absences in other branches of the law."[40] Therefore, tax law does not necessarily have to wait for other legal areas in order to devise a definition of the term "robot" for tax purposes. There is also the "prevalence of concepts derived from tax legislation, that is, from the definition it provides, even if the term originated in another branch of the law or even another non-legal field."[41]

Consequently, the tax system can, through legislation, establish robot-related definitions without worrying if they coincide with those of other legal branches.

c Proposed Legal-Tax Definition of Robot

Considering the foregoing, I propose this general definition of a smart robot: "an autonomous self-learning program, with or without a physical support, which, by means of sensors, processors, and actuators, impacts and interacts with its environment."

I do not believe that corporeality should be a requirement (as set out in the European Parliament resolution of February 16, 2017), considering the technological advances and impact of AI programs and softbots on the economy and the job market. However, I do think that true robots interact with and affect their surroundings. A simple computer program with no connection to the outside world cannot be considered a robot. Additionally, a smart robot should have self-learning capabilities.

Yet this definition must be adapted to the specific case of each tax law when describing the elements of the levy. The definition of robot is less relevant than the impact robots have on the labor market as such, or on the economy and redistribution of wealth.[42] And that impact is what legislators should consider

region of Álava, but only regarding the taxation of situations where no capital gains were realized. The sentence concluded, "Finally, it should be noted that the manner of determining whether a capital gain is taxable is the sole prerogative of tax lawmakers, in their recognized legislative freedom."

40 José Antonio Fernández Amor, "Derecho tributario y cuarta revolución industrial: análisis jurídico sobre aspectos fiscales de la robótica," *Nueva fiscalidad*, 1, 2018, p. 87.

41 Ramón Falcón y Tella, *Derecho Financiero y Tributario (Parte General)*, *op. cit.*, p. 146.

42 Xavier Oberson, *Taxing Robots*, *op. cit.*, p. 16.

when creating new taxes, or adapting existing ones, that affect robots, their use, or the income they generate.

B Existing Robot Types

1 *Criteria for Possible Robot Classification*

Robots can be classified in many ways, according to one or several of their properties.[43] These classifications may be legally relevant for tax purposes, as they could be part of the taxable element. Robots can be divided by complexity,[44] components, uses, humanoid qualities, mobility,[45] autonomy, or other aspects.

Today there are various types of robots that are having an increasing impact on our society. The following section lists the most common and/or important robots, grouped by use and by characteristics, that should be considered when creating tax legislation. Smart robots, such as military drones or service androids, may be included in more than one category.

2 *Robotic Archetypes by Characteristics*

a Drones

A drone is generally defined as an unmanned aircraft. However, there are many terms with subtle nuances[46] to distinguish between the different types of unmanned aircraft. These vehicles, which can operate without a pilot on board, are either controlled remotely or fly with total autonomy thanks to AI.[47] The former are mere tools or machines, operated by human pilots from a distance, but the latter fall under the category of smart robots.

43 Juan García-Prieto Cuesta, "¿Qué es un Robot?," in Moisés Barrio Andrés (dir.), *Derecho de los Robots, op. cit.*, p. 40.

44 Martha M. Conde Canaviri, "Generaciones de La Robótica," *RITS* [*online*], 2008, n.1, pp. 129–131.

45 Elena García Armada, *Robots, op. cit.*, p. 14.

46 Moisés Barrio Andrés, "Drones. Concepto. Clases e historia. Usos Actuales. El Derecho de los drones," in Moisés Barrio Andrés (dir.), *Derecho de los drones*, La Ley, Wolter Kluwer, Madrid, 2018, p. 33. See also, Fernando González Botija, *Los drones y el Derecho de la Unión Europea: Reglamento (UE) nº 2018/1139 y propuestas de EASA*, Atelier, Barcelona, 2019. On the topic of drones and the law, see Pam Storr and Christine Storr, "The Rise and Regulation of Drones: Are We Embracing Minority Report or WALL-E?," in Marcelo Corrales, Mark Fenwick and Nikolaus Forgó (eds.), *Robotics, AI and the Future of Law*, in the "Perspectives in Law, Business and Innovation" Collection, Springer, 2018, pp. 105–122.

47 Moisés Barrio Andrés, "Prologue," in Moisés Barrio Andrés (dir.), *Derecho de los drones, op. cit.*, p. 23.

Drones have a wide range of potential uses in both the public and private sectors. Emergency services are increasingly finding them helpful (for rescues, finding missing persons, or fighting fires, for example), and they have been used in the military for several decades. They also have interesting applications in logistics and distribution (last-mile delivery drones).

Additionally, land offices and tax authorities are using drones to detect undeclared structures. Therefore, even if it were not deemed necessary to create a specific tax regime for smart robots, and specifically for autonomous drones, these already play an important role in tax law and would need to be brought in line with existing regulations.

b Autonomous Vehicles

These vehicles, especially cars in development right now, can operate without human guidance. Self-driving cars are swiftly becoming a reality, with major corporations testing them on roads in Germany, the United States, and other countries. This category includes the Teslas with autopilot already on the market.[48]

These robotic cars will have a considerable impact on the job market and the economy in general if – or, more accurately, when – they become a common sight on our roads.

c Softbots and Artificial Intelligence

Software robots or softbots "are robots that consist solely of computer programs and have no connection to the physical support on which said programs are executed."[49] For example, "they are often used to carry out financial transactions."[50]

Artificial intelligence, on the other hand, is defined as "any data processing technology characterized by the ability to make calculations on certain information in a virtual dimensional space constructed by means of (generally non-linear) operations effected within the algorithm itself to take advantage of

48 On the subject of liability derived from the actions of autonomous vehicles, see Ivó Coca-Vila, "Self-driving Cars in Dilemmatic Situations: An Approach Based on the Theory of Justification in Criminal Law," in *Criminal Law and Philosophy: An International Journal for Philosophy of Crime, Criminal Law and Punishment*, 12, 1, 2018, pp. 59–82.

49 Juan García-Prieto Cuesta, "¿Qué es un Robot?," in Moisés Barrio Andrés (dir.), *Derecho de los Robots, op. cit.*, p. 42.

50 Erica Palmerini, "Robótica y Derecho: sugerencias, confluencias, evoluciones en el marco de una investigación europea," *cit.*, p. 59.

different properties of highly dimensional spaces."[51] Another definition might be "the capacity of software to develop processes similar to the human brain."[52]

Even though robots "represent a physical emanation of AI"[53] or "are the implementation of AI in the market,"[54] for tax purposes there should be no distinction between robots and softbots as long as they have a similar impact on the economy and job market.

d Humanoid Robots: Androids and Cyborgs

The term "android" was coined in the nineteenth century and refers to non-human beings with a skin-like outer layer, like the robots in *R.U.R.*[55] In general culture, it is defined as an automaton with a human form: in other words, a humanoid robot. The most obvious example is the female android Sophia, mentioned earlier in this chapter. These robots are expected to enter the service industry, for instance as wait staff or store clerks.

Cyborgs, on the other hand, are cybernetic organisms made of both biological and electronic matter. The term "cybernetic" was first used by Norbert Wiener, a professor at the Massachusetts Institute of Technology (MIT), in the 1960s.[56] The potential impact of cyborgs is uncertain.

3 *Robotic Archetypes by Use*

a Industrial Machinery

"Industrial robots are essentially programmable machine tools that perform a sequence of actions, typically in assembly-line scenarios,"[57] although they may also move finished goods in distribution centers.[58] These industrial or manipulator robots are common in food and pharmaceutical manufacturing and widespread in the automotive industry.[59] Of all smart robots, these are expected to have the greatest impact on the economy and especially on the job market. They are also one of the most numerous types, with a global average of 74 robots per 10,000 employees in 2018, according to the International

51 Juan García-Prieto Cuesta, "¿Qué es un Robot?," in Moisés Barrio Andrés (dir.), *Derecho de los Robots*, *op. cit.*, p. 46.
52 Xavier Oberson, *Taxing Robots*, *op. cit.*, p. 6.
53 *Ibid.*, p. 6.
54 *Ibid.*
55 John Jordan, *Robots*, *op. cit.*, p. 51.
56 *Ibid.*
57 *Ibid.*, p. 73.
58 *Ibid.*, p. 74.
59 Elena García Armada, *Robots*, *op. cit.*, p. 14.

Federation of Robotics.[60] When people talk about taxing robots, these are often what they have in mind.

b Healthcare Robots

A healthcare robot can be described as a powered, computer-controlled manipulator with artificial sensing that can be programmed to move and position tools to carry out a wide range of surgical, medical, and healthcare tasks.[61] This category includes various robots associated with medical and other types of care. Although I have lumped them all together under the general heading of "healthcare robots," there are significant differences between types. All of these robots need clearer, more specific regulation[62] – and not just with regard to taxation – given their intimate and sensitive interaction with human beings.

i *Prosthetic and Rehabilitation Robots*

Prosthetic robots are smart prostheses that use brain-computer interface technology to replace missing or damaged body parts,[63] while rehabilitation robots provide accelerated rehabilitation therapy tailored to each patient's needs.[64]

ii *Service and Care Robots*

These are basically robotic orderlies or nurses, programmed to perform simple tasks such as cleaning (personal hygiene and grooming) or dispensing medication. They can be used to care for senior citizens or individuals with disabilities. Given our aging population, it comes as no surprise that the demand for such robots is on the rise.[65]

This category can also include robots that provide more generic services to the general population, from domestic cleaning robots – such as the Roomba and similar robotic vacuum cleaners – to robotic helpers like Amazon's Alexa voice assistant.

---

60 IFR press release, Frankfurt, February 7, 2018.

61 Blake Hannaford (dir.), *Surgical Robotics: Systems Applications and Visions*, Springer, New York, 2011.

62 Eduard Fosch Villaronga, "ISO 13482:2014 and Its Confusing Categories. Building a Bridge Between Law and Robotics" (pp. 31–44), in Philippe Wenger, Christine Chevallereau, Doina Pisla, Hannes Bleuler and Aleksandar Rodić (eds.), *New Trends in Medical and Service Robots*, Springer, Cham, 2016.

63 Roberto García Portero, "Los robots en la sanidad," in Moisés Barrio Andrés (dir.), *Derecho de los Robots, op. cit.*, pp. 207 and 208.

64 *Ibid.*, p. 208.

65 *Ibid.*, pp. 208 and 209.

iii *Surgical Robots*

Surgical robots, like the Da Vinci, are sophisticated systems controlled by surgeons from a console, allowing them "to perform highly precise actions and operate on a very small scale, without the inevitable visual or manual difficulties they would otherwise face,"[66] and to intervene in cases requiring superhuman strength or precision.[67]

In the near future, as robotics advances and the 5G rollout continues, we can expect to see a transition from remote-assisted surgery, in which a surgeon is aided by an expert not physically present in the OR, to fully remote robotic surgery, where the expert performs the entire operation from a distance (in another city or country) with the help of a surgical robot.[68]

c Space and Military Robots

It is common knowledge that the armed forces[69] and space agencies of various countries have been using robots for some time. These robots range from drones to motorized vehicles like the Mars Rover. The impact of these machines is not always apparent to the general public.

C Conclusions

The need for a clear definition of what exactly constitutes a "smart robot" was made patent in the opening lines of the European Parliament resolution of February 16, 2017, with recommendations to the Commission on Civil Law Rules on Robotics. That definition is the basis for developing any type of robot regulation, especially with regard to taxation.

As we have seen, smart robots can have a wide variety of features and uses. The differences between robot types may have legal relevance when establishing a specific definition for each class. For instance, the obvious distinctions between an autonomous vehicle and a surgical robot will naturally give rise to different regulation needs. Most definitions put forward in scholarly literature

66 Erica Palmerini, "Robótica y Derecho: sugerencias, confluencias, evoluciones en el marco de una investigación europea," *cit.*, p. 58. On this topic, see also the interesting work by Sero Andonian *et al.*, "Device failures associated with patient injuries during robot-assisted laparoscopic surgeries: A comprehensive review of FDA MAUDE database," *The Canadian Journal of Urology*, 15, 1, 2008, pp. 3912–3916.

67 Roberto García Portero, "Los robots en la sanidad," in Moisés Barrio Andrés (dir.), *Derecho de los Robots*, *op. cit.*, p. 209.

68 *Ibid.*, p. 210.

69 John Jordan, *Robots*, *op. cit.*, p. 136.

agree that a robot senses, decides, and acts. They also include self-learning as a feature that distinguishes robots (simple objects) from smart robots (a possible new category).

The following is my proposed general definition of a smart robot:

> an autonomous self-learning program, with or without a physical support, which, by means of sensors, processors, and actuators, impacts and interacts with its environment.

In my view, corporeality is not a requirement, but interaction with and alteration of the environment is. The impact of smart robots should matter more than their physical form, or lack thereof. Furthermore, when measuring their impact, it is not enough to merely consider the physical consequences (of an autonomous vehicle on the road, for instance); we also need to gauge how they affect the economy (in the case of computer programs that conduct high-frequency trading) and other areas.

CHAPTER 2

The Need for Public Intervention to Face the Challenges Posed by Robotics

A The Impact of Robotics

"Now that humankind stands on the threshold of an era [of] ever more sophisticated robots, bots, androids and other manifestations of artificial intelligence [...] it is vitally important for the legislature to consider its legal and ethical implications and effects, without stifling innovation."[1] The European Parliament understands that advances in robotics pose numerous legal and economic problems. The ultimate purpose of the law is to resolve conflicts, and advanced robotic technology will require regulation in order to settle the disputes that will inevitably arise in different existing legal fields.[2]

Robots are already ubiquitous.[3] In this fourth industrial revolution or Industry 4.0, the consequences of automation and robotization are far-reaching and varied.[4] More new products, new jobs, and, above all, new conflicts (legal

1 European Parliament, *Report with recommendations to the Commission on Civil Law Rules on Robotics (2015/2103(INL))*, session document A8-005/2017, January 27, 2017, Letter B of the Introduction to the Motion for a European Parliament *Resolution*.

2 On this new era and its challenges, see Néstor García Canclini, "How to research the communicational era of capitalism," in *Desacatos*, 56, 2018, pp. 90–105. Gérald Berthoud, "Los saberes hoy: desafíos y apuestas," in *Andamios*, Vol. 7, Issue 14, 2010, pp. 349–375.

3 "Today it is no longer fiction, as companies increasingly use robots on production lines or algorithms to optimize their logistics, manage inventory, and carry out other core business functions," in McKinsey Global Institute – MGI, *A Future that Works: Automation, Employment, and Productivity*, January 2017, Preface.

4 There is a broad consensus on this among authors and scholars. See: A. Ortega Klein, *La imparable marcha de los robots*, Alianza, Madrid, 2016. Joseph E. Stiglitz, "The coming great transformation," *Journal of Policy Modelling*, 39, 2017, pp. 625–638. John P. Sullins, "Introduction: Open questions in roboethics," *Philosophy and Technology*, 24, 3, 2011, pp. 233–238. R. Calo, "Robotics and the Lessons of Cyberlaw," *Cal. Law Review*, 103, 2015. María José Santos González, "Regulación legal de la robótica y la inteligencia artificial: retos de futuro," *Revista Jurídica de la Universidad de León*, 4, 2017. David Álvaro Pascual, *Inteligencia artificial: un panorama de algunos de sus desafíos éticos y jurídicos*, senior thesis, Universidad de Girona, Spain, 2017. A. Antón Antón and I. Bilbao Estrada, *Retos y oportunidades de la Administración en la era digital*, Thomson Reuters, 2019. Alejandro Sánchez del Campo Redonet, *Reflexiones de un replicante legal. Los retos jurídicos de la robótica y las tecnologías disruptivas*, Preface by Juan Pablo Nieto Mengotti, Thomson Reuters – Aranzadi, Cizur Menor, Navarra, 2016. *Id.*, "Cuestiones jurídicas que plantean los robots," *Revista de privacidad*

 | DOI:10.1163/9789004538511_003

and otherwise) are appearing every day. The law, as a tool for solving the problems that arise in society, must adapt to the new realities created by advancing technology.[5]

One of the greatest fears with robotics is the loss of jobs and consequent increase in public spending, in the form of unemployment benefits and other welfare expenses. This would be compounded by a simultaneous loss of revenue, as fewer jobs mean less income from work-related taxes. If robots are brought into labor and contractual settings, we need to create new regulations (or modify existing ones) on occupational health and safety, the definition of disabled persons, extra-contractual and criminal liability, etc. These new legal issues must be studied by experts in each pertinent branch of law to come up with an adequate response to this phenomenon.

"The impact of automation technologies on employment has been a highly debated topic since the beginning of the First Industrial Revolution. While previous technological advances have destroyed jobs in some sectors, job losses were usually offset by newly created jobs in other sectors in the medium to long term."[6] This is the greatest fear today: that this fourth revolution[7] will not create enough new jobs, in the medium and long term, to compensate for the

y Derecho digital, 2, 2016. Ugo Pagallo, Marcelo Corrales, Mark Fenwick and Nikolaus Forgó, "The Rise of Robotics & AI: Technological Advances & Normative Dilemmas," in Marcelo Corrales, Mark Fenwick and Nikolaus Forgó (eds.), *Robotics, AI and the Future of Law*, in the "Perspectives in Law, Business and Innovation" Collection, Springer, 2018, pp. 1–13. Mark Fenwick, Erik P. M. Vermeulen and Marcelo Corrales, "Business and Regulatory Responses to Artificial Intelligence: Dynamic Regulation, Innovation Ecosystems and the Strategic Management of Disruptive Technology," in Marcelo Corrales, Mark Fenwick and Nikolaus Forgó (eds.), *Robotics, AI and the Future of Law, op. cit.*, pp. 81–103. Ugo Pagallo, *The Laws of Robots. Crimes, Contracts, and Torts*, in "Law, Governance and Technology Series 10," Springer, Dordrecht-Heidelberg-New York-London, 2013.

5 For a fascinating read, see N. Nevejans, "Comment proteger l'homme face aux robots?," *Archives de Philosophie du Droit*, 59, 2016, pp. 131–163.

6 David Klenert, Enrique Fernández-Macías and José-Ignacio Antón, *Do Robots Really Destroy Jobs? Evidence from Europe*, Seville, European Commission, 2020, JRC118393, p. 7.

7 On the fourth industrial revolution in general, see: Luis Joyanes Aguilar, *Industria 4.0 La cuarta revolución industrial*, Marcombo, 2020. E-book. Klaus Schwab, *La cuarta revolución industrial*, Debate, Barcelona, 2016. Esteban Vegas Lozano and Ferrán Reverter Comer (authors), Antonio Monleon (dir.), *Big Data: hacia la cuarta revolución industrial*, Universitat de Barcelona, Barcelona, 2017. Miguel Ángel Gómez Salado and Francisco Vila Tierno (eds.), *Cuarta revolución industrial y su impacto sobre la productividad, el empleo y las relaciones jurídico-laborales: desafíos tecnológicos del siglo XXI*, Aranzadi, Cizur Menor, Navarra, 2021. Francisco Javier Braña Pino, *Cuarta revolución industrial, automatización y digitalización: una visión desde la periferia de la Unión Europea en tiempos de pandemia*, Instituto Complutense de Estudios Internacionales (ICEI), 2020.

ones "destroyed" by robots. Some even worry that robots will end up replacing all, or virtually all, human workers, although such a pessimistic and remote possibility falls outside the scope of this book.

Bill Gates[8] predicted that, by 2030, robots will have taken over most jobs and should therefore pay taxes to keep revenue up.[9] He suggested using robot productivity to generate more revenue, either by taxing the profits derived from increased efficiency or directly levying a robot tax of some kind. If we go this route, we will undoubtedly need to address the issue of legal personality in relation to robot taxation.[10]

1 *Repercussions of Robotics for the Labor Market*

The destruction of jobs by robots has been discussed at length[11] since the first automated machines were introduced in industrial manufacturing. With more

8 "There are many ways to take that extra productivity and generate more taxes. Exactly how you'd do it, measure it, you know, it's interesting for people to start talking about now. Some of it can come on the profits that are generated by the labor-saving efficiency there. Some of it can come directly in some type of robot tax. I don't think the robot companies are going to be outraged that there might be a tax. It's OK," in Kevin J. Delanay, "The robot that takes your job should pay taxes, says Bill Gates," February 17, 2017, *Quartz* (qz.com).

9 This has been the subject of various press articles, including: Juande Portillo, "¿Deben pagar impuestos los robots?," *Cinco Días*, September 7, 2019. Anonymous, "Podrían imponer impuestos a robots," *NOTIMEX*, September 16, 2017. "¿Llegará el día en que los robots sean sujetos de Derecho?," *Infobae*, December 26, 2020. "¿Deben los robots pagar impuestos?," *CE Noticias Financieras*, September 27, 2019. "Robot-lución: el gran reto de gobernar y convivir con las máquinas," *El País*, August 24, 2019. "Según Bill Gates, los robots deberían pagar impuestos," *CE Noticias Financieras*, February 22, 2017. "Proponen que robots paguen impuestos para financiar pensiones," *El Universal*, October 8, 2018. "Ways for robots to pay taxes," *CE Noticias Financieras*, January 31, 2021. "Esclavicemos a los robots y liberemos a los pobres," *El Comercio*, February 16, 2014. "El robot que pague," *El País*, June 5, 2019. Gabriel Calzada, "Los robots nos van a chupar la sangre," *Actualidad Económica*, July 1, 2017, p. 10. Marimar Jiménez, "¿Y habrá impuesto a robots que no sustituyan a humanos?," *Cinco Días*, February 21, 2017. J. Guerreiro, S. Rebelo and P. Teles, "Should robots be taxed?," *Northwestern University mimeo*. J. M. Durán Cabré, "Hola, soy un robot: ¿tengo que pagar impuestos?," *La Tributación de los Robots*, IEB Report 2/2019. U. Thuemmel, "¿Tiene sentido que los robots tributen?," *La Tributación de los Robots*, IEB Report 2/2019.

10 The initial difficulty revolves around the special tax capacity of robots, legal personality as a decisive factor for identifying robots as taxable objects or tax-paying entities, the capacity of robots to pay taxes and to act, and the possibility of creating a "capacity of representation" for robots. All these issues are discussed in Chapter 3 – Personhood of Robots.

11 As the following studies prove: J. Rifkin, *El fin del trabajo. Nuevas tecnologías contra puestos de trabajo: el nacimiento de una nueva era*, Editorial Booket, Madrid, 2014. C. Benedikt and M. A. Osborne, "The future of employment: How susceptible are jobs to computerization?," *Oxford Martin*, 114, 2013. Jesús R. Mercader Ugina, *El futuro del trabajo en la era de la*

and more robots in factories and other workplaces, the debate is livelier than ever. However, the medium and long-term consequences of the mass introduction of robots in the job market are not yet clear. Obviously, "technological change is a major driver of growth and development, yet it is equally associated with labour market change."[12] The most pressing question is what that change will look like.

In hindsight, today we realize that the Industrial Revolution brought increased productivity as well as more jobs, creating new products and industries.[13]

"However, it is becoming increasingly clear that creating jobs as new technologies disrupt industries will be far more challenging than in previous eras."[14] If we compare the first and fourth industrial revolutions, two major differences are immediately apparent. The first is the speed at which changes occur. "While the prevailing evidence of past technological developments suggests that waves of technological change result in short-term job destruction followed by the creation of new and better jobs, today's technological advances are emerging at an unprecedented rate and changing work in ways not seen before."[15] This faster pace is a result of globalization, digitization, a

digitalización y la robótica, Tirant lo Blanch, Valencia, 2017. *Id.*, "El impacto de la robótica y el futuro del trabajo," *Revista de la Facultad de Derecho de México*, Mexico, UNAM, vol. LXVII, Issue 269, September-December 2017. Miguel Ángel Gómez Salado, "Robótica, empleo y Seguridad Social. La cotización de los robots para el actual Estado de Bienestar," *Revista Internacional y Comparada de Relaciones Laborales y Derecho del Empleo*, Adapt University Press, Vol. 6, Issue 3, July-September 2018. Instituto Cuatrecasas de Estrategia Legal en RRHH, *Robótica y su impacto en los recursos humanos y en el marco regulatorio de las relaciones laborales*, Wolters Kluwer, Madrid, 2018. G. Graetz and G. Michaels, "Robots at work," *The Review of Economics and Statistics*, 100, 5, 2018. R. Abbott and B. Bogenschneider, "Why we should start taxing the robots that are taking human jobs," *The Conversation*, February 28, 2018. C. B. Frey and M. A. Osborne, "The future of employment: How susceptible are jobs to computerization?," in *Technological Forecasting and Social Change*, 114, January 1, 2017.

12 International Labour Organization – ILO, *Inception Report for the Global Commission on the Future of Work*, International Labour Office, Geneva, 2017, p. 10.

13 "Historical evidence shows that new technologies destroyed jobs, but they always created new jobs by driving the development of new activities, generating new products and new industries," in International Labour Organization – ILO (Irmgard Nübler), *New technologies: A jobless future or golden age of job creation?*, Research Department Working Paper No. 13, Geneva, November 2016, p. 10.

14 M. Mustafa Erdoğdu and Coşkun Karaca, "The Fourth Industrial Revolution and a Possible Robot Tax" (Chapter 5, pp. 103–122), in Irem Berksoy, Kutlu Dane and Milenko Popovic (eds.), *Institutions & Economic Policies: Effects on Social Justice, Employment, Environmental Protection & Growth*, IJOPEC Publication, London, 2017, p. 109.

15 International Labour Organization – ILO (Irmgard Nübler), *New technologies: A jobless future or golden age of job creation?*, Research Department Working Paper No. 13, Geneva,

larger population, and the exponential growth of innovation and scientific and industrial improvements.

The second difference is the fact that robots are already present in the workplace, and their numbers are growing. "The use of robots is increasing rapidly in both developed and emerging countries."[16] "For instance, since 2010, the number of operational industrial robots has increased by 9 per cent on average per year, reaching some 1.6 million units at the end of 2015"[17] and more than 2.7 million by 2019, although that year registered the first drop in global robot installations after six consecutive years of growth.[18] Additionally, in 2019 over 23 million personal or domestic service robots were sold.[19]

Faced with the real and immediate possibility of robots replacing people in many more job positions than before, "the big question is whether increased productivity and competitiveness result in an increase in employment and a rise in wages"[20] or, on the other hand, the techno-pessimists' fears prove to be founded. The legislation we choose to pass will be a decisive factor in this respect.

"[Some] economists argue that product innovation, diversification and structural transformation are the main drivers of job creation,"[21] all of which stem from the robotization inherent to the new revolution. But "automation does indeed substitute for labor – as it is typically intended to do,"[22] at least in the short term. "However, automation also complements labor, raises output in ways that lead to higher demand for labor, and interacts with adjustments

---

November 2016, quoted in International Labour Organization – ILO, *Inception Report for the Global Commission on the Future of Work, op. cit.*, p. 10.

16 International Labour Organization – ILO, *Robots worldwide: The impact of automation on employment and trade*, International Labour Office, Research Department Working Paper, No. 36, October 2018, p. 11.

17 International Labour Organization – ILO, *Inception Report for the Global Commission on the Future of Work, op. cit.*, p. 10.

18 International Federation of Robotics – IFR, *Executive Summary World Robotics 2020 Industrial Robots.*

19 International Federation of Robotics – IFR, *Executive Summary World Robotics 2020 Service Robots.*

20 International Federation of Robotics – IFR, *The Impact of Robots on Productivity, Employment and Jobs: A positioning paper by the International Federation of Robotics*, April 2017, p. 5.

21 International Labour Organization – ILO (Irmgard Nübler), *New technologies: A jobless future or golden age of job creation?*, Research Department Working Paper No. 13, *op. cit.*, p. 10.

22 David Autor, "Why Are There Still So Many Jobs? The History and Future of Workplace Automation," *Journal of Economic Perspectives*, Vol. 29, Issue 3, 2015, p. 5.

in labor supply."[23] In other words, it creates skilled jobs that did not exist. This is already happening and is expected to continue on a larger scale in the future.

At this early stage in the fourth revolution, we do not have enough information to answer that "big question," which is why experts are still studying the real effects of robotization in the medium and long term.

a Percentage of Automation

Several studies on the percentage of job automation have been published in recent years, presenting data and findings that are contradictory in some cases. "Figures suggest that 9 % of OECD jobs are potentially automatable" and, specifically in the United States, "only 9% of jobs rather than 47%, as proposed by Frey and Osborne, face a high automatability."[24]

These reports all highlight one incontrovertible fact: robots will "destroy" certain jobs currently held by humans. But it remains to be seen how many jobs will disappear and when. This does not necessarily mean net job loss; as stated above, new and more skilled positions will probably be created.

Other studies contain telling data: An analysis of more than 2,000 work activities across 800 occupations revealed that "about half the activities people are paid almost $15 trillion in wages to do in the global economy have the potential to be automated" and although "less than 5 percent of all occupations can be automated entirely, about 60 percent of all occupations have at least 30 percent of constituent activities that could be automated." We are clearly facing a major paradigm shift. Fortunately, "more occupations will change than will be automated away,"[25] at least in the short and medium term.

In the specific case of Spain, up to 36% of existing jobs are likely to be automated. The fourth industrial revolution will clearly accelerate the robotization of many tasks, and this may pose a threat to the security and stability of the Spanish labor market,[26] still in critical condition after the pandemic.

23 David Autor, "Why Are There Still So Many Jobs? The History and Future of Workplace Automation," *cit.*, p. 5.

24 Melanie Arntz, Terry Gregory and Ulrich Zierahn, *The Risk of Automation for Jobs in OECD Countries: A Comparative Analysis*, OECD Social, Employment and Migration Working Papers, No. 189, OECD Publishing, Paris, 2016, p. 25. Available at http://dx.doi.org/10.1787/5jlz9h56dvq7-en.

25 McKinsey Global Institute – MGI, *A Future that Works: Automation, Employment, and Productivity*, January 2017.

26 Observatorio Económico BBVA, "¿Cuán vulnerable es el empleo en España a la revolución digital?," *Observatorio Económico*, March 19, 2018. In English: BBVA Research, "How vulnerable is Spanish employment to the digital revolution?," working paper.

The global outlook is not much brighter, as we can glean from the following table:

Organization	Estimate
University of Oxford (Frey & Osborne)	47% of workers in the United States are at high risk of having their jobs replaced by automation
PWC	38% of jobs in the United States, 30% of jobs in the United Kingdom, 21% in Japan and 35% in Germany are at risk of automation
ILO (Chang & Huynh)	ASEAN-5: 56% of jobs are at risk of automation in next twenty years
McKinsey	60% of all occupations have at least 30% technically automatable activities
OECD	OECD average: 9% of jobs are at high risk. There is a low risk of complete automation, but a substantial share (between 50% and 70%) of automatable tasks are at risk
Roland Berger	Western Europe: 8.3 million jobs will be lost in industry and 10 million new jobs created in services by 2035
World Bank	Two-thirds of all jobs in developing countries are susceptible to automation

Now let us take a look at the estimated impact of automation technology on employment:[27]

"Great care, however, should be taken in interpreting these estimates, since many of the studies look at the probability that a job *could* be automated, not the probability that it (or the tasks therein) *will* be automated."[28] In other words, automation is not a foregone conclusion just because a job is automatable. These estimates, which vary from study to study (depending on methodology and different interpretations of data) and can therefore be contradictory, are merely informed economic guesses. There is a margin of error, as they do

27 Table published in International Labour Organization – ILO, *Inception Report for the Global Commission on the Future of Work, op. cit.*, p. 25.

28 *Ibid.*, p. 30.

not always take into account the enormous differences between countries,[29] all the pertinent economic and social variables, or the unpredictability of certain developments (such as the recovery and long-term effects of a disastrous global pandemic).

Moreover, "many workers in occupations that have been classified as vulnerable to automation in these studies may in fact be less exposed to automation than previously thought," because these workers "often perform a substantial share of non-routine interactive tasks, which are known to be less automatable,"[30] especially in unstructured environments.

b Speed and Intensity of Automation

"Technical, economic, and social factors will determine the pace and extent of automation."[31] It is vital that we begin to regulate robotics, weighing the impact of development and the risks it entails.

Back in 2017, a McKinsey Global Institute report predicted that "half of today's work activities could be automated by 2055, but this could happen up to 20 years earlier or later depending on the various factors, in addition to other wider economic conditions."[32] The wisest course of action would be to regulate robotics at an early stage, without waiting for the undesirable consequences of this fourth revolution to manifest.

c The Offshoring and Reshoring Phenomenon

One new phenomenon linked to the growth of robotics is reshoring, which is essentially the opposite of offshoring.[33] In a nutshell, offshoring is the relocation

---

29 "Many more jobs can now be automated, and the shares of these recently automatable jobs vary greatly from country to country," in European Commission, *Robots at work: A report on automatable and non-automatable employment shares in Europe*, Publications Office of the European Union, January 2018, p. 6.

30 Melanie Artnz, Terry Gregory and Ulrich Zierahn, *The Risk of Automation for Jobs in OECD Countries: A Comparative Analysis*, OECD Social, Employment and Migration Working Papers, No. 189, *op. cit.*, p. 25. Available at http://dx.doi.org/10.1787/5jlz9h56dvq7-en.

31 McKinsey Global Institute – MGI, *A Future that Works: Automation, Employment, and Productivity*, January 2017.

32 *Ibid.*

33 For general information on this subject, see: Joannis Bournakis, Michela Vecchi and Francesco Venturini, "Off-shoring, Specialization and R&D," *Review of Income and Wealth*, Vol. 64, Issue 1, March 2018, pp. 26–51. Claire Joubioux and Evelyne Vanpoucke, "Towards right-shoring: a framework for off- and re-shoring decision making," *Operations Management Research: Advancing Practice through Theory*, Vol. 9, Issues 3–4, 2016, pp. 117–132. Lisa M. Ellram, "Offshoring, Reshoring and the Manufacturing Location Decision," *Journal of Supply Chain Management*, Vol. 49, Issue 2, April 2013, pp. 3–5.

of business processes – production, manufacturing, services, or R&D + i – from one country to another, usually one where costs (especially those related to labor) are cheaper. The result is normally a loss of jobs in developed countries, as these are moved to developing countries where standards tend to be lower. Robotization makes it possible for technologically progressive countries to reshore processes that were offshored in the past and, consequently, bring back the jobs related to those processes, which may be quite varied. However, while automation undoubtedly boosts output and productivity, it also requires less labor.[34]

The impact of the "drop in global employment of 1.3% between 2005 and 2014" has been "rather small in developed countries, -0.54%, but much more pronounced in emerging countries with about 14%."[35] Countries with high robot density, such as Germany and South Korea, and those "where the accumulation of robots has been rapid, such as China, experienced an increase, or only a small decline, in the share of manufacturing in total employment."[36]

Robotics clearly reduces the offshoring trend and the destruction of manufacturing jobs in developed countries that often goes with it. At the same time, however, "robotization in developed countries negatively affects employment in emerging countries,"[37] where fewer new jobs are created, altering the global map of economic activity.

---

34 "Evidence also shows that where reshoring to developed countries has occurred, it has fallen short of expected employment effects. Reshoring has mostly been accompanied by capital investment, such as in robots, with the little job creation that has occurred concentrated in high-skilled activities (De Backer *et al.*, 2016). This means that jobs that 'return' with reshored production will not be the same as those that have left. Indeed, reshoring is likely to be more about manufacturing output rather than employment, given the positive relationship between manufacturing output growth and productivity growth," in United Nations Conference on Trade and Development, *Trade and Development Report 2017, Beyond Austerity: Towards a Global New Deal, Chapter III: Robots, Industrialization and Inclusive Growth*, United Nations, New York and Geneva, 2017, p. 51.

35 International Labour Organization – ILO, *Robots worldwide: The impact of automation on employment and trade, op. cit.*, p. 11.

36 United Nations Conference on Trade and Development, *Trade and Development Report 2017, Beyond Austerity: Towards a Global New Deal, Chapter III: Robots, Industrialization and Inclusive Growth, op. cit.*, p. 52.

37 "We confirm the result of De Backer *et al.* (2018) with a more robust approach and show that robots reduce the trend in off-shoring. In this regard, we find that robotization in developed countries negatively affects employment in emerging countries, providing the first evidence of cross-country effects via robot-driven re-shoring," in International Labour Organization – ILO, *Robots worldwide: The impact of automation on employment and trade, op. cit.*, p. 11.

2 *Repercussions of Robotics for the Economy*

"Like past waves of innovation, AI will create both benefits and costs. The primary benefit of previous waves of automation has been productivity growth; today's wave of automation is no different."[38] This fourth revolution is similar to the three which preceded it: the short-term effect is economic disparity, but in the long run it will boost productivity.[39] It has been estimated that "automation could raise productivity growth globally by 0.8 to 1.4 percent annually."[40]

Another anticipated benefit of this revolution is reduced environmental impact. "The technologies associated with the Fourth Industrial Revolution can bring significant ecological benefits."[41] Robots will be able to perform tasks that were once impossible, and they may even cut back on pollution as technology improves over time.

a Economic Inequality

Although automation is likely to increase productivity and create wealth, not all of its effects are positive. One of the most serious negative consequences will be greater economic inequality. Labor will be sacrificed for capital (robots), making the rich richer and the poor poorer. "Recent automation is not divisive along demographic lines (like age and gender) when it comes to substituting for jobs,"[42] but it does discriminate by level of skill or qualification, and consequently by financial capacity.

Robotics will have the greatest impact on unskilled workers in low-income jobs, as the tasks they perform are most likely to be automated, while highly

---

38 Executive Office of the President, National Science and Technology Council, *Preparing for the Future of Artificial Intelligence*, October 2016, p. 29.

39 On the impact of robots on the labor market, see the following studies: María Yolanda Sánchez-Urán Azaña and María Amparo Grau Ruiz (authors), *El impacto de la robótica, en especial la robótica inclusiva, en el trabajo: aspectos jurídicos-laborales y fiscales.* Archive material. *Id., Robotics and Work: Labor and Tax Regulatory Framework*, Routledge, 2028-05. María Luz Rodríguez Fernández, *Humanos y robots: empleo y condiciones de trabajo en la era tecnológica*, Bomarzo, Albacete, 2020. J. M. D. Rodríguez, "El Derecho del Trabajo ante el futuro (presente) tecnológico y económico: Robots, Plataformas digitales, nuevos trabajos y viejos tiranos," *Trabajo y Derecho*, 40, 2018.

40 "Automation also contributes to productivity, as it has done historically. [...] Based on our scenario modeling, we estimate automation could raise productivity growth globally by 0.8 to 1.4 percent annually," in McKinsey Global Institute – MGI, *A Future that Works: Automation, Employment, and Productivity*, *op. cit.*

41 World Economic Forum – WEF, *Impact of the Fourth Industrial Revolution on Supply Chains*, October 2017, p. 16.

42 European Commission, *Robots at work: A report on automatable and non-automatable employment shares in Europe*, Publications Office of the European Union, January 2018, p. 7.

qualified workers will be less affected as their AI-complementing skills will be in greater demand.[43] "The greatest losers in the advent of technology are likely to be low skilled individuals who currently earn a low wage,"[44] exacerbating existing economic disparity.

"Historically, inequality has largely been seen as a social and normative issue but is now increasingly recognized as an economic issue. There is growing evidence that excessive inequality negatively affects economic performance in various ways."[45] The economic consequences of inequality range from political instability and economic uncertainty to high debt and financial instability. Inequality can also depress consumption and weaken aggregate demand, discourage investment, and slow job creation. Furthermore, high inequality often generates public resistance to pro-growth policies such as trade and technology.[46] Measures must be taken to ensure that robots do not unnecessarily contribute to growing inequality, for no economic benefit is worth the risk of such devastating effects on society as a whole, particularly its most vulnerable members.

The recent "stagnation of earnings, despite rising productivity, and the shrinkage of the middle class, because of soaring inequality, are without precedent in our economic history."[47]

This is due to the fact that "capital's share of national income has risen, while labor's share has fallen"[48] as a result of the digitization, automation, and robotization of the economy. Robot regulation should ensure that all citizens, not just those who own capital, reap the benefits of economic growth.[49] We must try to protect and preserve the vast majority of the population's ability to make a living through work. This may require a revision of the current system

43 "AI's central economic effect in the short term will be the automation of tasks that could not be automated before. This will likely increase productivity and create wealth, but it may also affect particular types of jobs in different ways, reducing demand for certain skills that can be automated while increasing demand for other skills that are complementary to AI," in Executive Office of the President, National Science and Technology Council, *Preparing for the Future of Artificial Intelligence, op. cit.*, p. 2.

44 European Commission, *Robots at work: A report on automatable and non-automatable employment shares in Europe, op. cit.*, p. 7.

45 International Labour Organization – ILO, *Inception Report for the Global Commission on the Future of Work, op. cit.*, p. 24.

46 *Ibid.*, p. 28.

47 International Labour Organization – ILO (Irmgard Nübler), *New technologies: A jobless future or golden age of job creation?, op. cit.* p. 18.

48 *Ibid.*

49 This is discussed in I. Cevasco, J. G. Corvalán and E. M. Le Fevre Cervini, *Artificial Intelligence and Work: Building a New Employment Paradigm,* Editorial Astrea, CABA, 2019.

of taxes on capital ownership and gains in order to harness the benefits of robotization.

B On the Need to Regulate Robots

As we have seen, the impact of robots on the labor market and the economy is considerable and will continue to grow in coming years. But this is not just a macroeconomic issue. Robots will create works of art, posing new copyright dilemmas; robots will commit crimes, requiring new solutions in criminal law;[50] robots will make automated decisions that affect people, and this in turn will create problems of justice and fairness ... Robots are going to affect every area of our lives, and the law must be prepared to address[51] the new legal challenges that will arise in each of them.[52] The real question is not whether robots need to be regulated, but how to implement that regulation.

We must decide "how to distribute human rights and responsibilities that arise from the actions of nonhumans,"[53] as we will be the ones using "robots and AI entities to create new things and to violate the legally protected interests of other human beings"[54] and corporations.

50 On this subject, see Gonzalo Quintero Olivares, "La robótica ante el Derecho penal: el vacío de respuesta jurídica a las desviaciones incontroladas," *Revista Electrónica de Estudios Penales y de la Seguridad*, Editorial Jurídica Continental, Costa Rica, Vol. 1, 2017.

51 On the law and robots, see Ugo Pagallo, "Robotrust and legal responsibility," *Knowledge, Technology & Policy*, 23, 2010, pp. 367–379. *Id.*, "The human master with a modern slave? Some remarks on robotics, ethics, and the law," in M. Arias-Oliva, T. W. Bynum, S. Rogerson and T. Torres Corona, *Backwards, forwards and sideways*, Universitat Rovira I Virgili, Tarragona, 2010. Silvia Díaz Alabart, "Robots y responsabilidad civil," in *Los robots y el Derecho*, 2018, pp. 99–114.

52 On these new legal challenges, see, among other sources: Isabel María Zurita Martín, *La responsabilidad civil por los daños causados por los robots inteligentes como productos defectuosos*, Reus, Madrid, 2020. Georg Kofler, Katerina Pantazatou and Alexander Rust (eds.), *Tax and the digital economy: challenges and proposals for reform*, Kluwer Law International, Netherlands, 2019. Covadonga Mallada Fernández, *Nuevos retos de la ciberseguridad en un contexto cambiante*, Aranzadi, Cizur Menor, Navarra, 2019. Migle Laukyte, "Social Robots: Boundaries, Potential, Challenges: Marco Norskov (ed.), (Ashgate, Dorchester, 2016)," *NanoEthics: Studies of New and Emerging Technologies*, Vol. 11, Issue 3, pp. 273–275. Fernando Miró Llinares, "Inteligencia artificial y justicia penal: más allá de los resultados lesivos causados por robots," *Revista de Derecho Penal y Criminología*, 20, 2020, pp. 87–130.

53 Moisés Barrio Andrés (dir.), *Derecho de los robots*, *op. cit.*, p. 85.

54 *Ibid.*

As Balkin, quoting Calo, reminded us, "We are still a long way from treating robots and AI agents as self-conscious rights-bearing or responsibility-bearing entities."[55] In the initial regulatory phase, we must focus on the automation of systems and decision-making by robots in lieu of human beings. "Therefore the key question for law – at least at this early point in history – is how to allocate rights and duties among human beings when robots and AI entities create benefits or cause injuries,"[56] rather than trying to come up with a whole new kind of legal responsibility for robotic systems.

At present, it seems unlikely that we will have fully autonomous smart robots in the immediate future. It would be unfortunate if legislators, trying to anticipate the conflicts arising from robotization, were to focus on such a distant and uncertain horizon. Today's robots may not be fully autonomous, but they are beginning to make decisions and engage in actions that clearly have the potential to benefit or harm people.

1 *The Legal Framework of Robots*

The legal framework that currently applies to robots was not designed with them in mind, and legislative amendments are needed in order to address potential conflicts. "Social change, whether technological or ideological, entails a change in the legal system. By this I do not mean that the system needs to be changed, but that it already has changed. When legislators reform the law, they are acting as notaries: certifying or bearing witness to the fact that something already happened. And when legislators do nothing, they are merely allowing tools of adjustment to spontaneously emerge in social life."[57]

Clearly, then, the duty of the legislator is to identify changes that are taking place, determine how they affect the legal system, and adapt it to those changes in an efficient, effective, consistent way.

a Adapting the Legal System to New and Emerging Realities

Adaptation of the law is a slow but steady process. A legal system cannot be overhauled in a day; it takes time to carefully modify and adjust legal concepts and jurisprudence, create new laws, or amend existing ones. "To lessen the negative repercussions of technological progress on present and future employment, it is vital for economic agents (both public and private) to manage the

55 *Ibid.*
56 *Ibid.*
57 Luis Díez-Picazo, *Experiencias jurídicas y Teoría del Derecho*, Ariel, Barcelona, 1973, p. 319.

challenges of the digital revolution. To achieve this, action must be taken on three fronts: education, the labour market, and redistributive policies."[58]

At this time, broad regulation of AI research or practice would be inadvisable as its impact cannot be predicted. However, it seems important to adapt existing regulation as necessary to account for the effects of AI and robots.[59]

Yet the changes made in each branch of the law will differ in terms of both scope and timeline, depending on when advances are made and how profound their effects are.

b The Need for Legal Certainty

The increasing prevalence of robotics and AI in everyday life and work raises a host of ethical and legal issues, which need to be identified and addressed in order to maximize the societal benefits of these technologies while also mitigating their potential risks.[60]

Many people are concerned about the unintended consequences of the widespread adoption of these new technologies. "Use of AI to make consequential decisions about people, often replacing decisions made by human-driven bureaucratic processes, leads to concerns about how to ensure justice, fairness, and accountability."[61]

One of the biggest concerns is safety – not putting people's health or lives at risk – when using AI to control equipment in the physical world, "especially as systems are exposed to the full complexity of the human environment."[62] Accidents could be caused by complex robots whose actions we cannot easily foresee, and legislators must therefore regulate the use of "kill switches" or opt-out mechanisms, as recommended in the annex to the motion for a resolution with recommendations to the Commission on Civil Law Rules on Robotics.[63]

One basic goal of regulating robotics is to "ensure that AI technology is operating as intended and that unwanted, or unpredictable, behaviours are

---

58 Observatorio Económico BBVA, "¿Cuán vulnerable es el empleo en España a la revolución digital?," *op. cit.*, p. 13 [p. 17 in English].

59 Executive Office of the President, National Science and Technology Council, *Preparing for the Future of Artificial Intelligence*, October 2016, p. 17.

60 House of Commons, Science and Technology Committee, *Robotics and artificial intelligence*, Fifth Report of Session 2016–17, October 12, 2016, p. 16.

61 Executive Office of the President, National Science and Technology Council, *Preparing for the Future of Artificial Intelligence*, *op. cit.*, p. 2.

62 *Ibid.*

63 European Parliament, *Report with recommendations to the Commission on Civil Law Rules on Robotics* (*2015/2103*(*INL*)), session document A8-005/2017, January 27, 2017.

not produced, either by accident or maliciously."[64] It is in the legislator's hands to impose an obligation of due diligence on designers and producers, so that they will strive to create safer robots.

Moreover, lawmakers should protect users by establishing a specific civil liability regime for cases in which robots do harm, despite all safety measures, by making decisions that are beyond the control or even the expectations of their creators. To date, the question of liability has mainly been discussed in the context of autonomous vehicles and autonomous weapons systems[65] (obvious cases of physical harm to people and even loss of life), but there are probably situations where the damage done to individuals is less apparent.

It may even be necessary to program smart robots with an explanation for their decision-making.[66] Transparency in the process of determining robot choices will be fundamental for helping us understand and perhaps even assign liability for their actions, especially considering that "instances of bias and discrimination being accidentally built into AI systems have recently come to light. [...] It is not clear how much attention the design of AI systems – and the potential for bias and discrimination to be introduced – is receiving."[67] Without a system of transparency, it will be impossible to effectively rid decision-making processes of all biases unintentionally given to robots by their designers or owners.

"There are inherent challenges in trying to understand and predict the behavior of advanced AI systems,"[68] because "it is currently rare for AI systems to be set up to provide a reason for reaching a particular decision."[69] Due to self-learning, it is not always possible to know why a robot reaches a given conclusion.[70] This is one of the things that set these new technologies apart: they

64 House of Commons, Science and Technology Committee, *Robotics and artificial intelligence*, Fifth Report of Session 2016–17, *op. cit.*, p. 16.

65 *Ibid.*, p. 20.

66 Executive Office of the President, National Science and Technology Council, *Preparing for the Future of Artificial Intelligence*, *op. cit.*, p. 2.

67 House of Commons, Science and Technology Committee, *Robotics and artificial intelligence*, Fifth Report of Session 2016–17, *op. cit.*, p. 18.

68 Executive Office of the President, National Science and Technology Council, *Preparing for the Future of Artificial Intelligence*, *op. cit.*, p. 2.

69 House of Commons, Science and Technology Committee, *Robotics and artificial intelligence*, Fifth Report of Session 2016–17, *op. cit.*, p. 17.

70 A case in point is the AlphaGo program developed by Google DeepMind. It managed to beat Lee Sedol in March 2016 by making a highly unusual move that led commentators and AlphaGo developers to think it had malfunctioned. AlphaGo was not programmed to explain the reason for that move, and therefore we cannot fully understand how the machine won against the game's best player. *Ibid.*, p. 17.

are designed, not to effect a simple action-reaction, but to analyze input and make decisions based on that analysis which are not predetermined in a linear way.

Transparency must become a fundamental feature of smart robots if we hope to successfully address liability and safety issues. The High-Level Expert Group on Artificial Intelligence, set up by the European Commission in June 2018, reached the same conclusion in its Ethics Guidelines for Trustworthy AI, listing[71] transparency as one of their seven key requirements.[72]

2 *Objectives of Robot Taxation*

While some industry representatives believe "recent calls for the introduction of a robot tax are unwarranted,"[73] due to the positive impact of robotics or the absence of negative impact, we must remember that taxation is not a form of punishment or reward meted out by lawmakers. Countless other activities with both positive and negative effects are currently being taxed, because taxes can serve non-fiscal purposes even though their primary objective is to raise revenue for public expenditure.

There are several possible reasons for creating a new robot-specific tax. The first is the state's eternally pressing need for more revenue to cover its growing expenses. There are two sides to this argument: one is the constant growth of public spending in a welfare state (regardless of the impact of robots), and the other is the increase in public spending and loss of revenue specifically caused by robots.

The second reason for taxing robots is the need to establish and maintain order, using taxes to implement policies that are not specifically fiscal in nature. In this case, the tax revenue would be used to encourage or deter certain types of behavior, with regard to robots, among taxpayers.

---

71 European Commission, *Ethics Guidelines for Trustworthy AI*, High-Level Expert Group on Artificial Intelligence, April 2019.

72
1. Human agency and oversight
2. Technical robustness and safety
3. Privacy and data governance
4. Transparency
5. Diversity, non-discrimination, and fairness
6. Environmental and societal well-being
7. Accountability.

73 "The IFR believes recent calls for the introduction of a robot tax are unwarranted given the proven positive impact of robotics on employment and wages," in IFR, International Federation of Robotics, *The Impact of Robots on Productivity, Employment and Jobs: A positioning paper by the International Federation of Robotics*, April 2017, p. 2.

a Non-fiscal Purposes

The term "non-fiscal" only has meaning in opposition to the fiscal or financial.[74] In general, it "refers to anything unrelated to the fiscal or revenue-generating purpose of taxation"[75] – in other words, anything beyond simply raising revenue.

Non-fiscal or extra-fiscal levies are an aspect of taxation rather than a particular tax category.[76] They serve the primary purpose of taxation by generating revenue, but they also serve a secondary purpose of giving direction and order, as one more tool that lawmakers can use to intervene in the market and society. Sometimes the non-fiscal aspect only applies to part of a levy. Tax incentives are a textbook example of fiscal norms frequently used for non-fiscal purposes, as long as the purpose is constitutionally defensible.[77]

Financial capacity can be modulated for constitutionally protected reasons, which explains why taxes with non-fiscal purposes can exist in our legal system. Various rulings issued by Spain's Constitutional Court – STC 122/2012 of June 5 (TOL2.579.439),[78] STC 37/1987 of March 26

---

74 María Amparo Grau Ruiz, *Sostenibilidad global y actividad financiera. Los incentivos a la participación privada y su control*, preface by Jacques Malherbe, Thomson Reuters – Aranzadi, Cizur Menor, Navarra, 2019, p. 44. Other noteworthy works by the same author include: "Responsabilidad social de la empresa: impacto financiero y tributario," in Isaac Merino Jara (dir.), *Entidades con valor social: nuevas perspectivas tributarias*, preface by Rafael Calvo Ortega, Ministerio de Hacienda y Función Pública, Instituto de Estudios Fiscales, Madrid, 2017, pp. 693–713. *Id.*, "Tributación y robótica responsables para una economía digital sostenible," Documento Jornada científica *Derecho Financiero, servicios digitales y robótica*, May 17, 2019, Málaga. *Id.*, "La adaptación de la fiscalidad ante los retos jurídicos, económicos, éticos y sociales planteados por la robótica," *Nueva Fiscalidad*, 4, 2017. *Id.*, "El Derecho artificial y la artificiosidad de los derechos," in María José Falcón y Tella and Juan Antonio Martínez Muñoz (eds.), *Estudios Jurídicos Multidisciplinares. José Iturmendi Morales, Maestro Complutense. Homenaje*, *op. cit. Id.*, "Empleo y robótica: la legitimidad de adoptar medidas extrafiscales para la urgente capacitación tecnológica funcional," in C. Molina, *La transformación digital de la economía y del trabajo y su impacto en los sistemas de protección social: Retos de futuro inmediato* (forthcoming).

75 María Amparo Grau Ruiz, *Sostenibilidad global y actividad financiera. Los incentivos a la participación privada y su control*, *op. cit.*, p. 44.

76 *Ibid.*

77 Elizabeth Gil García, *Los incentivos fiscales a la I + D + i*, Tirant lo Blanch, Valencia, 2017, pp. 149–150.

78 "Unlike taxes with a fiscal or revenue-raising purpose, in a primarily non-fiscal tax 'the *intentio legis* is not to create a new source of public income for strictly fiscal or redistributive purposes' (STC 37/1987 of March 26, TOL79.746), not merely to levy an outward sign of wealth or financial capacity, but also to dissuade taxpayers from engaging in certain behavior, shirking certain obligations, or, to put it in more positive terms, to stimulate or encourage a certain way of acting."

(TOL79.746)[79] and STC 186/1993 of June 7 (TOL82.209) – have confirmed that the tax system can serve extra-fiscal purposes, even though these are not the system's primary function, as one of the multiple tools the state can use to achieve the economic and social propositions enshrined in our constitution.

The robot tax has some similarities to non-fiscal "compensatory" levies, such as environmental taxes, which "are not based on the principle of supporting public expenditure in proportion to one's wealth, but on the notion that whoever harms the environment must compensate for the damage done by making a financial contribution that will cover, generically or specifically, part of the cost of environmental protection."[80]

A similar argument can be posited with regard to the negative externalities of robotization. Robot taxes could be designed to internalize those negative effects, so that the social costs of replacing workers with robots would be largely borne by the company making the replacement.

The revenue generated by such taxes could be used to finance a universal basic income or help workers adapt to the new job market. Yet this does not mean that it should be levied for these specific purposes. I believe it would be best to avoid this mechanism for controlling future spending, as it "violates the principle of solidarity enshrined in the universality of the budget."[81] Resource vulnerability, fiscal populism, and inflexibility[82] cannot be overcome by transparency alone, whose "benefits can be achieved by means other than taxation."[83]

---

79 "While the non-fiscal function of the state tax system is not explicitly recognized in the Constitution, said function may be directly derived from the constitutional precepts that establish the guiding principles of social and economic policy (particularly Articles 40.1 and 130.1), given that both the tax system as a whole and each specific tax concept are part of the instruments at the state's disposal for fulfilling constitutionally regulated economic and social purposes. Furthermore, said function is expressly stated in Article 4 of the current General Tax Act, according to which 'taxes, in addition to being a means of bringing in public revenue, must also serve as instruments of general economic policy, meet the demands of social progress and stability, and ensure a better distribution of the domestic product.' Nor is this contravened by the principle of financial capacity established in Article 31.1 of the Constitution, as lawmakers may consider extra-fiscal factors when regulating the *de facto* situation of a tax and not violate said principle."

80 María Teresa Soler Roch, "El principio de capacidad económica y la tributación medioambiental," *Tratado de Tributación Medioambiental*, vol. 1, Thomson Aranzadi Iberdrola, Cizur Menor, 2008, p. 101. María Amparo Grau Ruiz, *Sostenibilidad global y actividad financiera. Los incentivos a la participación privada y su control, op. cit.*, p. 44.

81 María Amparo Grau Ruiz, *Sostenibilidad global y actividad financiera. Los incentivos a la participación privada y su control, op. cit.*, p. 99.

82 *Ibid.*, p. 101.

83 *Ibid.*, p. 102.

Non-fiscal purposes may be legitimate, but they must be pursued in a consistent and coherent manner. It makes little sense to apply tax cuts for creating jobs while simultaneously offering tax incentives for research and innovation in robots that may end up destroying jobs. Research and innovation in robotics need to be socially responsible, and incentives of this kind should be contingent, in one way or another, on maintaining employment.

b Revenue Needs

The basic and ultimate goal of taxation is to raise funds to "help defray public expenditure"[84] and maintain the social services of the welfare state.

Aside from the general need for revenue, there is a specific need linked to the impact of robots themselves. "If the mass workplace for the people disappears in the future" due to the influence of robots, "from a tax perspective a double negative effect could occur. Firstly, significant tax and social security revenues would be lost," as there would be fewer salaries on which to levy personal income and social security taxes. Social spending would also soar, given the need "to support the growing number of unemployed people."[85] A robot tax could be one way to make up for "the decline in tax revenues that governments collect on wages."[86]

If tax revenue from wages decreases and social expenditure increases, "the conclusion is clear: governments will soon find themselves technically bankrupt."[87] If the mass arrival of increasingly technologically sophisticated robots means a reduction in current revenue for tax authorities or an increase in spending, the need for additional revenue should logically be met by the robots that caused it.

The possible impact of robots on tax revenue and government spending is still uncertain, as we have yet to determine exactly how they will affect the economy and labor market. However, we are undoubtedly facing a potentially serious problem. The following paragraphs explore some of the proposed

84 STC of October 28, 1997 (TOL9.382): "Taxes, from a constitutional perspective, are coercive payments made directly or indirectly to public agencies for the purpose of helping defray public expenditure," in Luis María Cazorla Prieto, *Derecho Financiero y Tributario*, 18th edition, Thomson Reuters – Aranzadi, Cizur Menor, Navarra, 2018, p. 195.

85 M. Mustafa Erdoğdu and Coşkun Karaca, "The Fourth Industrial Revolution and a Possible Robot Tax" (Chapter 5, pp. 103–122), in Irem Berksoy, Kutlu Dane and Milenko Popovic (eds.), *Institutions & Economic Policies: Effects on Social Justice, Employment, Environmental Protection & Growth, op. cit.*, p. 111.

86 *Ibid.*, p. 112.

87 Mario Segura Alastrue, "Los robots en el Derecho Financiero y Tributario," in Moisés Barrio Andrés (dir.), *Derecho de los robots, op. cit.*, p. 177.

solutions, such as measures for adapting to the new job market or a universal basic income.

i *Universal Basic Income*

Universal basic income has gone from being a controversial theoretical policy to a highly relevant economic and political topic,[88] with proposals tabled by everyone from US conservatives to the European Parliament,[89] practical experiments in Finland[90] and Ontario,[91] and even the rejected referendum in Switzerland.[92] In Spain, as a consequence of the pandemic-induced crisis, the coalition government of Unidas Podemos and PSOE established a guaranteed minimum income in Royal Decree-Law 20/2020 of May 29. This is not the same as a universal basic income, although there are many similarities. The biggest difference is that the UBI is unconditional and universal; the entire population is eligible to receive it, with no restrictions or requirements.

We know that "millions of workers around the world are going to be replaced by robotic and artificial intelligence systems,"[93] and that rising unemployment will go hand-in-hand with burgeoning welfare expenditure (more benefits paid out over a longer period of time due to steadily increasing life expectancy).

In light of this prospect, some "have argued for the need to delink social protection from employment by creating a universal basic income that would provide a flat unconditional benefit to all citizens or residents of a country, regardless of income."[94] This would guarantee a minimum living standard, irrespective of employment status, maintaining consumption levels while also allowing workers to invest in acquiring skills and competences for future jobs.[95]

88 On this subject, see the study by Francesca Bria, "Ingreso básico y precariedad laboral en la economía de los robots," *Nueva Sociedad*, 279, January–February 2019, pp. 114–121. Also L. Moreno, "Robotization, Europeanization and minimum income (EuVisions)," *Research Gate*, January 18, 2019.

89 Mario Segura Alastrue, "Los robots en el Derecho Financiero y Tributario," in Moisés Barrio Andrés (dir.), *Derecho de los robots*, *op. cit.*, p. 177.

90 Xavier Oberson, *Taxing Robots*, *op. cit.*, pp. 163 and 239.

91 Mario Segura Alastrue, "Los robots en el Derecho Financiero y Tributario," in Moisés Barrio Andrés (dir.), *Derecho de los robots*, *op. cit.*, p. 178.

92 Xavier Oberson, *Taxing Robots*, *op. cit.*, p. 163.

93 Mario Segura Alastrue, "Los robots en el Derecho Financiero y Tributario," in Moisés Barrio Andrés (dir.), *Derecho de los robots*, *op. cit.*, p. 177.

94 International Labour Organization – ILO, *Inception Report for the Global Commission on the Future of Work*, *op. cit.*, p. 21.

95 "Finally, the most recent debate on the future of jobs has raised the issue of 'basic income' as a counterpolicy measure. This would guarantee minimum living standards for all, irrespective of employment status, thus maintaining the consumption demand.

The key elements of universal basic income are as follows: the subsidy must be unconditional,[96] basic (sufficient to meet basic needs), universal (for all citizens), and individual (regardless of marital status).[97] The difference between this and a guaranteed minimum income, like the one approved by Spain's coalition government, is that the latter is usually conditional.

Advocates of universal basic income see it as way to eradicate total poverty and a deterrent against low-quality work, forcing companies to improve both conditions and salaries. Moreover, the fact that it is universal and unconditional makes it less prone to corruption.[98]

However, not everyone is in favor of universal basic income. The first argument against it is the cost, one of the biggest obstacles,[99] and the difficulty of implementing such a system: it is hard to know how much income is enough to be effective,[100] and identifying basic needs is more of a political than an economic matter.[101] Secondly, many fear that a universal basic income would encourage people to indulge in leisure and laziness[102] and take away their

---

Moreover, basic income is expected to strengthen the bargaining position of workers and wage shares, and by providing social security, it may strengthen incentives for workers to invest in skills and competences that may be in high demand in future labour markets," in International Labour Organization – ILO (Irmgard Nübler), *New technologies: A jobless future or golden age of job creation?*, Research Department Working Paper No. 13, *op. cit.*, p. 18.

96 "Basic income is [...] an *unconditional* subsidy (payable to every citizen for the rest of their lives, regardless of income level). The defining trait of this measure is that it guarantees subsistence, irrespective of the beneficiary's work activity," in Mario Segura Alastrue, "Los robots en el Derecho Financiero y Tributario," in Moisés Barrio Andrés (dir.), *Derecho de los robots, op. cit.*, p. 179.

97 Xavier Oberson, *Taxing Robots, op. cit.*, p. 163.

98 "Proponents argue that a sufficiently large benefit can eliminate absolute poverty, is easy to administer and is less prone to leakage or corruption. By raising the reservation wage of workers, the benefit can also act as a deterrent against poor quality jobs, encouraging employers to improve pay and working conditions. The idea of universal basic income has received strong support among some experts," in International Labour Organization – ILO, *Inception Report for the Global Commission on the Future of Work, op. cit.*, p. 21.

99 Xavier Oberson, *Taxing Robots, op. cit.*, p. 165.

100 "Basic income also attracts many critics. They argue that, in order to be effective, benefit levels would need to be sufficiently high. They also argue that they would be costly, difficult to implement and would displace spending on necessary health and other social services," in International Labour Organization – ILO, *Inception Report for the Global Commission on the Future of Work, op. cit.*, p. 22.

101 Xavier Oberson, *Taxing Robots, op. cit.*, p. 165.

102 *Ibid.*, p. 164.

incentive to work without truly addressing the structural causes of poverty and inequality.[103]

I agree with Oberson that, "despite many drawbacks, the idea of a UBI is worth analyzing further" if automation ends up destroying more jobs than it creates. Universal basic income is one measure that could help workers adjust.[104]

In my opinion, that future is still too far away and the drawbacks, cost, and unforeseeable consequences of implementing a UBI (as we cannot predict how beneficiaries will behave) seem to outweigh the benefits, especially as universal basic income is not necessary to maintain demand. Therefore, for now it seems more logical to focus on measures for helping workers adapt to the new reality, at least in terms of robot taxation.

ii *Helping Companies and Workers Adapt to the New Labor Market*

"The discussion about jobs at risk has turned into a discussion about shifts in required jobs"[105] and, consequently, in the skills needed to perform them and how the workforce can acquire those skills.

"The main goal to be achieved through the taxation of robots and processes leading to automation is to finance the training costs necessary for job loss to adapt to new business areas,"[106] so that workers who have lost their jobs can adjust their skill set to meet the requirements of new jobs available in or related to robotics. Flexibility is vital if humans hope to work with the technology of the fourth industrial revolution.[107]

Robot tax or no, workers are already "re-shaping the profiles and skills needed" to perform the jobs of the future. "Human resources policies and

---

103 "Others fear that such a grant would deter individuals from working, that households with adequate income would receive an unnecessary benefit and that a universal basic income would not address the structural causes of poverty and inequality," in International Labour Organization – ILO, *Inception Report for the Global Commission on the Future of Work*, *op. cit.*, p. 22.

104 Xavier Oberson, *Taxing Robots*, *op. cit.*, p. 165.

105 "A new form of flexibility will be required for humans to work alongside Fourth Industrial Revolution technologies such as robots," in World Economic Forum – WEF, *Impact of the Fourth Industrial Revolution on Supply Chains*, October 2017, p. 16.

106 M. Mustafa Erdoğdu and Coşkun Karaca, "The Fourth Industrial Revolution and a Possible Robot Tax" (Chapter 5, pp. 103–122), in Irem Berksoy, Kutlu Dane and Milenko Popovic (eds.), *Institutions & Economic Policies: Effects on Social Justice, Employment, Environmental Protection & Growth*, *op. cit.*, p. 112.

107 "New job profiles will emerge. Significant demand has already emerged in the space of cyber risk, cybersecurity and resilience," in World Economic Forum – WEF, *Impact of the Fourth Industrial Revolution on Supply Chains*, *op. cit.*, p. 17.

programmes need to facilitate the change and support the transition process if disruptions are to be avoided"[108] in the job market and especially in our economy. We must cover the cost of "learning new skills and adapting our education system"[109] if we want to seize all the opportunities offered by robotics and AI. A simple tax would slow down the robotization process, driving costs up and efficiency down, although the revenue it generates could be used to mitigate the undesirable effects of robotization.

Fortunately, the public and private sectors seem to be moving in the same direction, and "one of the most important steps we must take is [to ensure] that current and future workforces are sufficiently skilled and well-versed in digital skills and technologies, particularly STEM [science, technology, engineering, and mathematics] subjects."[110]

However, it does not seem that merely investing more in education and training will be enough to bridge the huge gap between the workforce's existing skills and those which companies require. "A growing body of research at the ILO, CEDEFOP and OECD aims at explaining the phenomenon that despite high investment in education and training, many enterprises cannot find the right type of skills in the labour market."[111] Although taxing robots could supply the resources needed to help workers adapt, such efforts would have to be carefully directed and focused. "Anticipation of future skills needs has therefore become a main policy advice to cope with widening skills mismatch."[112] We will have to spend more – and, most importantly, spend better – on education and training.

108 "They are re-shaping the profiles and skills needed. Enhancing capabilities is no longer sufficient, as new skills need to be acquired to monitor the technologies and master new production processes. Human resources policies and programmes need to facilitate the change and support the transition process if disruptions are to be avoided," in *ibid.*, p. 17.

109 "Though we heard a wide range of views on how the nature of work may change, our witnesses generally agreed that learning new skills, and adapting our education system, would help to ensure that the UK realised the full range of opportunities presented by robotics and AI, while also managing its potential risks," in House of Commons, Science and Technology Committee, *Robotics and artificial intelligence*, Fifth Report of Session 2016–17, *op. cit.*, pp. 12–13.

110 *Ibid.*, p. 13.

111 International Labour Organization – ILO (Irmgard Nübler), *New technologies: A jobless future or golden age of job creation?*, Research Department Working Paper No. 13, *op. cit.*, p. 22.

112 *Ibid.*

C General Principles of the Legal Regulation of Robots

The widespread implementation of robots will bring profound social, cultural, labor, and economic changes, which in turn will give rise to new issues of privacy and data protection, civil and criminal liability,[113] consumer rights, safety, etc., that must be addressed by the legal system.

The law will have to react to and at least partially anticipate those changes, updating itself to reflect the new reality. "The law must provide a legal framework of reference" to give robot owners and users legal protection, as mentioned earlier in this chapter; but "at the same time, it has an obligation to create forward-looking regulations that can boost the deployment of robotics and ensure that this field develops in a manner consistent with the values of the existing legal system."[114] We need to make sure that technological advances take place within our established constitutional and legal parameters.

As Barrio points out,[115] a logical model for legislators intent on developing robot regulations is internet law. This is an excellent point of departure, as a precedent in which the law adapted to technological changes. Today, with the anticipated mass deployment of robotic technology on the horizon, experts are debating "the viability of creating a new and separate legal branch: robot law."[116]

There are three different ways to view the substantive quality of this "law of robots":[117]

The first considers how robots affect traditional legal concepts and principles and attempts to update them to fit the new circumstances.

The second calls for a new legal discipline with new principles and concepts, creating a new law for a new reality.

And the third approach denies the specificity of robotics and sustains that the new challenges they pose can be overcome by existing regulations – in other words, there is no need for a fundamental transformation of the law.

It seems fairly obvious that robotics entails unprecedented changes which require us to review the legal construction of hitherto inalterable concepts.[118]

---

113 On this subject, see: María del Carmen Núñez Zorrilla, *Inteligencia artificial y responsabilidad civil: régimen jurídico de los daños causados por robots autónomos con inteligencia artificial*, Reus, Madrid, 2019. Domingo Bello Janeiro, *Nuevas tecnologías y responsabilidad civil*, Reus, Madrid, 2020.

114 Moisés Barrio Andrés (dir.), *Derecho de los robots*, *op. cit.*, p. 63.

115 *Ibid.*, pp. 64–65.

116 *Ibid.*, p. 65.

117 *Ibid.*, pp. 81–82, citing Ugo Pagallo, *The Laws of Robots: Crimes, Contracts, and Torts*, Springer, Dordrecht, 2013.

118 *Ibid.*, p. 82.

These changes, which are happening incredibly fast in comparison with previous innovations that required updates to the law, also mean that "fundamental concepts are becoming problematic as boundary markers."[119]

The first and second approaches seem to me to be the most suitable. The legal problems posed by robotics can be solved by updating existing laws or creating new ones: "a robot law that simultaneously adapts the general law and, whenever necessary, generates a new law"[120] to address issues that cannot be properly solved by merely refreshing existing legislation.

As for the idea of a "separate branch to handle robots"[121] with "academic and legal autonomy,"[122] while acknowledging the economic-social importance of said robots and agreeing that in conjunction they call for an independent academic discipline of robot law, I do not believe this should be an autonomous legal field.

In my view, such a field would have no basic unifying characteristic other than the robotic object itself. Robot law would therefore be nothing but an amalgam of tax, criminal, administrative, labor, and civil regulations on the same object which, though highly specialized, has no truly unique general principles.

Falcón[123] explained, "The unity of the legal system means that tax regulations are integrated in that system just like any other norm, and the fact that they regulate economic activity has no special significance other than the greater requirement of legal certainty derived from the monetary nature of that activity,"[124] and I believe the same is true of robotic regulations, which can also be integrated in the legal system just like any other norm, under the same general common principles of law. The fact that these principles are applied across different legal branches[125] and even with varying degrees of intensity

119 *Ibid.*

120 *Ibid.*, p. 84.

121 *Ibid.*, p. 83.

122 *Ibid.*, p. 85.

123 "The autonomy of financial law, and the unity of its content, is fundamentally based on the monetary nature of financial activities, which requires a specific administrative and monitoring regime and increases the importance of legal certainty." Ramón Falcón y Tella, *Derecho Financiero y Tributario (Parte General)*, *op. cit.*, p. 23.

124 *Ibid.*, p. 27.

125 "Certain sectors of the legal system are overlapping areas, common to financial law and other branches, either because the regulated matter has aspects common to multiple disciplines, because financial law uses legal categories or institutions established in those other branches, or because it is based on the general principles of those other disciplines." *Ibid.*, p. 26.

within the same branch leads me to conclude that the unity of the legal system trumps any aspirations of legal autonomy.

Academic autonomy may be established for other reasons – such as the socio-economic importance of the subject, the need to teach it separately given its complexity, or internal connections – which is reasonable, in my view.

1 *Principles of Robot Law*

"When we speak of the general principles of law, we are referring, *prima facie*, to criteria or values which are neither legislated nor customary."[126] Depending on the scholar, these principles are believed to stem from positive law, natural law, or a combination of both.

From a positivist perspective, "the general principles of law are norms obtained, via a process of abstraction, from the laws themselves."[127] These scientific or systematic principles are inferred from the norms by something akin to inductive reasoning. However, we cannot obtain the general principles of robot law in this way, as there are no existing regulations from which to glean them.

From the iusnaturalist angle, in contrast, "the general principles of law are simply the rules of natural law."[128] As a large part of robot law will consist of regulations on matters that have nothing to do with natural law (being artificial elements or legal fictions), we will not be able to extract clear principles this way either, except perhaps by opposition, to set protective boundaries for the rights of human beings. It is hard to apply natural law to something unnatural, and robots are, by definition, artificial inventions of humankind. Even so, we can derive some principles from the intrinsic nature of robots (for instance, principles regarding data protection).

"The general principles of law are the fundamental ideas that inform our positive law, contained in legislation and customs, and ultimately those guidelines derived from the concept of justice as it is understood in our legal system."[129] New arrivals, such as smart robots, must adapt to the society in which they land, and society in turn must adjust to their novelty. The legal field will have to follow suit, seeking principles in other areas that can be adapted or applied to this new body of law. The goal is not to come up with a brand-new

126 Luis Díez-Picazo and Antonio Gullón Ballesteros, *Sistema de Derecho Civil. Volumen I*, 11th edition, Tecnos, Madrid, 2005, p. 141.

127 *Ibid.*, p. 143.

128 *Ibid.*

129 Manuel Albaladejo, *Derecho Civil I*, 17th edition, Edisofer, Madrid, 2006, pp. 100–101.

set of general principles, but to use those that already exist in our legal system as much as possible.

The principles of equality and good faith apply, to a greater or lesser degree, in every branch of the law and can be implemented in the new legislation without major alterations. Other specific principles will clearly apply (such as the use of data by robots), in compliance with the European Union's General Data Protection Regulation[130] and its implementation in Spain, Organic Law 3/2018 of December 5 on Personal Data Protection and Digital Rights. In particular, the principles of lawfulness, fairness, and transparency, purpose limitation, data minimization, accuracy, storage limitation, integrity and confidentiality, and accountability are all obviously applicable and would hardly need to be adapted at all.

The principle of protection that characterizes labor law could be adapted to protect not just workers but all human beings from robots, both physically and legally. Regulations should prevent robots from deceiving, harming, or using people, whether in a work setting or for financial gain.

In this respect, the annex to the European Parliament resolution with recommendations to the Commission on Civil Law Rules on Robotics stipulates that designers ought to "integrate obvious opt-out mechanisms (kill switches) that should be consistent with reasonable design objectives."[131] Security and safety must underpin all regulations governing robots.

The precautionary and prevention principles could also be borrowed from environmental law. As robots may give rise to risky situations, robot regulations should be designed according to the prevention principle, requiring adequate surveillance and precaution to avoid potentially negative consequences. The precautionary principle would be linked to prevention, requiring the adoption of protective measures when there is a reasonable suspicion of harm (for instance, that a robot might pose a serious public health or environmental risk) even in the absence of hard evidence.

The principle of ultimate responsibility tells us that the final responsibility always falls to a person rather than a robot, at least until such time as an "electronic personhood for robots" is created. AI cannot be used as a shield to

130 Regulation (EU) 2016/679 of the European Parliament and of the Council of April 27, 2016, on the protection of natural persons with regard to the processing of personal data and on the free movement of such data, and repealing Directive 95/46/EC (General Data Protection Regulation).

131 Annex to the European Parliament resolution of February 16, 2017, with recommendations to the Commission on Civil Law Rules on Robotics.

deflect accountability. After all, there is always a human being – designer, programmer, manufacturer, vendor, user, etc. – behind the robot.

2 *Principles Inherent to Tax Law*

The principles of our tax law are laid out in Article 31 of the Spanish Constitution of 1978, specifically in Part 1, Chapter 2, on "Rights and Freedoms,"[132] and in Article 3 of the General Tax Act.[133] These constitutional principles are consistently upheld in scholarly literature[134] and case law,[135] with numerous rulings on their scope and application. However, some authors believe it is "difficult to argue the existence of other principles common to all branches of financial law and different to those that govern other public law sectors."[136]

These can be divided into two groups: substantive legal principles and formal legal principles.[137] The first encompasses the principles of generality, equality, progressivity, non-confiscatory taxation, and ability to pay, while

132 Article 31 of the Spanish Constitution of 1978:
1. Everyone shall contribute to sustain public expenditure according to their financial capacity through a fair tax system based on the principles of equality and progressive taxation, which in no case shall be of a confiscatory scope.
2. Public expenditure shall make an equitable allocation of public resources, and its programming and execution shall comply with criteria of efficiency and economy.
3. Personal or property contributions for public purposes may only be imposed in accordance with the law.

133 Article 3. Principles of the regulation and application of the tax system:
1. The regulation of the tax system is based on each individual's financial capacity to pay taxes and on the principles of fairness, generality, equality, progressivity, equitable distribution of the tax burden, and non-confiscatory taxation.
2. The application of the tax system shall be based on the principles of proportionality, efficacy, and limitation of the indirect costs of complying with formal obligations, and shall ensure respect for the rights and liberties of taxpayers.

134 For instance, in Juan Martín Queralt, Carmelo Lozano Serrano, José M. Tejerizo López and Gabriel Casado Ollero, *Curso de Derecho Financiero y Tributario*, 22nd ed., Tecnos, Madrid, 2011, pp. 95ff.; Alejandro Menéndez Moreno (dir.), *Derecho Financiero y Tributario. Parte General*, 15th ed., Lex Nova, Thomson Reuters, Madrid, 2014, pp. 73ff.; and Fernando Pérez Royo, *Derecho Financiero y Tributario. Parte General*, 25th ed., Civitas Thomson Reuters, Cizur Menor, Navarra, 2015, pp. 63ff.

135 See, among other rulings: STC 37/1981 of November 16 (TOL110.839), STC 211/1992 of December 11 (TOL81.991), STC 27/1981 of July 20 (TOL110.830), STC 150/1990 of October 4 (TOL80.402), and STC 182/1997 of October 28 (TOL80.402).

136 Ramón Falcón y Tella, *Derecho Financiero y Tributario (Parte General)*, *op. cit.*, p. 23.

137 Alejandro Menéndez Moreno (dir.), *Derecho Financiero y Tributario. Parte General*, *op. cit.*, pp. 78 and 88.

second would include the principle of legality or *reserva de ley* (non-delegable legislation).

Of course, these principles should inform all tax laws governing robots. The following section will focus on specific aspects of the ability-to-pay principle as it applies to robot taxation.

PART 2

Personhood

CHAPTER 3

Personhood of Robots

A What Is Personhood?

In order to analyze the personhood of robots – in other words, the possibility of giving them a legal personality – we must consider the concept of personhood as well as its historical evolution.[1] At first, the notion of person-robots might seem like a legal aberration, but a quick survey of the past shows that personhood has changed dramatically over the centuries, giving us an inkling of how it might evolve and adapt to Industry 4.0.

1 *Concept of Personhood*

Plainly put, "personhood is the condition of being a person."[2] From a legal standpoint, "a person is any being which the law accepts as a member of the community," and personhood entails "recognition of the capacity to hold legal rights and obligations."[3] However, being a person is not necessarily the same as being human. There are physical or natural persons (human beings) and legal or corporate persons, which can be defined as "human organizations formed to achieve a purpose and which the law accepts as members of the community."[4]

Scholars have long debated the exact nature or essence of a person:[5] some see it as a category that precedes the law,[6] and others as a category exclusive to the law. However, this debate has no bearing on the matter at hand, as the

---

1 On these topics, see: Miguel L. Lacruz Mantecón, *Robots y personas: una aproximación jurídica a la subjetividad cibernética,* Reus, Madrid, 2020. Pin Lean Lau, "The extension of legal personhood in Artificial Intelligence," *Revista de Bioética y Derecho*, 46, pp. 447–466. Franco Alirio Ceballos Rocero, "Otros sujetos de Derecho o personas (?)," *Revista de Estudios Socio-Jurídicos*, Vol. 22, Issue 1, 2020, pp. 321–351.

2 Manuel Albaladejo, *Derecho Civil I, op. cit.*, p. 201.

3 *Ibid.*, pp. 202 and 358–359.

4 *Ibid.*, p. 360.

5 This subject is discussed at length in Rafael Casado Raigón and Ignacio Gallego Domínguez (coords.), *Personalidad y capacidad jurídicas, 74 contribuciones con motivo del XXV Aniversario de la Facultad de Derecho de Córdoba*, Vols. I and II, Servicio de Publicaciones, Universidad de Córdoba, Córdoba, 2005.

6 "Personhood is not a mere quality that can be arbitrarily assigned by the legal system, it is a requirement of human nature and dignity which the law has no choice but to acknowledge." Luis Díez-Picazo and Antonio Gullón Ballesteros, *Sistema de Derecho Civil. Volumen I, op. cit.*, p. 213.

 | DOI:10.1163/9789004538511_004

existence of legal (non-human) persons is well established and accepted in the world of law.

Today it seems self-evident that, "from a legal perspective, it must be argued that every man is a person."[7] Any point of view that denies the personhood of all human beings can hardly be taken seriously in our time. The law recognizes the personhood of human beings by "acknowledging their natural suitability as subjects of legal relations [...], whereas in the case of personified organizations, it is the law which, deeming it convenient that they should hold legal rights and obligations, grants them a personality that it could have just as easily withheld."[8]

Yet we should remember that positive law, Roman law, other laws in antiquity, and regrettably even some in modern times have treated certain human beings as objects rather than subjects of law, meaning that they were not considered persons. The very idea is abhorrent to us now, but it has not always been so.

The legal system recognizes a person's legal capacity and capacity to act. The former is the legal aptitude of a person to hold rights and obligations (to have legal relations), while the latter refers to a person's capacity or competence to effectively perform legal acts, i.e., the ability to acquire or exercise rights and take on obligations.[9] Furthermore, "all men have legal capacity, which begins and ends with their personhood" and "is an abstract capacity, identical for everyone," whereas the "capacity to act [...] is neither possessed by all men nor equal for all who possess it."[10]

2 *Historical Evolution*

Personhood is not an immutable concept. It has changed over time to encompass a growing quantity and variety of persons. Even today, outside the realm of robotics, the concept seems to be evolving and spreading to a wider range and greater number of persons.[11]

---

7 *Ibid.*

8 Manuel Albaladejo, *Derecho Civil I*, *op. cit.*, p. 202.

9 Manuel Albaladejo, *Derecho Civil I*, *op. cit.*, p. 202; also Luis Díez-Picazo and Antonio Gullón Ballesteros, *Sistema de Derecho Civil. Volumen I*, *op. cit.*, p. 214.

10 Manuel Albaladejo, *Derecho Civil I*, *op. cit.*, p. 218.

11 Such as animals, rivers, or lakes. A recent example is the Bangladeshi Supreme Court's decision to extend the legal status of other living things to the country's rivers, whose rights will be protected by Bangladesh's National River Conservation Commission. Reuters, "Fears of evictions as Bangladesh gives rivers legal rights" [available at https://www.reuters.com/article/us-bangladesh-landrights-rivers/fears-of-evictions-as-bangladesh-gives-rivers-legal-rights-idUSKCN1TZ1ZR, accessed 27/09/21].

a Legal Personality in Rome

i *Persons*

In Roman law, jurists used the term *persona* – originally the mask that theatrical actors donned to play different characters – to refer to human beings in general, whether freeborn or slave. In Justinian's time, however, it was limited to persons whom the law recognized as such, those with legal personhood.[12] So, although it initially applied to all human beings, later the word was reserved for legally acknowledged persons, thereby excluding slaves.

ii *Foundations and Associations*

"Roman jurists did not theorize or come up with a definition of a legal person.[13] Different social entities [which were given their own personality over time] were called by various names [...], but there was never a technical term that encompassed all existing realities."[14] While the *civitates*, *municipia*, *coloniae*, and other entities had legal personality, this was not the case of foundations and associations.[15] Over time, the law constantly personified them until they were eventually given the consideration of independent bodies with certain rights.[16]

It was not until the early modern age that the legal personality of companies made an entrance in relation to the evolving concept of personhood.

iii *Slaves*

Given the exceptional position of slaves, as human beings who were considered things under Roman law,[17] they were part of the *ius personarum*, according to Gaius, and part of the *res mancipi*, according to Ulpian.[18] This duality

12 Manuel Jesús García Garrido, *Derecho Privado Romano*, 16th edition, Ediciones Académicas, Madrid, 2008, p. 131.

13 Antonio Fernández de Buján, *Derecho Privado Romano*, 5th ed., Iustel, Madrid, 2012, p. 192. On this subject, see also Francesco Ferrara, *Teoría de las personas jurídicas*, translation of the second revised Italian edition by Eduardo Ovejero y Maury, Reus, Madrid, 1929. Francisco Capilla Roncero, *La persona jurídica: funciones y disfunciones*, Tecnos, Madrid, 1984.

14 Antonio Fernández de Buján, *Derecho Privado Romano, op. cit.*, p. 223.

15 On this subject, see: Isaac Merino Jara (dir.), *Entidades con valor social: nuevas perspectivas tributarias*, preface by Rafael Calvo Ortega, Ministerio de Hacienda y Función Pública, Instituto de Estudios Fiscales, Madrid, 2017. Aitor Orena Domínguez, "Fundaciones: cuestiones sobre su fiscalidad," in Isaac Merino Jara (dir.), *Entidades con valor social: nuevas perspectivas tributarias, op. cit.*, pp. 557–586.

16 Manuel Jesús García Garrido, *Derecho Privado Romano, op. cit.*, pp. 137–140.

17 See W. L. Westermann, *The Slave System of Greek and Roman Antiquity*, American Philosophical Society, Philadelphia, 1955.

18 Antonio Fernández de Buján, *Derecho Privado Romano, op. cit.*, p. 238.

meant they had certain capacities reserved for *personas*, even though they were technically not persons, and this situation could give us an idea of where to start in our efforts to regulate smart robotics. Talking about robots in ancient Rome is not as crazy than it sounds.[19]

"A person also had to have legal capacity, which was denied to enslaved individuals."[20] Even so, slaves were not considered mere things; consequently, "although slaves lacked legal personhood and were classified among the *res mancipi*, at the same time they were granted certain faculties by virtue of their human condition."[21]

An interesting fact to consider when contemplating the creation of a legal framework for robots is that "the slave, who had no rights, could conduct business transactions and perform acts that would increase or decrease his master's wealth."[22] A similar solution could be adopted with smart robots, allowing them to perform certain legal acts that benefit their owners, but not giving them rights or legal personhood.

We could even let robots own a small amount of property, like Roman slaves: "Social custom made it common practice to let slaves manage a *peculium*, with which some were even able to buy their freedom."[23] It seems unlikely that robots would ever buy themselves with such a scheme, but the idea could apply for the purposes of liability or paying taxes.

The master's third-party liability for the slave's actions also evolved over the years. Perhaps the liability regime that applied to slaves in Roman law can serve as a model for a system of robot liability, never forgetting the obvious differences between the two situations.

Roman law distinguished between civil obligations, "which could be enforced, as legally required, by bringing a personal suit before a judge," and natural obligations, "which cannot be enforced by any court action."[24]

The first examples of natural obligations arose from interactions between slaves[25] and third parties.[26] Until creditors were allowed to sue the *pater*

19 Guillermo Suárez Blázquez, *Derecho de empresas en la Roma clásica*, Dykinson, Madrid, 2014, p. 219.

20 Antonio Fernández de Buján, *Derecho Privado Romano, op. cit.*, p. 317.

21 Manuel Jesús García Garrido, *Derecho Privado Romano, op. cit.*, p. 338.

22 *Ibid.*, p. 336.

23 *Ibid.*, p. 338.

24 Antonio Fernández de Buján, *Derecho Privado Romano, op. cit.*, pp. 565–566.

25 "The first natural obligations were those derived from business relations between enslaved persons and those who were free or had their own *dominus*:" *Ibid.*, p. 566.

26 "Relations established with third parties regarding the assets contained in the *peculium*, which cannot be regarded as civil obligations, are considered to generate natural obligations:" Manuel Jesús García Garrido, *Derecho Privado Romano, op. cit.*, p. 338.

familias alongside, rather than in lieu of, his servant,[27] slaves could only change the situation of their *dominus* for the better, never for the worse. Moreover, the owner answered "for the private offenses and damages done by his slaves with an *actio noxalis*,"[28] which entailed paying a fixed penalty, handing the slave over to the victim, or punishing the slave.

Perhaps a similar regime would work for robots; a robot could be jointly liable with its owner (thus ensuring that creditors will not be left unpaid due to the robot's lack of assets), and there could even be a limit to that joint liability based on the value of the smart robot, a manufacturer's guarantee, or insurance coverage (which could be made mandatory). However, all of this will have to be carefully studied and planned when developing the necessary liability regime for robots.

It seems that "the computer robot of today has replaced the human slave robot of antiquity."[29] In other words, smart robots are our new technological slaves. Curiously, "modern robotics attempts to replace persons with machines equipped with artificial intelligence," while in the ancient world people were replaced with servants who acted as "tools endowed with natural intelligence." As we saw in the first chapter, when I mentioned Karel Čapek's play, "there is a direct connection between the slave-robot of ancient civilization and the modern computer robot. It is no coincidence that the original Czech word *robota* means 'servant'."[30]

In ancient Rome, slaves were not just used to perform the most strenuous, menial, or disagreeable jobs. Businessmen often used slaves to manage and run their companies.[31] In the past, we used automated machines as mere production tools to perform heavy or repetitive labor, but today we are using smart robots to carry out more complex, more human tasks.

The simile seems fairly adequate if we examine it from a purely legal and economic perspective, setting aside the inevitable moral considerations which arise from the fact that slaves in ancient Rome[32] were human beings whereas

27 "The creditors of the son or slave could also sue the head of the household for debts accrued by his children and chattels. Thus, the *pater familias* was held liable jointly with, rather than for, the person under his authority." *Ibid.*, p. 343.

28 *Ibid.*, p. 338.

29 Guillermo Suárez Blázquez, *Derecho de empresas en la Roma clásica, op. cit.*, p. 219.

30 *Ibid.*, p. 224.

31 *Ibid.*, pp. 225–228.

32 On slavery in Rome, see also: Ettore Ciccotti, *La esclavitud en Grecia, Roma y el mundo cristiano: apogeo y ocaso de un sistema atroz*, Círculo Latino, San Andrés de la Barca, 2006. M. I. Finley and Antonio Prometeo Moya, *Esclavitud antigua e ideología moderna*, Crítica, Barcelona, 1982. Myles Lavan, *Slaves to Rome: Paradigms of Empire in Roman Culture*, Cambridge University Press, Cambridge, 2013.

smart robots are not and never will be. After all, a smart robot is a more or less skilled instrument, and the same was true of a slave in Rome, who "as a man was an intelligent being" but "as a productive instrument, let us not forget, was also a machine controlled by his master."[33] One intelligence is natural and the other artificial, but both are directed by a higher authority.

In ancient Rome, slaves were considered "items or goods with a monetary market value" and, at the same time, "productive and intelligent machines that could be taught and instructed." Slaves were bought and sold; their labor was their product, and they could be trained and educated, adding to their economic value.[34] From a commercial perspective, we have a similar view of smart robots today: they are items or goods with a monetary market value (productive and intelligent machines capable of learning).

And, as Ercilla García rightly noted, just as "there was a legal status for slaves in Rome, since they represented a significant part of Roman society and were vital to the economy, so, in the near future, our economy will depend heavily on the labor of non-biological entities capable of making autonomous decisions, giving us a very good reason to create a legal status for said entities."[35] Whether that legal status should be personhood (one specific to robots or a variation on an existing type) or an entirely new category (somewhere between object and person) is the question analyzed in this chapter.

b Legal Personality of Companies

"A legal person is a social reality which the legal system acknowledges as having or assigns an individual entity, separate from its constituent members, and treats as a subject of rights and obligations, with the capacity to act through its bodies or representatives."[36]

Experts have historically defended different theories regarding the essence of legal persons, from the fiction theory endorsed by Innocence IV and Savigny, which holds that legal persons are nothing but a legal fiction with no basis in the real world, to the reality theory favored by Gierke, which argues that legal personalities are based in reality and are not mere ideal inventions. The first theory relies on a fiction and the second on an abstraction.[37]

33 Guillermo Suárez Blázquez, *Derecho de empresas en la Roma clásica*, *op. cit.*, p. 230.

34 *Ibid.*, pp. 231–233.

35 Javier Ercilla García, *Normas de Derecho Civil y Robótica: Robots Inteligentes, Personalidad Jurídica, Responsabilidad Civil y Regulación*, *op. cit.*, p. 19.

36 Luis Díez-Picazo and Antonio Gullón Ballesteros, *Sistema de Derecho Civil. Volumen I*, *op. cit.*, p. 586.

37 *Ibid.*, pp. 587–588.

An entity is considered a legal person in the eyes of the law – even though, from a natural point of view, it clearly is not a person – for reasons of convenience. In contrast, the law recognizes a human being as a person for reasons of justice.[38] Positive law does not aspire to make legal persons human: personhood is nothing more than a legal category. Although it is a legal fiction, we are not talking about a fictional human person but about the aptitude of an unnatural entity – the product of a social rather than a physical or spiritual reality – to hold legal rights and obligations.

Legal persons have "bodies for shaping what might be called the will of the entity, externalizing that will, making decisions, and interacting with third parties."[39] These bodies may be one-man or collegial.[40]

The current understanding is that bodies have a monist relationship with the legal person; in other words, when the body acts through a natural person, there is an act of the legal person, as it cannot act as a separate, independent person. In contrast, the represented party's position with regard to the representative is dualist; when the representative acts, the act belongs to the representative, even though he is acting on behalf of the represented party, because the representative acts as a different person.[41] It is therefore clear that legal persons have both legal capacity and capacity to act.[42] "In theory, the capacity of legal persons is general and not limited to the scope of their stated purpose."[43] In certain spheres legal persons do not have capacity, as they are limited by law or their very nature.

Within the category of legal persons, depending on their internal structure, we must differentiate between "associations" and "foundations."[44] The former

38 Manuel Albaladejo, *Derecho Civil 1*, *op. cit.*, pp. 361–362.

39 *Ibid.*, p. 364.

40 *Ibid.*

41 *Ibid.*, p. 365.

42 *Ibid.*, p. 408.

43 *Ibid.*, p. 410.

44 On the subject of associations and foundations, see: Asociación de Profesores de Derecho Civil, *Asociaciones y Fundaciones. Jornadas de Alicante, 11 a. 2004*, Servicio de Publicaciones, Universidad de Murcia, Murcia, 2005. José Manuel Martín Bernal, *Asociaciones y Fundaciones*, Civitas, Madrid, 2005. María Teresa Soler Cantalapiedra (ed.), *Asociaciones y Fundaciones*, 5th ed., Thomson Civitas, Cizur Menor, Navarra, 2007. Alejandro Blázquez Lidoy and Isidoro Martín Dégano, *Manual tributario de entidades no lucrativas (asociaciones y fundaciones)*, CEF D.L., Madrid, 2012. Miguel Gil del Campo, *Fiscalidad de fundaciones, asociaciones y del mecenazgo*, 2nd ed., Ciss, Valencia, 2005. Juan José Marín López, *Asociaciones, fundaciones y cooperativas*, Consejo General del Poder Judicial, Madrid, 1996. Tomás García Luis, *Fiscalidad de fundaciones y asociaciones*, Lex Nova, Valladolid, 1995. Alejandro Rebollo Álvarez-Amandi, *La nueva Ley de fundaciones*, Centro de Estudios Financieros, Madrid, 1994.

are made up of multiple "persons" that have come together to pursue a common goal, whereas the latter are organizations of "assets" united to likewise fulfill a certain purpose.[45] Scholars consider that a category of associations are companies. Sometimes these legal persons are viewed as a genre and subtype, or as two separate types. I consider them two separate categories, because companies are for-profit entities with the possibility of having a sole proprietor, whereas associations are not.[46]

There are also entities without personality which, at least superficially, are identical to entities with personhood and yet "are not legal persons because, for one reason or another, they have not been granted that status."[47]

It is safe to say that today the concept of legal personhood has been warped to the point of becoming a mere financial tool for keeping one's personal assets outside the scope of potential liability. Once a reality that required personification, the legal person is now simply a tool of modern capitalism.[48] To drive this point home, I will merely point out that a sole proprietorship is a legal person created for the sole purpose of separating the natural person from their business activity and, in the process, shirking part of the responsibility it entails.

c Animals: From Chattels to Sentient Beings

"Animals are essentially stuck between two allegedly exhaustive categories – objects (things) and subjects (persons) – yet belong to neither of them."[49] This may explain the general tendency in the legal systems of our neighbors to increasingly consider animals as sentient living beings rather than mere chattels. Our society is increasingly sensitive to animals and their needs.[50] However, "the gradual growth in public awareness that animals are sentient creatures which may have their own interest deserving recognition and respect

---

45 Manuel Albaladejo, *Derecho Civil I*, *op. cit.*, pp. 370–371.

46 Luis Díez-Picazo and Antonio Gullón Ballesteros, *Sistema de Derecho Civil. Volumen I*, *op. cit.*, pp. 601–602.

47 Manuel Albaladejo, *Derecho Civil I*, *op. cit.*, p. 423.

48 Luis Díez-Picazo and Antonio Gullón Ballesteros, *Sistema de Derecho Civil. Volumen I*, *op. cit.*, pp. 588–589.

49 Visa A. J. Kurki and Tomasz Pietrzykowski (eds.), *Legal Personhood: Animals, Artificial Intelligence and the Unborn*, Law and Philosophy Library 119, Springer, Cham, Switzerland, 2017, p. 56. Recommended reading on the topic of this section: S. M. Solaiman, *Legal personality of robots, corporation, idols and chimpanzees: a quest for legitimacy*, University of Wollongong, 2017. Rafal Michalczak, "Animal's Race against the Machines," in Visa A. J. Kurki and Tomasz Pietrzykowski (eds.), *Legal Personhood: Animals, Artificial Intelligence and the Unborn*, *op. cit.*, pp. 91–101.

50 Proposed bill amending the Civil Code, the Mortgage Act, and Law 1/2000 of January 7 on Civil Procedure, with regard to the legal regime of animals.

in the form of laws protecting them for their own sake undermines the image of the world composed only of persons and things."[51] Recent attempts to modify Spanish legislation are based on the idea that animals are only partly subject to the legal regime governing goods or things. Their aim is to maintain animals as procurable beings and objects of interpersonal trade, but underscoring the need to respect them, in the context of human-animal relations, as living things.

We are clearly still far from the legal personification of animals, but it is a step toward creating a new type of regime that distinguishes animals from persons and things and treats them as non-personal subjects (before the law). Certain rights are given to animals to protect them from people (not as things or persons but as sentient living beings).

Kate Darling has suggested that it might be convenient to grant robots certain rights, "just as we have done in legislation to prevent cruelty to animals."[52] The fact is that "social robots have a human or animal form and can exhibit autonomous behavior which seems quite lifelike, and this triggers an emotional response in us."[53] "Another cutting-edge technology that casts doubts on the traditional dichotomy between persons and things concerns the rise of autonomous artificial agents capable of flexibility adjusting their conduct and reactions to the environment."[54] In this case, the goal would be to protect the feelings of people affected by behavior that *feels* lifelike (even though animals are living things and robots are not). Or it might be to protect the intelligence, however artificial, of robots because it is a quality we *perceive* as distinctive and unique to living things.

d Robotic or Electronic Personhood

We need to consider "the possibility that these machines (robots) could have obligations or even some type of legally recognized personhood"[55] as their impact on the legal world increases exponentially.

---

51 Tomasz Pietrzykowski, "Chapter 4: The Idea of Non-personal Subjects of Law," in Visa A. J. Kurki and Tomasz Pietrzykowski (eds.), *Legal Personhood: Animals, Artificial Intelligence and the Unborn*, *op. cit*, p. 54. A similar idea is expressed in Rafal Michalczak, "Chapter 6: Animals' Race Against the Machines," in *ibid.*, p. 93.

52 Alejandro Sánchez del Campo Redonet, *Reflexiones de un replicante legal: Los retos jurídicos de la robótica y las tecnologías*, *op. cit.*, p. 23.

53 *Ibid.*

54 Tomasz Pietrzykowski, "Chapter 4: The Idea of Non-personal Subjects of Law," *cit.*, p. 54; and similarly Rafal Michalczak, "Chapter 6: Animals' Race Against the Machines," *cit.*, p. 93.

55 Alejandro Sánchez del Campo Redonet, *Reflexiones de un replicante legal: Los retos jurídicos de la robótica y las tecnologías*, *op. cit.*, p. 29.

There are "automated" answers that put an end to certain tax proceedings, as stipulated in Article 100.2 of the General Tax Act. In current practice, these "provisional settlements" include the digital signature of the competent civil servant who, in this way, "accepts" the content of the issued order as his own. Whether or not that person actually reviews what he is signing is another matter. Perhaps there is another way to confirm that these "automated responses" are official government communications without the signature of a specific employee, in cases where this administrative task could be carried out by a robot. Maybe the robot could be granted a certain capacity. In any case, taxpayers should be able to file a claim, in fact and in law, asking the civil servant in question to confirm or revise that automated response, which would therefore be understood as a mere proposal.

Examining the similarities and differences between natural and legal persons may be helpful for determining whether robots can fit in an existing category or require a new one. We should also consider whether the figure is "alien" to our legal system or something that has naturally evolved from legal personhood.

i *Comparison of Persons and Robots*

It is often said that giving robots personhood only makes sense if they are comparable to human beings.[56] This argument is partly rooted in non-legal fields, specifically in the comparative study of human versus artificial intelligence. Without downplaying the future possibilities of technology, the robots that exist today cannot be equated with human beings or their intelligence.

Robots do not have biological origins. Although robotics has evolved and robots have often rivaled or even surpassed human brains when performing certain tasks, human beings have a more complete array of features and capabilities. What is more, they are greater than the sum of their physical substance and skills. A human being is a person, not because the law says so, but by reason of natural justice, as we have already seen.

Article 30 of the Spanish Civil Code makes it quite clear: "Personhood is acquired at the moment of live birth, following complete detachment from the maternal womb." Robots, simply put, are not natural persons; they lack the basic requirement of life, and therefore cannot be considered physical persons.

On this matter, most legal scholars agree that "robots are things: they may be quite singular, but they cannot be persons, subjects of rights. They can

56 Carlos Rogel Vide, "Robots y personas," in Carlos Rogel Vide (coord.), *Los robots y el Derecho*, Reus, Madrid, 2018, p. 17.

only be objects of said rights, singularly the right to property and any other real right."[57] Consequently, "it is a mistake to put smart robots and persons on the same level."[58] Any comparison of robots with humans (natural persons), whether from a metaphysical, biological, or legal perspective, will inevitably prove that, at present, humans are something different, and robots cannot be likened to physical persons or granted personhood in the same terms.

However, in the legal world, personhood is not limited to human beings, i.e., natural persons. Companies and foundations, for instance, can have legal personhood. Therefore, before categorically asserting that smart robots cannot be considered persons, we should see how they compare to legal persons and try to determine if they might fit in that category of personhood.

"Clearly, robots are different in many important respects from corporations. However, there are also many important similarities."[59] Robots have more in common with legal persons than with natural persons. Legal persons have no "life," can be owned by other natural or legal persons, need representatives to act, and are created. Therefore, if at some point we must go to the extreme of creating a robot personality, it would necessarily be closer to legal than to natural personhood, although the solution could range from an adaptation of "traditional" legal personality to a "new" category of legal personhood. While robots are not legal persons, they theoretically could be in the future, for unlike natural persons, "a legal person is […] a fictional legal figure."[60] And as such, a simple legislative reform could grant personhood to robots by creating new types of legal persons, as we will see.

In the future, robots may be so highly evolved that they are more similar to humans than to other machines, and they may even demand recognition of their personhood and refuse to pay taxes without representation,[61] but for now that scenario is only science fiction.

57 *Ibid.*

58 María José Santos González, "Regulación Legal de la Robótica y la Inteligencia Artificial: Retos de Futuro," *Revista Jurídica de la Universidad de León*, 4, 2017, p. 40.

59 Peter M. Asaro, "A body to kick, but still no soul to dams: Legal perspectives on robotics," in Patrick Lin, Keith Abney and George A. Bekey (coords.), *Robot Ethics: The Ethical and Social Implications of Robotics*, MIT Press, Cambridge, Massachusetts, 2012, p. 182.

60 María José Santos González, "Regulación Legal de la Robótica y la Inteligencia Artificial: Retos de Futuro," *cit.*, p. 40.

61 Xavier Oberson, "Taxing robots? From the emergence of an electronic ability to pay to a tax on robots or the use of robots," *World Tax Journal*: *WTJ*, Vol. 9, Issue 2, 2017, p. 261.

ii *Traditional Legal Personhood versus a New Brand of Personhood: the Possibility of Using Existing Types of Legal Entities, such as Companies or Foundations*

One of the options on the table is using a type of personhood that already exists for robots. For example, we could set up a company whose assets include the robot and whose stated purpose is the commercial exploitation of that robot. We might even create a foundation for the purpose of maintaining and developing a robot, as long as the robot served public interest in some way.

Existing types of legal persons, such as companies or foundations, could in practice be used to separate the robot's activity from the goods necessary for that activity and its outcome, making the robot independent. However, the person liable for paying taxes would be the company or foundation. The real actors would be the bodies of that company (general shareholders meeting and director or executive board) or foundation (board of trustees), although those bodies could choose to follow the robot's instructions in areas where it can instruct them.

Naturally, this does not mean that the robot has legal capacity or personhood.[62] But the practical effect would be similar up to a point, although there is always the risk of such formulas being used to limit potential civil liability derived from use of the robot, which may not be desirable.[63]

In some cases, the problem of liability can be solved by requiring insurance.[64] A robot works much like a driverless car and should therefore have at least basic liability coverage like that required for any vehicle. But in other cases, legislators may need to intervene. For example, the law could limit robot exploitation to corporations, raise the minimum capital requirement in certain cases, require the company name to include some mention of the fact that robots are essential to their business, or establish any other sort of requirement.

Naturally, within the European Union any such regulation must be harmonized. Specific legislation governing robot companies or foundations is quite likely to appear in the near future.

---

62 For a discussion of the topic of capacity, see Rafael Mir Jordano, "Capacidad. Conjugación de palabras, ideas y conceptos," in Rafael Casado Raigón and Ignacio Gallego Domínguez (coords.), *Personalidad y capacidad jurídicas, 74 contribuciones con motivo del XXV Aniversario de la Facultad de Derecho de Córdoba*, Vol. II, *op. cit.*, pp. 881–891.

63 On these subjects, see Silvia Díaz Alabart, *Robots y responsabilidad civil*, Reus, Madrid, 2018.

64 María Amparo Grau Ruiz, "La búsqueda de alternativas para la tributación de los robots: la tasa californiana aplicable a los vehículos autónomos," in César García Novoa (dir.), *4ª Revolución industrial: la fiscalidad de la sociedad digital y tecnológica en España y Latinoamérica*, Thomson Reuters – Aranzadi, Madrid, 2019.

iii Robotic Personhood as an Evolution of Legal Personhood: the Possibility of Attributing General Legal Capacity to Robots, thereby Creating a New Type of Legal Person

Aside from the possibility (which already exists) of creating a company or foundation dedicated to exploiting a robot, the robot could also be considered a person in its own right.[65]

Here I must briefly mention the origins of the corporation. As we know, general and limited partnerships grew out of merchant associations in medieval Italian cities[66] and the fact that commercial activity was frowned upon by the nobility and the clergy (who resorted to *commenda* contracts as they could not openly engage in trade). However, corporations are rooted in public initiatives, as this type of company was formed thanks to a government authorization which granted partners the privilege of limited liability and the possibility of issuing shares. The rise of the corporation is linked to colonization efforts and long-distance expeditions, as it allowed capital to be concentrated, divided into fractional shares, and represented by negotiable instruments.

The corporation became quite a phenomenon among seventeenth-century Dutch merchants. As Garrigues noted, the bold commercial sector in

65 "We must not lose sight of the fact that the category of 'person' apparently does not depend solely on the nature of things. This obstacle could be overcome by legal reform, given that the law has already recognized not only the personhood of natural persons but also the legal personhood of certain organizations or groups of persons and assets. It is not preposterous to think that, if necessary, the law might also recognize the personhood of these sophisticated devices." José Antonio Fernández Amor, "Derecho tributario y cuarta revolución industrial: análisis jurídico sobre aspectos fiscales de la robótica," *Nueva fiscalidad*, 1, 2018, p. 87. An insightful study on the topic of robots as persons is Robert van den Hoven van Genderen, "Do We Need New Legal Personhood in the Age or Robots and AI?," in Marcelo Corrales, Mark Fenwick and Nikolaus Forgó (eds.), *Robotics, AI and the Future of Law*, in the "Perspectives in Law, Business and Innovation" Collection, Springer, 2018, pp. 15–55.

66 The "company" started out as a small family community, usually made up of parents and children or other relatives living in the same house (*cum pane*). The members of that basic community accepted reciprocal, unlimited liability for their business operations. The company was incorporated in writing, had a corporate purpose, and was entered in a trade registry signed by the partners. This new subject of law was invented to facilitate trade. With its appearance, the partners' individual creditors were held separate from the company's creditors. Medieval tradition favored unlimited liability for partners, as the company had originated in the *affectio societatis* shared by members of the same family. The *Siete Partidas* established regulations for a non-specific contractual company, whose particular content would be determined by the practice of its activity. See Juan Gigglberger, "Breves apuntes sobre la evolución de la sociedad comercial," *Revista Jurídica (Universidad de Ciencias Empresariales y Sociales, UCES)*, 14, 2010, pp. 43–58.

Amsterdam – the only free port open to all ideas – and daring Dutch seafarers blazed new trails for trade and industry. That adventurous spirit gave rise to new types of companies, consisting solely of capital contributions. In this way, the personal basis of the sole proprietorship and general partnership was replaced by the strictly capitalist basis of the corporation.[67]

These historical precedents suggest that a robotic personhood could eventually be established by specific legislation. That law would need to provide for cases when the robot cannot act, appointing a body to complete its capacity to act if necessary. This would entail creating a whole new type of person, neither natural nor legal but designed especially for smart robots.

If robots do acquire legal personhood someday, they would need to be able to operate in the legal world (and interact with tax authorities), which would probably require a supplement to their capacity, though always reserving the ability to respond to changes and unforeseen circumstances by reprogramming the robot if necessary. If the robot is exploited by a company or foundation, their acting bodies should be sufficient for these purposes. Thus, if robots do acquire their own personality, it seems that the law which creates that personality, or the applicable international treaty, ought to handle this matter, contemplating the need to complement the role of said machines.

iv *Robots' Capacity to Act and "Capacity of Representation"*

A more pressing question is whether or not robots could act on behalf of another person, even if they themselves lack personhood. If, in practice, a robot can make purchases in a person's name, perhaps – as a stopgap measure until another legal path is chosen – we could program that robot to use the person's digital signature, or even allow the robot to act on its owner's behalf.

While it may be expedient, this solution poses a number of legal issues. "No one can have a contractual relationship with a machine [...] because contractual obligations are personal legal relations"[68] and robots are not persons (in this scenario); consequently, here we would not be dealing with a contract but with a legal act.

---

67 The Dutch East India Company, established by merging eight shipping firms in 1602, was probably the first company to have the defining characteristics of a modern corporation. It was followed by the Dutch West India Company in 1621, the British East India Company in 1612, the Danish East India Company in 1616, and the French East and West India Companies in 1664. See Joaquín Garrigues, *Hacia un nuevo Derecho Mercantil*, Madrid, Tecnos, 1971, pp. 24ff.

68 José Ignacio Cano Martínez de Velasco, *La decadencia del contrato: El Derecho robot*, Bosch Civil, Barcelona, 2011, p. 136.

We can assume that someone who makes a deal with a robot is actually making it with the robot's owner or user, effectively treating the robot as a medium. This is based on the presumption that, when a person's digital signature is used, that person is acting through the robot. The same would be true of a robot making a cash purchase or selling an object. The person dealing with the robot assumes that they are actually dealing with another person who is behind the robot. When a machine is used to express the will of a contractual party – for instance, when we shop online – the result is a valid contract.

But this system is a fiction, because in reality it is the robot, not the person, who will decide what to buy, from whom, and at what price.[69] The problem is that there is no genuine consent or agreement. There can be no agreement because the person behind the robot is not exercising his or her will, and sometimes does not even know what is being agreed. Hence, no contract.

For this reason, it may seem preferable to have a more advanced regulation ground in reality that allows robots some sort of capacity of representation, which would be an improvement on the current situation where the representative is always either a natural or a legal person. This would give rise to a proper contract, lending greater security to legal transactions.

In this respect, it does not seem reasonable that a person who acquires a robot to do his shopping, maintain and repair his home, or manage his stock portfolio should be held liable, without limitation (including all current and future assets), as stipulated in Article 1.911 of the Civil Code, for obligations the robot incurs with his credit card when a software glitch or technical error racks up clearly unintentional expenditures.

It seems imperative to recognize this new legal regime of the robotic "capacity of representation" in positive law: the robot's ability to act for another, including the division of liability between the "represented" person and the robot's manufacturer or vendor; the proper way to accredit that representation (the willingness to accept actions performed via the robot); and the limits on the liability of the "represented" person and other liabilities that correspond to the manufacturer or supplier, or to whoever accepts responsibility for the robot's actions.

Therefore, the robot, like the slave under Roman law, would be considered a thing, a piece of property whose existence depends on the owner. Yet, again like the slave, as an autonomous and (artificially) intelligent entity, it would

69 I am not talking about merely following an order with specific parameters given by the person, as in that case the robot would simply be a medium, like the internet. I am talking about a situation where the robot decides, where it narrows down the general parameters given by a person or created by itself.

also be an instrument of its owner's legal activity, capable of conducting legal business for its owner (though not for itself).[70] All of this could be developed under a legal regime of robotic "capacity of representation," without going to the extreme of acknowledging robotic personhood.

B Do Robots Really Need Personhood?

1 *The Need to Give Robots Personhood*

Based on what we have seen so far, it seems fairly clear that "robots, given their interaction with natural persons in the real world, need their personhood to be acknowledged in the legal world, in order to be subjects of rights and obligations."[71] Or, if personhood is deemed unnecessary, they should at least have an appropriate legal framework. Both scenarios have more to do with ethics and legal theory than with practical or technical legislative matters. We must analyze each one separately to determine if robots really do need legal personhood.

Regarding the possibility of granting personhood to robots, the European Parliament uses the term "electronic person," but this is not entirely appropriate for a tax entity with a legal personality. "Cyber-natural person" or "electro-natural person" would be much more accurate for a smart robot.[72] I believe that the best term for a smart robot with a specific legal personality would be "robotic person," a new category to join the existing ones of natural person and legal person.

If we create a specific legal personality for smart robots, "we will also need to talk about specific content, namely, the legal rights and obligations that the cyber-natural person will *hold*."[73] This content will not only depend on the state of technology, and consequently the technological sophistication of the smart robot, but also on several fundamental questions which are at the root of the concept of personhood. I should mention some of them here, although the list is by no means exhaustive, and I will not discuss them in detail because they are incidental to the subject of this work and require an analysis of future events.

---

70 Javier Ercilla García, *Normas de Derecho Civil y Robótica: Robots Inteligentes, Personalidad Jurídica, Responsabilidad Civil y Regulación, op. cit.*, p. 23.

71 *Ibid.*, p. 18.

72 *Ibid.*, p. 26.

73 *Ibid.*, pp. 34–35.

Possible essential components of robot personhood include the subjective right to "physical integrity,"[74] the right to "legal capacity,"[75] the robot's "liability" and capacity for "guilt,"[76] and perhaps even "intellectual property rights" on the works they create.[77]

All these matters will have, if they are not already having, a huge impact on our lives with major social, economic, and legal consequences. But for the purpose of our analysis, we must focus on whether or not it is necessary to create a specific type of legal personality for robots in the field of tax law. The only rights and obligations of the robotic legal person that concern us here are the right to property (*ius patrimonio*) and the possible obligation to pay taxes. Both are highly relevant concepts from a legal perspective and merit in-depth discussion, but I will come back to them later.

In summary, "robots will eventually require a legal personality,[78] not only because of their autonomous capabilities, which allow them to make decisions based on self-learning or the world around them, but also, and above all, because in the near future, it will be impossible to ignore the social (citizens) and legal (liability) implications of their ubiquitous presence in a predominantly service-industry society with an increasingly aged population."[79]

2 *Robots as Taxpayers*

As long as they lack legal capacity, robots cannot be true taxpayers because there is not and cannot be a special tax capacity, as we will see. However, if robots are eventually granted legal personhood, they could be liable to pay taxes.[80] The following paragraphs will explore this possibility.

---

74 *Ibid.*, pp. 35–36.

75 *Ibid.*, pp. 36–37.

76 *Ibid.*, pp. 37ff.

77 *Ibid.*, pp. 54ff.

78 On the general subject of legal personality, see Rosa Moliner Navarro (coord. and author) and María José Reyes López (coord.), *La persona jurídica /Cuaderno IV*, Dykinson, Madrid, 2010. Francisco Capilla Roncero, *La persona jurídica: funciones y disfunciones*, Tecnos, Madrid, 1984.

79 Javier Ercilla García, *Normas de Derecho Civil y Robótica: Robots Inteligentes, Personalidad Jurídica, Responsabilidad Civil y Regulación*, *op. cit.*, p. 20.

80 Pablo García Mexía talks of "entes capaces no personales" (ECNP): "Entes Capaces No Personales. ¿Hacia una personalidad para los robots?," in https://www.automatas.tech/pablo-garcia-mexia-colaboracion.html (accessed May 2019), cited in María Amparo Grau Ruiz and María Yolanda Sánchez-Urán Azaña, "El impacto de la robótica, en especial la robótica inclusiva, en el trabajo: aspectos jurídicos-laborales y fiscales," UCM, 2018. [Available online at https://eprints.ucm.es/47523/]. Also *id.*, "Robotics and Work: Labor and Tax Regulatory Framework," in *International Congress on Technological Innovation*

a Robots as Entities with Personhood

If we want to give robots personhood and create a new type of legal personality, we must first make sure that they can effectively operate in the legal world and, specifically, interact with tax authorities.

If, as I said earlier, legal persons have gone from a reality requiring personification to mere tools of modern capitalism,[81] in the future the concept of legal personhood could become a mere financial tool for safeguarding private assets and placing the burden of liability on an independent robotic person.

For, as Díez-Picazo rightly pointed out, "personhood is attributed to entities other than human beings [...] for the sole purpose of defining those assets which creditors can claim [...] thereby limiting their liability."[82] In the same vein, Falcón y Tella asserted that "every type of person [...] has its own intrinsic characteristics which must be established according to the regulations that govern its actions and responsibility. But the attribution of legal capacity or personality by positive legislation always entails a certain autonomy of assets."[83]

Perhaps it would be more pertinent to ask if we want to limit the financial liability of robots to third parties. Do we really want to shield robot owners, manufacturers, or users from potential claims? Something similar can already be achieved simply by placing companies between the robot and its owner. In our case, the question is not whether we should grant personhood to robots in general, but whether they could be considered taxpayers if we do.

i *Legal Capacity*

Today's technology does not appear to require the personification of robots. They are still far from having all the capacities of a specific legal personality, at least from a technological standpoint.

Of course, the goal of robotic personhood would be to give robots the aptitude to hold rights and obligations (to have legal relations).[84] Such robots would be subject to pay any taxes levied upon them, just like corporations and

and Future of Work, April 5–6, 2018, Santiago de Compostela, Eprint UCM, 2018. [Available online at https://eprints.ucm.es/47718/].

81 Luis Díez-Picazo and Antonio Gullón Ballesteros, *Sistema de Derecho Civil. Volumen I, op. cit.*, pp. 588–589.

82 Ramón Falcón y Tella, "Los entes sin personalidad como sujetos pasivos en la Ley 58/2003, General Tributaria," in Rafael Casado Raigón and Ignacio Gallego Domínguez (coords.), *Personalidad y capacidad jurídicas. Vol. I, op. cit.*, p. 451.

83 *Ibid.*, p. 452.

84 Manuel Albaladejo, *Derecho Civil I*, op. cit., p. 202; also Luis Díez-Picazo and Antonio Gullón Ballesteros, *Sistema de Derecho Civil. Volumen I, op. cit.*, p. 214.

other legal persons. It would make no sense to give robots a legal personality and later not allow them to be taxable persons.

Tax laws would need to be amended to include robots as taxable persons (subject to existing taxes or new ones specific to robots).

ii *Capacity to Act*

Giving robots personhood does not necessarily mean they would have capacity to act,[85] which is a person's competence to effectively perform legal acts, acquire or exercise rights, and take on obligations.[86] We would have to consider the technological abilities, the state of technology, and, of course, the specific characteristics of each robotic person in order to determine the scope of their capacity to act.

If a robot is not capable of performing legal acts, it does not need the capacity to act (autonomously). It might be advisable to give robots a supplement to their capacity to act, as both a natural and legal person, thus ensuring that we would always be able to respond to changes and unforeseen circumstances in society and even reprogram the robot if necessary. The law that regulates the machine's creation should also require the appointment of a person to act for the robot when it is unable to do so by reason of its software or design.

b Robots as *de facto* Entities

If robots are not granted personhood, could we still introduce a tax on robots? Can robots be required to pay taxes without changing their status from thing to person?

We must see if tax law can and should move ahead of general legislation by giving robots a special tax capacity and determining if robots can have

85 For a general discussion of the capacity to act, see: María del Carmen Gete-Alonso y Calera, *La nueva normativa en materia de capacidad de obrar de la persona*, Civitas, Madrid, 1985. 2nd ed. 1992. José Ramón de Verda y Beamonte and Josefina Alventosa del Río, *Derecho civil I: (Derecho de la persona)*, Tirant lo Blanch, Valencia, 2016. Ignacio Fernández Sarasola and Eduardo Sánchez Álvarez, *Manual de Fundamentos de Derecho público y privado*, Tecnos, Madrid, 2017. Ángel Carrasco Perera and María del Carmen González Carrasco, *Introducción al Derecho y fundamentos de Derecho privado*, 2nd ed., Difusora Larousse – Editorial Tecnos, Madrid, 2018. E-book. María José Santos Morón, *Lecciones de Derecho Civil Patrimonial*, 2nd ed., Difusora Larousse – Editorial Tecnos, Madrid, 2018. E-book. Mariano Aramburo y Machado, *La capacidad civil: estudio de las causas que la determinan, modifican y extinguen, según la filosofía del derecho, la historia de la legislación y el derecho vigente en España*, Reus, Madrid, 1931.

86 Manuel Albaladejo, *Derecho Civil I*, *op. cit.*, p. 202; also, Luis Díez-Picazo and Antonio Gullón Ballesteros, *Sistema de Derecho Civil. Volumen I*, *op. cit.*, p. 214.

financial capacity in their own right, rather than merely being signs of the financial capacity of their owners or users.

i *Special Tax Capacity: a Tax Levied on Robots or on Robot Owners? Critique of the Theory of Special Tax Capacity*

Under current Spanish legislation, certain robots already have to pay some taxes, such as the municipal motor vehicles tax. This tax is levied on all cars, autonomous or not,[87] unless legislators choose to modify the consolidated text of the Law on Local Tax Administrations (approved by Legislative Royal Decree 2/2004 of March 5) by increasing the tax burden on driverless vehicles or reducing or even eliminating it as an incentive to buy them. The same is true of VAT, to which robots are subject when they are bought or sold.

So, there is already some taxation on robots. But should the robots themselves have to pay tax? Can they pay, without some kind of legal personality? In the case of an autonomous vehicle, the taxpayer would not be the robot but the natural or legal person "in whose name it is registered," as Article 94 of the aforementioned consolidated text clearly states. But what happens if, when these cars are allowed to drive, they are registered to themselves rather than to a person? The taxpayer would probably be the owner or user. However, this raises the question of whether the car or, more broadly, any type of smart robot, could be considered an entity for the purposes of Article 35.4 of the Spanish General Tax Act – in other words, could there be a special kind of tax capacity for robots?

The old theory of special tax capacity states that, in addition to natural and legal persons, other entities without legal capacity under general ordinary law but specifically identified in tax law can be considered taxable persons. To put it another way, tax legislation can give entities lacking legal capacity a special capacity which allows them to be taxpayers.

At first glance, this special tax capacity might seem like the ideal way to tax robots and require payment from them as well. However, I do not believe this special tax capacity actually exists. It simply cannot exist. And without it, robots cannot be taxable persons unless they are first granted personhood. This is true for two reasons, which Berliri pointed out years ago.[88] Firstly, from

87 In California, the 2018 Transportation Assistance Funding Act made it possible to create specific taxes on driverless cars.

88 Luigi Vittorio Berliri, "Note alla Decisione della Commissione centrale per le imposte dirette" (November 22, 1939), no. 19.471, *Giurisprudenza delle Imposte Dirette*, 1940, pp. 495ff.; *Id.*, "Capacità giuridica tributaria o concurso di debitori d'imposta?," *Rivista Italiana di Diritto Finanziario, 1940*, p. 237. A similar opinion was expressed by Antonio Berliri, *Principi*, vol. 1, Giuffrè, Milan, 1952, pp. 180ff., although this author later changed

a practical perspective, it makes no sense to say that someone has special tax capacity (the obligation to pay taxes) if, under ordinary law, they are unable to own the money and assets necessary to pay those taxes or incur debt if they fail to pay.[89] Secondly, from a theoretical point of view, the concepts of personhood and legal capacity pertain to the realm of general legal theory and, as such, have unambiguous meaning in every branch of the law. It therefore seems that "there is nothing peculiar or unique in the field of tax law regarding recognition of the legal capacity or personality of robots."[90]

The fact that Spain's "tax law has expressly granted taxpayer status to entities without legal personhood" reflects a "commendable zeal to quickly adapt to the new economic reality so that no sign of wealth can avoid taxation under the pretext of lacking personality."[91]

Yet this "haste has led tax legislators to lump together all entities without personality, while the private field has wisely devised a legal regime of action and liability tailored to each type of *subject*."[92]

These entities without personality are always natural or legal persons, albeit under a special regime of action and liability. *De facto* entities "are also, and fundamentally, subjects of private legal relations. And if there is one criticism to be made of tax law, it is not that it expands the scope of legal capacity in comparison with ordinary law (which it does not), but rather its ignorance of the relations that prevail in other sectors of the legal system."[93] Obviously, "*de facto* entities do not materialize in our society and economy for the purpose of paying taxes. Tax legislation does not create them." Entities without personality "already exist in the relations governed by private law," and "if tax legislators take notice of them [...] it is only because those entities [...] own assets,

---

his mind in *Il testo unico delle imposte dirette*, Giuffrè, Milan, 1960, in light of Article 8 of this legal text, similar to Article 35.4 of Spain's current General Tax Act.

89 "It makes no sense to impose tax obligations on an entity which, in accordance with ordinary law, cannot own money or assets with which to satisfy the debt." Ramón Falcón y Tella, "Los entes sin personalidad como sujetos pasivos en la Ley 58/2003, General Tributaria," in Rafael Casado Raigón and Ignacio Gallego Domínguez (coords.), *Personalidad y capacidad jurídicas. Tomo I*, *op. cit.*, p. 453.

90 *Ibid.*, p. 469.

91 *Ibid.*, p. 449.

92 *Ibid.*, p. 450.

93 Ramón Falcón y Tella, *Derecho Financiero y Tributario (Parte General)*, *op. cit.*, p. 223. *Id.*, "Los entes de hecho como sujetos pasivos de la obligación tributaria," *Civitas. Revista española de derecho financiero*, 88, 1995, pp. 657–670.

contract with third parties, earn income" and are generally "active in the civil and commercial sphere."[94]

In reality, these entities without personality are, in some cases (classic examples would be informal joint ownership or an unchartered company), simply two or more "persons who possess a common asset on which an initial tax must be paid." In other cases (such as when an heir is deciding whether to accept or refuse an inheritance), they are "temporarily indeterminate persons who own certain assets that are part of a separate estate (in the example provided, that separate estate is the sum of inherited assets pending acceptance)".[95] Tax law uses "inaccurately the term 'taxpayer' to refer to a *de facto* entity or inheritance pending acceptance, when it actually means "the personal or subjective element that gives rise to tax liability." The law assigns taxpayer status to "the natural or legal persons comprising that entity"[96] or the temporarily indeterminate heir[97] in order to clearly delimit which assets will be used to fulfill the obligation.

As we can see, robots do not fit either of these categories. A robot is not a group of two or more persons, nor is it a temporarily indeterminate person. It is something else entirely. Therefore, robots are not and cannot be grouped with the entities without personality mentioned in Article 35.4 of the General Tax Act, much less assigned a special tax capacity that does not even exist. We cannot adopt this highly questionable legislative solution, for although the case of robots may seem similar at first glance, with artificial intelligence the problem is not identifying assets to fulfill a tax obligation but personification.

ii *Owners, Users, and Manufacturers as Taxpayers*

It would be a different matter if a law established a tax on smart robots and specifically assigned tax liability to its owners, users, or manufacturers. There is no impediment to levying such a tax, beyond the usual obstacles (double taxation, for instance) that legislators face when creating a new tax.

In the current scenario, and without further regulatory amendments, if lawmakers establish that certain smart robots must pay a tax, this would be

94 Ramón Falcón y Tella, "Los entes sin personalidad como sujetos pasivos en la Ley 58/2003, General Tributaria," in Rafael Casado Raigón and Ignacio Gallego Domínguez (coords.), *Personalidad y capacidad jurídicas. Tomo I*, *op. cit.*, p. 449.

95 Ramón Falcón y Tella, *Derecho Financiero y Tributario (Parte General)*, *op. cit.*, p. 224.

96 Ramón Falcón y Tella, "Los entes sin personalidad como sujetos pasivos en la Ley 58/2003, General Tributaria," in Rafael Casado Raigón and Ignacio Gallego Domínguez (coords.), *Personalidad y capacidad jurídicas. Tomo I*, *op. cit.*, p. 454.

97 *Ibid.*, p. 460.

interpreted as a tax payable by their owners, authorized users, or other persons. This would be a quick and easy way of designating a taxable person, either natural or legal. It could boil down to a simple issue of legislative interpretation, because ultimately a person would always be liable to pay the tax.

iii *Financial Capacity and Ability to Pay*

We have already ruled out the possibility of robots acquiring legal capacity, in the short or medium term, without giving them a specific legal personality (which does not seem necessary yet). But they could acquire it in the future. Today robots can already be taxed, at least indirectly, by taxing their owners or users, including the companies or foundations established for that purpose.

This raises the question of whether robots should pay a levy similar to personal or corporate income tax.[98] More specifically, are robots able to contribute, in the sense of Article 31.1 of the Spanish constitution,[99] and therefore obligated to pay taxes?

The answer is no, in my opinion. Business owners who use robots increase their profits thanks to the machines' "work" and high productivity, but they already pay personal or corporate income tax on those additional earnings.[100] As we will see in later chapters, robots are already "levied" via personal, corporate, or non-resident income tax; like any other asset, the tax liability of robots depends on how they circulate and operate in the legal and economic system.

It makes no sense to create a tax on robots merely because they replaced workers who stopped paying income and social security tax. However, there may be compelling social, political, or budgetary arguments for creating a tax on "robot income" to serve perfectly valid non-fiscal purposes.

---

98 This is what Bill Gates seemed to be suggesting in Kevin J. Delanay, "The robot that takes your job should pay taxes, says Bill Gates," February 17, 2017, *Quartz* (qz.com) [available at https://qz.com/911968/bill-gates-the-robot-that-takes-your-job-should-pay-taxes/] (accessed May 2019).

99 Art. 31.1 "Everyone shall contribute to sustain public expenditure according to their financial capacity through a fair tax system based on the principles of equality and progressive taxation, which in no case shall be of a confiscatory scope."

100 "Robots are simply capital goods, tangible assets, and should be taxed and treated accordingly in accounting. If a robot replaces a human worker, from the fiscal point of view a salary expense is replaced by a depreciation expense, which can always be worked into a fiscal plan by taking advantage of free depreciation incentives or accelerated depreciation through financial leasing contracts." César García Novoa, "La tributación de los robots y el futurismo fiscal," *Taxlandia*, April 17, 2018. [Available at https://www.politicafiscal.es/cesar-garcia-novoa/la-tributacion-de-los-robots-y-el-futurismo-fiscal] (accessed May 2019).

Finally, I must point out that, while robots have no financial capacity of their own, they do show clear signs of the financial capacity of their owners, users, buyers, and sellers. Like any other asset with market value, robots are indicators of wealth.

The ability to pay is an individual attribute of a natural person. If companies and other legal persons and entities are taxed, it is largely because otherwise income could remain in the company indefinitely and thus avoid or defer taxation without just cause. Therefore, I can only conclude that, if robots one day acquire legal personhood – i.e., general tax capacity – and are able to accumulate wealth in their own name, they will probably need to be taxed to make sure that robots are not used to defer or evade taxation. But until that happens, I see no solid justification for levying such a tax.[101]

In reality, those who support the creation of a robot tax do not base their argument on a special tax capacity or "electronic ability to pay,"[102] but on its usefulness as a non-fiscal means of keeping tax revenue up despite the loss of jobs, and perhaps even of creating a universal basic income.

The benefits of this approach are debatable. Facts show that unemployment is relatively lower in countries with more robots, like Germany and Japan. As stated in the previous chapter, although the impact of robots is obvious, their consequences are less so. If it comes to that, the law will have to determine how to structure and implement that tax in order to frame it correctly in our tax legislation system, with no problems of anachronism, jurisdiction, or legal certainty.

Designing that robot tax will also be a daunting challenge, given the difficulty of measuring the labor replaced by a robot.[103] We will take a closer look at this issue in the following chapters.

---

101 Even if an exception were made and one robot was granted personhood (for instance, a robot sent on a space colonizing mission), legislators might deem it preferable to grant a tax exemption in that case, to ensure that all generated wealth would be put toward the robot's goal, which is presumably in the public interest. Income tax only seems necessary if robots are generally granted legal personhood, which right now is a very remote possibility.

102 Phrase coined by the Geneva-based Professor Xavier Oberson, "Taxing robots? From the emergence of an electronic ability to pay to a tax on robots or the use of robots," *Aktuelle Juristische Praxis* (AJP) / *Pratique Juridique Actuelle* (PJA), 2, 2017, pp. 232–239; and *Id.*, "Taxer les robots? L'émergence d'une capacité contributive électronique," *World Tax Journal*, WTJ, Vol. 9, Issue 2, 2017, pp. 249–261; translated into Spanish by Antón Beiras, in *Taxlandia,* May 16 and 22, 2018.

103 "The idea of establishing the taxable base of this robot tax with reference to the salary of the worker being replaced is a proposal that does not consider how technology is incorporated in companies. A robot rarely steps in for a specific worker; the substitution is usually

C Conclusions

Just as a specific legal status was granted to slaves under Roman law, so the proposal of granting a specific legal personality to robots takes into account their "autonomous" abilities as well as their steadily growing impact on social and economic life.

The regulation of slavery in ancient Rome can serve as a basis for constructing a legal regime that grants robots a "capacity of representation" (for conducting certain legal business) while continuing to recognize these artificial agents as goods. This solution would shatter the traditional dichotomy between persons and things.

Robots are not comparable to natural persons and cannot be granted personhood in those terms. Robotic personhood would need to be either an adaptation of traditional legal personhood or a new type of legal personality, which is theoretically possible as juridical personhood is a legal fiction. Moreover, we would have to make sure that they can effectively operate in the legal world, which would probably require supplementing their capacity to act.

If robots do acquire personhood, they could become taxable persons and therefore liable to pay taxes levied on them. Without a legal personality they cannot be treated as taxpayers, as there is no special tax capacity in this case. If legislators refer to them as taxpayers in a legal text, this should be understood as an abbreviated allusion to a person, not to the robots themselves.

---

made by production sectors and often affects auxiliary companies, which are separate taxpayers, instead of the company incorporating the robot. Therefore, it is no easy feat to determine exactly which worker a robot displaces. But the biggest drawback is that this measure would have the perverse effect of encouraging companies to replace less skilled workers with robots. Such workers are paid less, meaning the company would have to pay less tax when their jobs are replaced." César García Novoa, "La tributación de los robots y el futurismo fiscal," *Taxlandia*, April 17, 2018. [Available at https://www.politicafiscal.es/cesar-garcia-novoa/la-tributacion-de-los-robots-y-el-futurismo-fiscal] (accessed May 2019).

PART 3

Taxation and Robotics

CHAPTER 4

Current Tax Treatment of Robots

In this chapter, I will analyze the incorporation of persons and robots in the production process, comparing the different tax effects of using robots and hiring human workers. I will also try to identify the consequences of those differences and determine whether they reflect the legislator's intent in accordance with constitutional mandates. This chapter attempts to summarize all tax aspects that currently apply to robotics.[1]

A Comparison of the Tax Situations of Robots and Workers

"Worker automation is often thought of as a matter of efficiency, where efficiency refers to the *ratio* of useful output to total input."[2] This means that, if

1 On the subject of taxation and robots, see the recent work by Fernando Serrano Antón (dir.), *Fiscalidad e inteligencia artificial: administración tributaria y contribuyentes en la era digital*, Thomson Reuters – Aranzadi, Cizur Menor, Navarra 2020. With the following articles: – Chapter 1. "Fiscalidad y Robótica: funcionalidades disruptivas en el Derecho tributario," by Fernando Serrano Antón. – Chapter 2. "Robot y persona: Reflexiones sobre la capacidad económica atribuible a robots inteligentes," by Israel Santos Flores. – Chapter 3. "Soluciones fiscales a los problemas derivados de la robotización: especial referencia a España," by Jesús Rodríguez Márquez. – Chapter 4. "La sustitución de trabajadores por robots: impacto en las contribuciones a la Seguridad Social y su posible financiación por tributos," by Miguel de Haro Izquierdo. – Chapter 5. "Inteligencia Artificial y Administración tributaria," by Ubaldo González de Frutos. – Chapter 6. "Big Data y la gestión tributaria," by Javier Hurtado Puerta. – Chapter 7. "Algunas aplicaciones de la inteligencia artificial en la Administración tributaria," by Santiago Segarra. – Chapter 8. "El uso de la Inteligencia Artificial y el análisis de información en la Agencia Tributaria," by José Borja Tomé. – Chapter 9. "Derechos y garantías de los contribuyentes en la cuarta revolución industrial: Aproximación desde las transformaciones de la relación jurídica tributaria en la era de la inteligencia artificial," by Adolfo A. Iriarte Yanicelli. – Chapter 10. "El uso del big data y la inteligencia artificial por las Administraciones tributarias en la lucha contra el fraude fiscal. Particular referencia a los principios que han de regirla y a los derechos de los contribuyentes," by Cristina García-Herrera Blanco. – Chapter 11. "Operaciones en red, impacto del blockchain y los smartcontract: Oportunidades de negocio, uso de las plataformas en red, en la era de las aplicaciones, y la tecnología 5G," by Ramón Bonell Colmenero. See also Juan José Hinojosa Torralbo and Ignacio Cruz Padial (dirs.), Guillermo Sánchez-Archidona Hidalgo (coord.), *Tributos, servicios digitales y robótica*, Thomson Reuters – Aranzadi, Cizur Menor, Navarra, 2020.

2 Ryan Benjamin Abbott and Bret Bogenschneider, "Should Robots Pay Taxes? Tax Policy in the Age of Automation," *Harvard Law & Policy Review*, Vol. 12 – 1, 2018, p. 163.

 | DOI:10.1163/9789004538511_005

a worker costs the company the same as a robot but is less productive (or if a worker costs more than a machine but creates the same output), that worker is less economically efficient. To measure this efficiency correctly, we must factor in all costs associated with the robot: not only the money spent to acquire, repair, maintain, and upgrade it, but also interests (if applicable), operating costs (electricity, etc.), and, of course, all applicable tax benefits.[3]

A specific type of benefit, tax abatement, is defined in *Black's Law Dictionary* as a "reduction or exemption of tax granted by government for a set period to encourage investment activities," and must always be approved by law. As we will see, such benefits mean that the tax system is not neutral when it comes to choosing robots or people to perform work,[4] and in fact drives firms toward automation. "This is not to say that corporate income tax is deliberately designed to favor robotization over job creation,"[5] but it still has undesirable results. Giving robots an advantage over workers is not a non-fiscal goal pursued by legislators but an involuntary consequence of the fact that our tax system has not "adapted to a world where the technological innovation of robotics is capable of replacing a company's traditional human workforce."[6] We must therefore take a closer look at the laws currently in force.

1 *Current Accounting Situation of Robots*

Under Spanish tax law, robots are production assets that contribute to the turnover and profits of corporations and enterprises. Consequently, the activities of robots are already subject to taxation, but only at the level of the enterprises that own, control, or use them.[7]

In order to analyze the situation of robots under current tax law, we must begin with their legal classification for the purposes of corporate income tax. As Professor Fernández Amor rightly stated, "they must be categorized as assets."[8] Within the category of PP&E (plant, property, and equipment), robots can be considered plant, if they are permanently installed in or attached to

3 *Ibid.*
4 *Ibid.*
5 José Antonio Fernández Amor, "Derecho tributario y cuarta revolución industrial: análisis jurídico sobre aspectos fiscales de la robótica," *Nueva fiscalidad*, 1, 2018, p. 68.
6 *Ibid.*
7 Xavier Oberson, *Taxing Robots, op. cit.*, p. 44.
8 José Antonio Fernández Amor, "Derecho tributario y cuarta revolución industrial: análisis jurídico sobre aspectos fiscales de la robótica," *cit.*, p. 57.

a property (Civil Code Art. 334.3),[9] or equipment (Civil Code Art. 335).[10] As such, they are subject to acquisition (Civil Code Art. 333)[11] and the "exercise of different rights, such as the right to property or possession via different forms of temporary conveyance"[12] (rental, finance lease, regular lease, etc.), and are "therefore part of the total assets assigned to a business,"[13] thus becoming "simply another element of corporate equity."[14]

Including a robot among a company's assets would result in a conversion (of its own or third-party resources) rather than a decrease in the assets assigned to the business.[15] In the case of an "ordinary or operating lease, as defined in the Spanish General Accounting Plan" (hereafter SGAP), the corporate lessee would recognize it as an expense rather than asset; the corporate lessor would incorporate it as an asset, but "clarifying that it will be an object used to carry out its business activity" unlike the other objects not destined for regular commercial use.[16] And the society that owners the robot, having recognized it as an asset, gives rise to a situation similar to the inclusion in the production process of the workers it replaced.

The classification as a PP&E asset or an intangible asset will depend on the nature of the robot in question. As mentioned in the first chapter, I do not believe that robots necessarily require a minimal physical structure; the only requirement should be that they have an impact on the physical world, so applications and software can also be robots.

As long as a robot has some physical element, according to International Accounting Standard (hereafter IAS) 16 it can be considered property, plant, and equipment, "insofar as it is a tangible item held for use in the production or supply of goods or services, for rental to others, or for administrative purposes for more than one period."[17] If the robot is a softbot, i.e. a computer

9 Article 335 of the Spanish Civil Code defines plant as "anything permanently attached to a property in such a way that it cannot be removed without breaking the material or damaging the object."

10 Article 334.3 of the Spanish Civil Code says: "Equipment is any object subject to acquisition not included in the previous category, and in general all those that can be moved from one place to another without harming the property with which they may be associated."

11 Article 333 of the Spanish Civil Code states: "Anything that is or can be acquired shall be considered fixed assets (property, plant, or equipment)."

12 José Antonio Fernández Amor, "Derecho tributario y cuarta revolución industrial: análisis jurídico sobre aspectos fiscales de la robótica," *cit.*, p. 58.

13 *Ibid.*

14 *Ibid.*

15 *Ibid.*

16 *Ibid.*

17 *Ibid.*, p. 59.

program, IAS 38 tells us that we are clearly dealing with an intangible asset,[18] which would fall under SGAP account 206 (computer software).

The problem arises when a robot has both intangible software and a tangible physical support. The fourth point of IAS 38 addresses this dual nature.[19] Specifically, it states that "in determining whether an asset that incorporates both intangible and tangible elements should be treated under IAS 16 *Property, Plant and Equipment* or as an intangible asset under this Standard, an entity uses judgement to assess which element is more significant." The SGAP's definition of account 212 (technical installations) also seems to support recognition as PP&E: "Complex units for specialised use in the production process, comprising [...] machinery [...], including information systems which, even if they can be separated by nature, are clearly interrelated in terms of use and are subject to the same rate of depreciation." In my view, this account is more appropriate for robots than SGAP account 213 (machinery).

2 *Corporate Expenses*

As part of the production process, robots help generate corporate income and, although they also incur expenses, "contribute to the realization of the turnover of the enterprise and, as a consequence, of its profits."[20] Therefore, the profits to which robots specifically contribute could be calculated by subtracting their expenses from the income generated by those robots' involvement in the production process. Two of the biggest expenses are operating costs and depreciation. The latter is particularly relevant to our discussion, as none of the costs generated by workers are comparable to the cost of depreciation, making it a distinguishing feature.

As workers, persons are also part of the corporate production process, and therefore generate income and expenses for their employers, the most significant costs being salaries and social security contributions.

---

18 As argued by Xavier Oberson, *Taxing Robots, op. cit.*, p. 45.

19 IAS 38, 4: "Some intangible assets may be contained in or on a physical substance such as a compact disc (in the case of computer software), legal documentation (in the case of a licence or patent) or film. In determining whether an asset that incorporates both intangible and tangible elements should be treated under IAS 16 *Property and Equipment* or as an intangible asset under this Standard, an entity uses judgement to assess which element is more significant. For example, computer software for a computer-controlled machine tool that cannot operate without that specific software is an integral part of the related hardware and it is treated as property, plant and equipment. The same applies to the operating system of a computer. When the software is not an integral part of the related hardware, computer software is treated as an intangible asset."

20 Xavier Oberson, *Taxing Robots, op. cit.*, p. 46.

a Robot Depreciation

As PP&E, a robot is "subject to depreciation, meaning that accounts must reflect its decreasing value as a result of use in the production process."[21] This process "spreads the cost of acquiring or producing the element over its useful life,"[22] representing "the decrease in the asset's value due to wear,"[23] which will "reduce the accounting result of the business activity."[24]

Depreciation is tax deductible when it corresponds to the "effective depreciation which different element suffer due to operation, use, enjoyment, or obsolescence," according to Article 12 of Law 12/2014 of November 27 on Corporate Income Tax (hereafter LIS). This article establishes several effective depreciation methods. Adapting to them is one of the corrections to which Article 10 of the LIS refers when explaining how to determine the taxable base: "The taxable base shall be calculated by applying the precepts of this law to correct the accounting result determined according to the norms set out in the Code of Commerce" and its enabling regulations, including the SGAP.

Acceptable tax depreciation methods are set out in Article 12 of the LIS: straight line,[25] declining balance,[26] sum of the years' digits,[27] a depreciation plan approved by the authorities, justification of the depreciated amount,[28] and free depreciation.[29] It is important to note that "free depreciation is not applicable in all cases,"[30] but certain robots could be subject to free depreciation, which is why I mention it.

The depreciation methods applicable to robots give companies the freedom to decide when to reduce business profits and, consequently, the amount

21 José Antonio Fernández Amor, "Derecho tributario y cuarta revolución industrial: análisis jurídico sobre aspectos fiscales de la robótica," *cit.*, p. 59.

22 *Ibid.*

23 *Ibid.*

24 *Ibid.*, p. 60.

25 Regulated in Art. 12.1 a) LIS and Art. 4 RIS (Corporate Income Tax Regulation). There is a certain freedom of choice, within the set parameters of maximum depreciation rate and maximum number of years, both reflected in a table. As I see, robots could be classified in three groups: Machinery, Electronic equipment, and, of course, Other elements. Each has a different maximum depreciation rate and maximum number of years, which are shown on the relevant tables. Classification in one group or another will depend on the characteristics of the robot in question. There is even an argument for classifying an autonomous vehicle as Outdoor transportation element, like a regular car.

26 Regulated in Art. 12.1 a) LIS and Art. 5 RIS.

27 Regulated in Art. 12.1 a) LIS and Art. 6 RIS.

28 Regulated in Art. 12.1 a) LIS and Art. 7 RIS.

29 Regulated in Art. 12.3 LIS.

30 José Antonio Fernández Amor, "Derecho tributario y cuarta revolución industrial: análisis jurídico sobre aspectos fiscales de la robótica," *cit.*, p. 62.

of taxes payable. The company recognizes the expense (depreciation) and decides when to pay tax on the profit.

Accelerated depreciation allows companies to claim a tax deduction earlier than its actual economic depreciation, which is obviously a tax benefit.[31] As Professor Gil García observed, "Depreciation is merely a financial means of delaying payment of tax, i.e., a deferral,"[32] with enormous fiscal repercussions.[33] Therefore, "the choice of one method or another will not be based solely on how efficiently it represents effective wear and tear, as one must also consider the tax advantage of applying margins of freedom, spreading depreciation out over time, or using a specific regime which may not even correspond to the accepted accounting regime."[34]

Consequently, depreciation is deductible even when there is no real depreciation, either because the economic depreciation is less or because the robot's value has increased due to inflation.[35] In the latter case, like PP&E, it is presumed for tax purposes that the robot will wear out, but in reality the robot does not depreciate and actually increases in nominal value. This increased value only becomes a taxable profit at the moment of the asset's disposal, if that time ever comes.[36] In contrast, workers' salaries can only be deduced for the tax year in which they are paid.

This situation is compounded by the effect of indirect taxes. The most important in Spain and other European Union countries is VAT. Professors Abbott and Bogenschneider have pointed out that "employers are thought to bear some of the incidence of indirect tax, as worker salaries and retirement benefits must be increased proportionately to offset the indirect tax,"[37] but they avoid that burden altogether by using robots.[38]

31 Ryan Benjamin Abbott and Bret Bogenschneider, "Should Robots Pay Taxes? Tax Policy in the Age of Automation," *cit.*, p. 164.

32 Elizabeth Gil García, *Los incentivos fiscales a la I + D + i*, Tirant lo Blanch, Valencia, 2017, p. 157.

33 Juan José Rubio Guerrero, "Incentivos fiscales a la inversión empresarial en el Impuesto de Sociedades," *Clm.economía Revista económica de Castilla – La Mancha*, 16, 2010, p. 262.

34 José Antonio Fernández Amor, "Derecho tributario y cuarta revolución industrial: análisis jurídico sobre aspectos fiscales de la robótica," *cit.*, p. 63.

35 Ryan Benjamin Abbott and Bret Bogenschneider, "Should Robots Pay Taxes? Tax Policy in the Age of Automation," *cit.*, p. 165.

36 *Ibid.*, pp. 165–166.

37 *Ibid.*, p. 166.

38 *Ibid.*

b Salaries and Social Security Contributions

Human workers generate salary and social security expenses for their employers. I would like to point out that there are many ways of incorporating people in the production process, although for now I will focus on employees rather than freelancers or the dependent self-employed.

"That employment relationship generates an expense for the company, normally called salary,"[39] which is recognized in accounts group 64 according to the SGAP. The employer's mandatory contribution to the social security administration (Art. 141.2 a) of Legislative Royal Decree 8/2015 of October 30, ratifying the consolidated text of the General Social Security Act for that worker is also entered in the same accounts. It is therefore a deductible expense which will reduce company profits.

The social security contributions required from employers are substantial: 23.60 percent for common contingencies, 1.25 percent for occupational accidents and illness, 5.50 percent for unemployment insurance, 0.20 percent for the salary guarantee fund (FOGASA), and 0.60 percent for professional training.[40]

Professor Fernández Amor stated that robots "do not have the added cost of contributions to social security or other social welfare systems,"[41] which favors their incorporation in the production process. His argument is partly based on the idea that social security payments are merely a para-fiscal demand established by law, with no direct relationship to corporate profits. I do not share this opinion, because the different nature of salaries and social security contributions is not an automatic argument in favor of using robots instead of workers.

While those contributions do represent an additional expense for the employer – nearly one third of the worker's salary – , their nature is not relevant to an analysis of this question, which ought to be a simple analysis of economic efficiency. The employer must weigh the productivity and expenses of each, regardless of whether they come from salaries and social security (in the case of workers) or electricity, maintenance, and repairs (in the case of robots), and compare their respective sum totals. It would make no sense to

39 José Antonio Fernández Amor, "Derecho tributario y cuarta revolución industrial: análisis jurídico sobre aspectos fiscales de la robótica," *cit.*, p. 64.

40 Order TMS/83/2019 of January 31, enabling the legal regulations governing contributions to social security, unemployment insurance, salary guarantee fund, and professional training for fiscal year 2019.

41 José Antonio Fernández Amor, "Derecho tributario y cuarta revolución industrial: análisis jurídico sobre aspectos fiscales de la robótica," *cit.*, p. 65.

do a segmented comparison of expenses, as with robots these could be higher than the combined cost of salaries and social security obligations.

However, robots do have one important advantage: significantly more flexibility in recognizing deductible costs, especially depreciation, than those associated with workers. Through depreciation, the cost of introducing robots in the production process (capital outlay) has a legal regime that allows companies greater leeway in tax planning,[42] which is undoubtedly a benefit that makes robots preferable to people.

A final argument in favor of introducing robots in the workplace is that acquiring a robot is a conversion of assets,[43] an investment, whereas hiring a worker uses the company's resources. From an accounting and tax perspective, robots offer companies greater flexibility in planning their use.

B Subject of Subsidies, Deductions, and Tax Incentives for Research, Development, and Innovation (R&D + i)

"R&D + i is a business activity [...] that will benefit society by bringing scientific-technical progress and benefit the producer and distributor of that activity's results by giving them an economic advantage."[44] That potential benefit explains why our tax system has a series of subsidies and incentives to encourage such activities. According to Spain's Court of Auditors, a tax incentive is any tax element that entails a reduction in tax revenue and differs from the definition of the tax liability, taxable base, taxable entity or taxpayer, chargeable event, basic tax rate or general tax rate, if applicable, tax management system, tax payment periodicity, and moment of accrual.[45]

R&D + i is particularly important in robotics, as innovation is what drives the field forward, and we must therefore take a closer look at these types of incentives. "The OECD recognizes in particular that it is important to follow carefully the development of AI and robots"[46] in order to determine how incentives in favor of research, development, and innovation should evolve.

42 *Ibid.*, p. 64.

43 We should remember that robots also have operating costs, in addition to depreciation, so they are not a straightforward conversion of company resources.

44 Elizabeth Gil García, *Los incentivos fiscales a la I + D + i, op. cit.*, pp. 25–26.

45 Court of Auditors, "Informe de Fiscalización de las actuaciones de la Agencia Estatal de Administración Tributaria en relación con los beneficios fiscales, ejercicio 2015," p. 20.

46 Xavier Oberson, *Taxing Robots, op. cit.*, p. 46.

1 *Types*

a Direct and Indirect Financing

Research, development, and innovation can be promoted by directly – by funding or subsidizing such activities – or indirectly – by creating tax abatements or incentives linked to such activities that reduce the amount of revenue collected by tax authorities.[47]

If the state aims to boost research by using tax abatements, "these represent a negative income and an unpaid cost,"[48] and are therefore tax expenses. From an economic perspective, tax incentives and direct financing can achieve the same results, but in practice, the former tend to be politically easier to implement. Tax incentives do not entail doling out public resources,[49] even though they still are an expense because they reduce the state's revenue.[50] "Reducing tax revenue is the same as using government funds for fiscal spending."[51] They are merely two sides of the same coin.

I will not get into the question of which is more suitable for boosting R&D + i in robotics here, as subsidies and tax advantages are both valid options for lawmakers to consider from an economic and political point of view. However, my primary interest here is in the indirect financing method of tax incentives.

b Direct and Indirect Tax Incentives

A tax incentive encourages certain voluntary conduct or activity with measures that alter the usual tax regime, either by reducing the tax burden with a special regime, or by making certain profits exempt.[52] Tax incentives can be direct or indirect.

Direct incentives are "patent box" regimes, special tax rate reductions based on income earned, investments made, or expenses incurred.[53] Indirect incentives are those that "eliminate levies in the state of origin, grant subjective exemption under sponsorship laws, or allow free depreciation for newly incorporated companies."[54] These types of incentives are not expressly designed to promote the activity in question, but they still benefit it or its results.[55]

---

47 Felipe Alonso Murillo, *Fiscalidad de la I + D + i. Tratamiento de los gastos en el Impuesto sobre Sociedades*, Netbiblo, La Coruña, 2010, p. 14.

48 Elizabeth Gil García, *Los incentivos fiscales a la I + D + i, op. cit.*, p. 140.

49 *Ibid.*, p. 142.

50 *Ibid.*, p. 143.

51 *Ibid.*

52 *Ibid.*, pp. 151–152.

53 *Ibid.*, p. 155.

54 *Ibid.*

55 *Ibid.*

The following section takes a closer look at direct tax incentives for R&D + i in robotics as well as some indirect incentives, such as depreciation, that are particularly effective in this area.

c Input and Output Incentives

Tax incentives can be granted for R&D + i activity or for the results it achieves.[56] Incentives for activity are generally called "input incentives," and those for the income it generates are known as "output incentives."[57]

Input incentives "cover the cost of engaging in R&D + i and usually include expenses incurred at every stage of the technological research, transfer, and innovation process," in an attempt to make R&D + i a more appealing and profitable venture for companies.[58] In Spanish legislation, LIS Article 35 regulates deductions for research and development and technological innovation activities.

Output incentives cover "the development and application of results obtained during the R&D + i process" to encourage patent registration and the commercialization of new products.[59] These are regulated in Spanish law by LIS Article 23, which stipulates a reduced tax rate on income from certain intangible activities, effectively creating a patent box regime.

2 *Tax Incentives in Spain's Corporate Income Tax Law* (LIS)

a Reduction of Taxable Income Derived from Certain Intangible Assets

The patent box or IP box regime reduces the tax burden of economic actors that develop new products and processes protected by intellectual property rights.[60] In Spain, the taxable base can only be reduced if the requirements set out in LIS Article 23 are met. Law 45/2015 of October 29, which approved Spain's federal budget for the year 2016,[61] introduced the "modified nexus approach" described in the final report on Action 5 of the OECD BEPS project.

56 María Amparo Grau Ruiz, "La adaptación de la fiscalidad ante los retos jurídicos, económicos, éticos y sociales planteados por la robótica," *Nueva fiscalidad*, 4, 2017, pp. 35–61.

57 Elizabeth Gil García, *Los incentivos fiscales a la I + D + i, op. cit.*, p. 161.

58 *Ibid.*, pp. 161 and 265.

59 *Ibid.*, pp. 161 and 381.

60 *Ibid.*, p. 384.

61 María Amparo Grau Ruiz, "La adaptación de la fiscalidad ante los retos jurídicos, económicos, éticos y sociales planteados por la robótica," *cit.*, pp. 35–61; and Elizabeth Gil García, *Los incentivos fiscales a la I + D + i, op. cit.*, p. 392.

b Deduction for Research and Development and Technological Innovation Activities

If robots are included in the production process, they could be eligible for a deduction for research and development and technological innovation activities under LIS Article 35.

This article specifies two types of deductions: one for research and development activities, regulated in section one, and the other for technological innovation activities, addressed in section two.

In Spain, the former type allows companies to deduce 25 percent of their research and development expenses and 8 percent of their investments in tangible and intangible assets, excluding buildings and land, as long as they are used solely for research and development activities.

The deduction for technological innovation is 12 percent. However, it is more restrictive, as only certain costs related to patents, licenses, or know-how can be deducted.[62]

"This does not mean, naturally, that merely incorporating robots is sufficient to enjoy the tax benefit."[63]

In fact, Binding Resolution V2647-11, issued by the General Directorate of Taxes on November 7, 2011,[64] ruled that a pharmacy which had purchased a robot for smart drug storage and dispensing could not apply the deduction for technological innovation activities. And Binding Resolution V0030-01, issued by the same body on May 21, 2001,[65] determined that the deduction did not apply to a series of robots which had been installed to increase production by operating 24 hours a day.

Even so, the possibility of applying the deduction for research and development and technological innovation (provided the necessary conditions are met) gives robots another clear tax advantage over human workers.

---

62 José Antonio Fernández Amor, "Derecho tributario y cuarta revolución industrial: análisis jurídico sobre aspectos fiscales de la robótica," *cit.*, p. 66.

63 *Ibid.*, pp. 65–66.

64 "The present case does not represent a technological advance in the sense of obtaining new products or production processes, or of making substantial, technologically significant improvements to existing products or production processes. What the complainant has done is purchase and subsequently integrate a robot in their pharmaceutical activity to perform automated medication storage and dispensing tasks, which does not qualify as technological innovation for the purposes of Article 35 of the TRLIS."

65 "Investments in elements of the company's fixed assets which are part of its production process and do not represent a technological improvement of the same cannot be considered scientific research and technological innovation activities."

c Free Depreciation under LIS Article 12.3

In certain cases, taxpayers can choose to declare a depreciation expense higher than the book value, regardless of how much it has actually depreciated.

There are two situations in which free depreciation is permitted for R&D + i in robotics, although it should be noted that newly incorporated companies are also eligible. LIS Article 12.3 b) states that tangible and intangible fixed assets associated with R&D activities may be freely depreciated, and Article 12.3 c) says the same applies to R&D expenses activated as intangible fixed assets.

Free depreciation gives companies more flexibility when designing their tax and market strategies, allowing them to recognize the depreciation expense whenever it suits them best (in other words, for reasons other than real depreciation).

3 *Tax Incentives for Research, Development, and Innovation (R&D + i) in Comparative Law*

a France

Our neighbor to the north offers tax incentives for R&D + i input and output.

There are currently two input incentives in France: firstly, a tax credit based on the volume of R&D expenditure, and "an incentive for innovation expenses;"[66] and secondly, an accelerated depreciation scheme for investments in scientific and technical research machinery equipment.[67]

In the area of output incentives, "France has established an IP box regime limited to patents, patentable inventions, and even improvements made on these elements."[68] Young and innovative firms can also apply for an exemption from social security contributions.[69]

b Austria

In Austria, the "invention premium" is an R&D incentive that allows companies to deduct their expenses for research and development activities.[70]

c Netherlands

Dutch tax authorities offer the "possibility of deducting R&D expenses as well as input and output incentives."[71] The WBSO tax credit scheme, designed to

66 Elizabeth Gil García, *Los incentivos fiscales a la I + D + i, op. cit.*, p. 355.

67 *Ibid.*, p. 372.

68 *Ibid.*, p. 417.

69 OECD, *R&D Tax Incentives: France 2017*, Directorate for Science, Technology and Innovation, April 2018.

70 Elizabeth Gil García, *Los incentivos fiscales a la I + D + i, op. cit.*, pp. 357–358.

71 *Ibid.*, p. 359.

stimulate research, development, and innovation, reduces personnel costs of R&D projects, among other expenses.

d Portugal

Our eastern neighbor has a patent box scheme for patents, designs, and industrial models derived from R&D activities.[72] In 2016 the scheme was modified and adapted to OECD guidelines on the nexus approach.[73]

e United Kingdom

In the UK, the patent box system introduced by the Finance Act in 2012 is "confined to patents, regulatory data protection, plant variety rights, and supplementary protection certificates"[74] but "excludes other usual forms of industrial property and has one of the most limited scopes, along with Belgium and the Netherlands."[75]

There are also R&D tax reliefs for expenses directly related to an R&D project,[76] which vary depending on the size of the company (SME or large enterprise) and project outsourcing.[77]

f Italy

This Mediterranean country offers R&D + i tax incentives in the form of tax credits or deductions, as well as incentives for innovative SMEs and start-ups.[78]

The Italian patent box scheme "was one of the first to align with international standards;"[79] however, "the objective scope of the Italian regime is much broader than that defined by the OECD,"[80] even extending to trademarks. It is an optional regime which, once chosen, cannot be revoked, for a renewable term of five years.[81]

---

72 *Ibid.*, p. 421.

73 *Ibid.*, p. 455.

74 *Ibid.*, p. 424.

75 *Ibid.*

76 HM Revenue & Customs, Research and Development (R&D) tax reliefs. Retrieved from https://www.gov.uk/guidance/corporation-tax-research-and-development-rd-relief.

77 OECD, *R&D Tax Incentives: United Kingdom, 2017*, Directorate for Science, Technology and Innovation, April 2018.

78 Modesto J. Fabra Valls and Paolo Falchi, "Los incentivos fiscales para el fomento de la innovación empresarial en España e Italia," *Quincena Fiscal Aranzadi*, 9, 2017, pp. 59–110.

79 Elizabeth Gil García, *Los incentivos fiscales a la I + D + i, op. cit.*, p. 425.

80 *Ibid.*

81 *Ibid.*, p. 453.

g Chile

The Chilean R&D tax incentive regime is governed by the Law on Tax Incentives for Private R&D Investment,[82] which aims to promote the development of innovative firms and make them more competitive. The 2012 reform of R&D tax credits "extended their scope to include in-house expenses, raised the annual tax ceiling, simplified bureaucratic procedures, and facilitated national and international cooperation."[83] Even so, the general level of support for innovation in this country remains quite low.[84]

4 *Coexistence of Tax Incentives and the Robot Tax*

One of the questions that arises when considering a robot tax is the potential conflict between existing tax incentives and the new levy. "We need to rethink the relationship between robotization and R&D + i tax incentives."[85] One argument against a robot tax is that it would pose a hindrance or obstacle to research and progress.

As we have seen, the OECD and many other countries around us[86] regard research and innovation as valid objectives in their own right, especially in the field of robotics, and tend to favor such tax incentives.[87] At first glance, it would seem illogical to have a policy that encourages technological innovation and, at the same time, a tax that deters it. However, I believe it is perfectly possible for R&D + i incentives to coexist with certain robot taxes in our tax system. There are two possible paths. The first is the so-called "Korean model" and the second is simple coexistence.

"The Korean model of robot taxation has basically consisted in reducing or eliminating tax incentives for technological innovation."[88] In other words, in order to increase the tax burden on robots, they chose to reduce tax benefits rather than levy new taxes. South Korea is the first country to "take steps toward

---

82 Law 20.241, published in the *Diario Oficial de Chile* on January 19, 2008, amended by Law 20.570 on March 6, 2012.

83 OECD, *Estudios Económicos de la OCDE: Chile, 2018*, February 2018, p. 55.

84 *Ibid.*, p. 55.

85 César García Novoa, "La tributación de los robots y el futurismo fiscal," *cit.* [available at https://www.politicafiscal.es/cesar-garcia-novoa/la-tributacion-de-los-robots-y-el-futurismo-fiscal].

86 OECD (2019). *Compendium of R&D tax incentive schemes: OECD countries and selected economies*, 2018, http://oe.cd/rdtax, accessed 07/01/2020.

87 Xavier Oberson, *Taxing Robots*, *op. cit.*, p. 46.

88 César García Novoa, "La tributación de los robots y el futurismo fiscal," *cit.* [available at https://www.politicafiscal.es/cesar-garcia-novoa/la-tributacion-de-los-robots-y-el-futurismo-fiscal].

'taxing' the use of robots in automated industrial processes,"[89] although the "tax" is really just curbing tax incentives on investment in automated machinery. The plan is to reduce the corporate income tax deduction for companies that invest in automated industrial equipment by two percentage points.[90]

The second option would be to simply maintain existing R&D tax incentives and introduce new taxes on robots (or modifying existing taxes). Although it might seem like this could give rise to a conflict of laws, we must remember that merely automating processes or installing robots does not automatically entitle a company to tax incentives on robot R&D. In my opinion, they are two closely related yet separate things. While fiscal policy encourages research in automation, it also creates new taxes as it seeks a fair distribution of the tax burden, modulating pressure for non-fiscal reasons.

Therefore, regardless of which path we ultimately take, there will be no conflict between a hypothetical future robot tax and existing research incentives.

5 *Tax Incentives for Research, Development, and Innovation in Robotics as a Solution*

Research and innovation in robotics is desirable, because R&D + i investments are "vital to productivity and growth, constituting the basis of a country's progress and social welfare,"[91] and robotics is the technology of the future. Tax incentives aim to increase an economy's technological sophistication and competitiveness. Yet research and innovation must be pursued responsibly, as automation can have both positive and negative consequences.

Tax incentives are often used for non-fiscal purposes, as long as they are constitutionally defensible,[92] in accordance with STC 122/2012 of June 5 (TOL2.579.439), STC 37/1987 of March 26 (TOL79.746), and STC 214/1994 of July 14 (TOL82.619).[93]

Tax incentives can promote socially responsible research and innovation in robotics. As fiscal tools at the legislator's disposal, they can be transitory measures designed to help workers catch up with technology by receiving additional training, so that they will have a share in some of the profits derived

89 María Amparo Grau Ruiz, "La adaptación de la fiscalidad ante los retos jurídicos, económicos, éticos y sociales planteados por la robótica," *cit.*, pp. 35–61.

90 *Ibid.*

91 Elizabeth Gil García, *Los incentivos fiscales a la I + D + i*, *op. cit.*, p. 121.

92 *Ibid.*, pp. 149–150.

93 These Supreme Court rulings confirmed that the tax system can serve extra-fiscal purposes, even though these are not the system's primary function, as one of the multiple tools the state can use to achieve the economic and social propositions enshrined in our Constitution.

from the use of robots while also protecting existing jobs. If such measures are well-designed, they could go a long way toward mitigating the negative effects of the fourth industrial revolution.

We should consider the possibility of making existing research and innovation incentives – such as the deduction for R&D + i activities regulated in Article 35 of the LIS, or the reduction of taxable income derived from certain intangible activities in Article 23 of the same law – contingent on compliance with the principles of responsible research and innovation (RRI).[94]

Specifically, these R&D + i incentives could come with the obligation to pursue research, development, and innovation in a way that anticipates and assesses their possible implications with regard to social expectations. Both incentives could be used to promote socially responsible research and innovation in robotics. If robot-specific incentives are created, they should be modeled on the ones that already exist and carefully consider how they might interact with potential robot taxes.

Socially responsible research and innovation may be able to prevent widespread job destruction, one of the most feared consequences of robotization. Tax deductions for research, development, and innovation are usually contrasted with the deduction for job creation contemplated in Article 37 of the Corporate Income Tax Law.[95] Yet the two types of deductions are not necessarily opposed. It would be possible to promote responsible research and innovation in robotics by making technological R&D + i tax incentives contingent on creating or maintaining a certain level of employment in the same field. In other words, the deductions could be combined; at the very least, the technological R&D + i deduction could be designed to ensure that the activity benefiting from the deduction is not used to eliminate jobs.[96] The potentially negative externalities of mass robot deployment in our economy and society

94 María Amparo Grau Ruiz, Laura Aymerich Franch, Eduard Fosch Villaronga, Juliana Chaves Chaparro, Helena Ancos Franco, Álvaro Falcón Pulido, and Mohamad Nadim Adi, *Self-coaching tools for conducting responsible research and innovation (RRI) with social robots (International Workshop at ICSR, Madrid 2019)*. In Self-coaching tools for conducting responsible research and innovation (RRI) with social robots, November 26, 2019, Eleventh International Conference on Social Robotics (ICSR2019). E-print UCM, 2019, p. 9.

95 These deductions are contrasted in José Antonio Fernández Amor, "Derecho tributario y cuarta revolución industrial: análisis jurídico sobre aspectos fiscales de la robótica," *cit.*, p. 66.

96 "Automation has the potential to create widespread benefits [...]. But without oversight, automation will also exacerbate unemployment and economic inequality," in Ryan Benjamin Abbott and Bret Bogenschneider, "Should Robots Pay Taxes? Tax Policy in the Age of Automation," *cit.*, p. 147.

might even make it advisable to link incentives to measures designed to prevent pollution, energy waste, gender inequality, or other problems.

However legitimate the non-fiscal purposes may be, they must be pursued in a coherent way to ensure responsible research and innovation in robotics. Perhaps an incentive of this type should be made conditional on employability.

Of course, I do not mean to suggest that robotics research and innovation should be forced to maintain existing jobs. That would be illogical, as robots will necessarily take over certain tasks from workers. However, it is important to consider the new responsibilities that will be given to workers, such as supervising, controlling, or directing robots. Responsible research and innovation could restructure tasks in a way that improves productivity without destroying jobs, at least on a macroeconomic level. In this respect, I think it would be reasonable to revise or improve regulations to make existing incentives contingent on maintaining a certain level of employment, by training workers in new technologies and helping them adapt to a job market that robotics is changing.

When it comes to research and innovation incentives, the priority should be to ensure responsible implementation rather than simply create more of them. The tax incentive would not be fully applicable if jobs are lost, but it would in cases of responsible research and innovation.

Similarly, incentives designed to give workers better training and skills could also be redefined, "ideally in such a way that the worker's own investment (however involuntary), made when the robot was introduced in the workplace, could be economically quantified."[97] The idea is to assess the contribution of workers to research and innovation for the purpose of profit-sharing. As Professor Grau Ruiz explained, "This contribution could be quantified based on the hours invested by a given worker (or the correlated savings for the employer from using robotics), plus their efforts to train the robot to perform tasks while sharing the workload." She continued, "The time and experience contributed by workers could be weighed up somehow in order to recognize their partial claim to certain intellectual property rights, as they helped train the robot, and their share in future profits, in a manner proportional to their sacrifice. Once the robot was fully trained, the person who helped train it would continue to reap the rewards of that effort (although this small measure would only affect those who had a hand in the robot's initial implementation)."[98]

97 María Amparo Grau Ruiz, "La adaptación de la fiscalidad ante los retos jurídicos, económicos, éticos y sociales planteados por la robótica," *cit.*, pp. 35–61.

98 *Ibid.*

When designing an incentive for research and innovation in robotics, it is important to consider if workers are involved and if they will receive any form of compensation for their efforts, so the incentive also encourages that kind of personal involvement within companies.

CHAPTER 5

The Question of Taxing Power in Spanish Law

In Spanish law, the unique distribution of powers would complicate the creation of a new robot tax.[1] The power to introduce levies based on new taxable events is not centralized but divided among several legislative bodies. The distribution of taxing power in our system could give rise to problems of competitiveness and material fairness,[2] in the event of a conflict between regional and federal authorities where both try to tax the same thing in relation to robots, as occurred with the Tax on Deposits in Credit Institutions (hereafter IDEC).[3]

This tax was first introduced in the region of Extremadura via Law 14/2001 of November 29, which was appealed on the grounds of unconstitutionality by the president of Spain on March 27, 2002. Nearly eleven years later, on

1 On this subject, see the recently published Juan José Hinojosa Torralbo and Ignacio Cruz Padial (dirs.), Guillermo Sánchez-Archidona Hidalgo (coord.), *Tributos, servicios digitales y robótica*, Thomson Reuters – Aranzadi, Cizur Menor, Navarra, 2020. With the following articles, among others: "De la economía digital a la robótica: algunas cuestiones tributarias," by Ignacio Cruz Padial, pp. 203–232; "Inteligencia artificial, robótica y Derecho Tributario. Los presupuestos del cambio de paradigma," by Pedro Ángel Colao Marín, pp. 233–259; "¿Sueñan los androides con impuestos finalistas?," by Norberto Miras Marín, pp. 261–288; "El impuesto sobre los robots: revisión de sus perfiles y encaje jurídico," by José Antonio Fernández Amor, pp. 289–311; "La tributación de los robots en el marco de la búsqueda de nuevas formas de gravamen," by César García Novoa, pp. 313–325; "El actual dilema fiscal por el impacto de la robótica: ¿innovación o empleo?," by María Amparo Grau Ruiz, pp. 327–346; and "Avances tecnológicos versus mercado laboral y pensiones públicas," by Miguel Gutiérrez Bengoechea, pp. 347–373. See also César García Novoa (dir.), *4ª Revolución Industrial: la fiscalidad de la sociedad digital y tecnológica en España y Latinoamérica*, Thomson Reuters – Aranzadi, Cizur Menor, Navarra, 2019. With the following articles, among others: "Los grandes retos fiscales de la economía digital desde la perspectiva europea," by César García Novoa, pp. 25–67; "Alternativas para la tributación de la economía digital: el establecimiento permanente virtual," by Saturnina Moreno González, pp. 69–105; "El impuesto sobre determinados servicios digitales como opción para gravar la nueva economía digitalizada," by Cristina García-Herrera Blanco, pp. 107–130; "Soluciones unilaterales para la fiscalidad de la economía digital. Especial referencia al 'equalization tax'," by Soraya Rodríguez Losada, pp. 131–154; "La búsqueda de alternativas para la tributación de los robots: la tasa californiana aplicable a los vehículos autónomos," by María Amparo Grau Ruiz, pp. 155–174; and "Retos fiscales de la digitalización. Perspectiva desde Chile," by Christian Blanche, pp. 303–318.

2 José Antonio Fernández Amor, "Derecho tributario y cuarta revolución industrial: análisis jurídico sobre aspectos fiscales de la robótica," *cit.*, p. 74.

3 In the region of Andalusia, this tax is known as the Tax on Client Deposits in Credit Institutions, but its regulation is essentially the same.

 | DOI:10.1163/9789004538511_006

November 14, 2012, STC 210/2012 (TOL2.701.003) dismissed that appeal,[4] tacitly recognizing the power of regional governments to establish a tax of this type.[5] Meanwhile, a similar levy had been introduced by the regional authorities of Andalusia (effective on January 1, 2011)[6] and the Canary Islands (effective on July 1, 2012).[7]

The central government reacted to this situation by creating a similar federal tax,[8] applicable to Spanish credit institutions and branches in Spain of foreign credit institutions, but with a rate of 0%, which "can be interpreted as a statement of its intention to reserve the right to tax bank deposits."[9] The same intention can be inferred from the preamble to Law 16/2012, according to which the tax is justified "by the aim of ensuring a harmonized tax treatment that will allow the financial system to operate more efficiently."

---

4 STC 210/2012 of November 14. Appeal on grounds of unconstitutionality no. 1894/2002, opinion of the Constitutional Court delivered by Justice Luis Ignacio Ortega Álvarez (TOL2.701.003) and published in the BOE on December 13. Upholding the constitutionality of the regional tax is "difficult to justify from an economic perspective," according to the report of the Committee of Experts for Tax Reform, p. 329. As we will see in section 3, the ruling is also debatable from a legal point of view.

5 By the time this ruling was given, Extremadura had already repealed the initial law, but its content was incorporated in Title IV of the consolidated text on regional taxes of Extremadura, approved by Legislative Decree 2/2006 of December 12 and later amended by Law 19/2010 of December 28 on fiscal and administrative measures, Law 2/2012 of June 28 on urgent measures in taxation, finance, and gambling, and Law 6/2013 of December 13 on tax measures to stimulate the economy. However, the repeal did not eliminate the object of the constitutional proceedings, as the appeal referred to legislative powers [in this respect, the decision alludes to the precedent set in ruling 204/2011 of December 15, F J 2 a (TOL2.347.798)]. Furthermore, after some amendments and the incorporation mentioned above, the tax ended up being regulated in the previously cited consolidated text in terms quite similar to the original law. On these matters, see José Luis Martín Moreno, "Constitucionalidad del impuesto sobre depósitos de las entidades de crédito: STC 210/2012, de 14 de noviembre," *Aletheia Cuadernos Críticos de Derecho*, 2, 2012, p. 73.

6 Article 6 of Decree-Law 4/2010 of July 6 on tax measures to reduce the government budget deficit and ensure sustainability, amended by Law 17/2011 of December 23, which amended the consolidated text of provisions regarding ceded taxes established by the Region of Andalusia, and which adopted measures regarding the Tax on Customer Deposits in Credit Institutions in Andalusia (Art. 3 and 1st temporary provision).

7 Article 41 of Law 4/2012 of June 25 on administrative and fiscal measures.

8 Article 19 of Law 16/2012 of December 27, which adopted various tax measures designed to consolidate public finances and stimulate the economy (BOE no. 312, December 28). The federal IDEC has been challenged by the Catalan Parliament (appeal 1808/2013), the regional government of Catalonia (appeal 1873/2013), and the regional government of Asturias (appeal 1881/2013). The filing of all three appeals was officially recognized in the BOE on May 13.

9 Report of the Committee of Experts for the Reform of the Spanish Tax System, February 2014, p. 349.

After the federal IDEC was approved, but before it took effect, Catalonia[10] and Asturias[11] each created their own taxes on bank deposits. Additionally, over the course of 2013, the provincial government of Vizcaya[12] and the regional government of Navarre,[13] on the one hand, and the regional authorities of Valencia,[14] on the other, approved the same tax with effect from 2014, which the federal government reacted to with more appeals. And, effective as of January 1, 2014, Law 18/2014 of October 15, which approved urgent measures for growth, competitiveness, and efficiency, raised the federal tax rate from zero to 0.03 percent. Though debatable, as we will see, this solution was upheld by STC 30/2015 of February 19 (TOL4.765.297 and TOL4.775.455).

---

10 The tax was created by Decree-Law 5/2012 of December 18, regarding the tax on deposits in credit institutions, which took effect when it was published in the BOGC the following day (December 19, 2012), although financial institutions had to provide the necessary information for charging the tax from October 1, 2012, according to the second additional provision. That decree-law was ratified and passed as a draft bill, eventually giving rise to Law 4/2014 of April 4 on the tax on deposits in credit institutions, which took effect on April 10 but could be applied retroactively unless the aforementioned decree-law was more favorable. Said tax was appealed before the Constitutional Court, although Order 123/2013 of May 21 lifted the suspension, and Order TC 153/2013 of July 9 dismissed the federal government's petition to reverse the lifting of that suspension, effectively allowing the tax to be levied.

11 The tax was created in Article 41 of Law 3/2012 of the Government of the Principality of Asturias of December 28, approving the general budget for 2013. The levy became applicable when it was published in the BOPA on December 29, 2012, although the rest of the law did not take effect until January 1 of the following year. The tax has been appealed by the central government, although the suspension was lifted by Order TC 154/2013 of July 9.

12 This Basque institution approved the IDEC in Article 2 of Regional Regulatory Decree 2/2013 of February 26, which introduced new taxes in the historical territory of Bizkaia (BOB of March 5). The article established that the law applied to taxable events within the territory, and that "until this tax has been agreed with federal authorities, the regulations set out in the aforementioned precept will apply and have the same effect." The central government reacted by lodging an appeal on grounds of unconstitutionality (case no. 3406–2013), but after the Joint Committee for Economic Accord reached an agreement on January 16, 2014 (which later gave rise to a draft bill amending the Accord, ratified by the federal government on March 7, 2014), it decided to withdraw that appeal (Decision of the Council of Ministers, May 30, 2014). As for the Basque region of Álava, it simply ratified that initial agreement of the Joint Committee in Regional Regulation 4/2014 of February 26.

13 The IDEC was approved by Regional Law 6/2014 of April 14, regarding the law on deposits in credit institutions (published in the BON on April 28, 2014), which establishes a rate of 0.03 percent in its eighth article.

14 Article 161 of Law 5/2013 of December 23 on fiscal, administrative, and financial management, and organization of the Regional Government of Valencia.

This is clearly "a textbook case of colliding federal and regional regulations," as the Committee of Experts for Tax Reform stated in their report.[15] A conflict of this scale and magnitude over robot taxation would seriously undermine the competitiveness of Spanish firms in a globalized economy. We must therefore analyze the taxing powers of different public entities and where they might overlap, the reasons for averting potential conflicts between regional and federal tax authorities, and possible solutions to adopt, preferably before a conflict arises. I will use the IDEC as a model for exploring the different roads we might take with regard to robot taxation.

A The Division of Taxing Powers Set out in the Spanish Constitution

In the Spanish legal system, taxing power[16] is attributed exclusively to the central government in Article 133.1 of the Spanish Constitution of 1978 (hereafter SC).[17] It is therefore an original constituent power, though not in the traditional sense of the term. Nor can the taxing power of regional and local governments be understood as derived from the traditional form.[18] "The exercise of their taxing powers may be regulated by federal organic law (Art. 157.3 of the Constitution),"[19] and SC Article 133.2 expressly mentions their ability to impose and collect taxes in accordance with the Constitution and other laws. As Professor Falcón y Tella wrote, the taxing power of the federal government is only limited by the Constitution, whereas the "taxing power of the regional governments" and that of local authorities "is determined not only by the Constitution but also by federal laws, both organic and ordinary."[20] Thus,

15 Report of the Committee of Experts for the Reform of the Spanish Tax System, February 2014, p. 349.

16 Professor Cazorla Prieto defines taxing power as "the ability of certain representative bodies of government entities to establish or approve taxes, through the pertinent legislative channels, as a means of obtaining the revenue needed to finance their activities," in Luis María Cazorla Prieto, *Derecho Financiero y Tributario*, Thomson Reuters – Aranzadi, Cizur Menor, Navarra, 2018, p. 72.

17 Therefore, we see that taxing power is the "distribution of the power or ability to levy taxes among different territorial government entities," in Fernando Pérez Royo, *Derecho Financiero y Tributario. Parte General*, 25th edition, Civitas Thomson Reuters, Cizur Menor, Navarra, 2015, pp. 86–87.

18 Ramón Falcón y Tella, *Derecho Financiero y Tributario (Parte General)*, *op. cit.*, quoting from the 2017 edition, p. 94.

19 Ramón Falcón y Tella, in Santiago Muñoz Machado (ed.), *Comentario mínimo a la Constitución española*, Crítica, Barcelona, 2018, p. 551.

20 Ramón Falcón y Tella, *Derecho Financiero y Tributario (Parte General)*, *op. cit.*, quoting from the 2017 edition, p. 94.

"the differences in the taxing powers of said entities" reside "in the limitations placed upon each"[21] and not in their origin, which is always constitutional.

According to Article 6.1 and 6.2 of the Regional Financing Law (hereafter LOFCA), "regional governments may not impose taxes on taxable events levied by the state." This limitation refers to the particular taxes of each region.[22] According to STC 289/2000 (TOL81.382), "the scope of taxation is broader than that of the taxable event referred to in section 2, Art. 6, of the LOFCA." And this rule "does not necessarily prevent regional authorities from establishing their own taxes on taxable items or sources already taxed by the state (STC 186/1933) (TOL82.209); what Art. 6.2 prohibits, in its own terms, is an exact coincidence of taxable events (STC 37/1987) (TOL79.746)."[23] From this we infer that taxes for non-fiscal purposes can be established, as long as the taxable event is different, within the limitations set by LOFCA Art. 6.2.[24]

One interesting thing to consider is the possibility of establishing fees, as stipulated in LOFCA Art. 7, creating new government services or activities related to robots or cutting costs in services or activities already subject to fees.

As for surcharges on federal taxes (LOFCA Art. 12 and SC Art. 1571), while "the regional governments have hardly ever used this option,"[25] if any surtaxes are established in the future, they would be contingent on the federal tax. Consequently, there would be no conflict, because the national government would determine the characteristics and structure of the tax.

In short, Spanish regions have the power to levy and collect taxes on the same taxable items with regard to robots.

---

21 Fernando Pérez Royo, *Derecho Financiero y Tributario. Parte General, op. cit.*, pp. 86–87.

22 Spain's regions also obtain revenue from ceded taxes (LOFCA Arts. 10 and 11 and SC Art. 157.1); however, these are not pertinent to the present discussion, as such taxes are coordinated by federal and regional authorities and cannot give rise to inter-jurisdictional conflict.

23 Ramón Falcón y Tella, *Derecho Financiero y Tributario (Parte General), op. cit.*, quoting from the 2017 edition, p. 99.

24 See J. Daubanis and Y. P. Yanni, "La imposición óptima de los robots," in *La tributación de los robots,* IEB Report 2/2019. A. G. Ayala Sanhueza, "Incentivos fiscales a la innovación en robótica: una necesaria reformulación," *Revista General de Legislación y Jurisprudencia*, 2, 2019, pp. 207–260. G. Sánchez Archidona Hidalgo, "La tributación de la robótica y la inteligencia artificial como límites del Derecho Financiero y Tributario," *Quincena Fiscal*, 12, June 2019, pp. 69–96. M. Segura Alastrue, "Los robots en el Derecho Financiero y Tributario," in *El Derecho de los robots,* Wolters Kluwer, Las Rozas, Madrid, 2018, pp. 167–188. U. Thuemmel, "Optimal Taxation of Robots," *CEifo Working Paper*, April 3, 2018, pp. 31 and 32.

25 Ramón Falcón y Tella, in Santiago Muñoz Machado (ed.), *Comentario mínimo a la Constitución española, op. cit.*, p. 678.

However, "while regional governments have legislative power, local and provincial councils do not."[26] This means that local governments only have derived taxing power, meaning it is derived from original legislation; therefore, they can "only levy taxes or decide on the regulation of their essential elements if a law specifically empowers them to do so."[27] That law is Legislative Royal Decree 2/2004 of March 5, which approved the consolidated text of the Law on Local Tax Administrations (hereafter LHL). Local authorities can have a greater impact on robotics than one might initially think. LHL Article 59, which lists the type of taxes they can levy, includes the municipal motor vehicles tax. This tax could be very relevant for robots classed as autonomous vehicles. The tax on business activities could have a smaller yet still significant impact. In conclusion, although local authorities cannot create new taxes without an amendment to the LHL, they can modify certain existing taxes with potentially enormous repercussions for robot taxation.

B The Need to Avoid the Proliferation of Regional Taxes in Robotics

The current division of taxing powers in Spain means that regional governments can, in theory, levy taxes on robots. To do so, experts must "determine the most appropriate level on which to establish such taxes."[28] It is too early to know if the solution to the problems and challenges posed by robotics will entail creating specific robot taxes or simply adapting existing taxes to this new situation. It is important to examine the issue from a national and global perspective, in light of the numerous taxes (like the IDEC) that have cropped up in recent years.

Clearly, our response to robotization cannot be the uncoordinated creation of seventeen different taxes, one for each region. Regional governments are not the most suitable authorities for taxing robots, due to the jurisdictional problems that would inevitably arise. For example, mobility is an intrinsic feature of certain types of robots, like driverless cars. Industrial robots could also be moved from one region to another with more favorable legislation.

---

26 Fernando Pérez Royo, *Derecho Financiero y Tributario. Parte General, op. cit.*, p. 96.

27 Alejandro Menéndez Moreno (dir.), *Derecho Financiero y Tributario. Parte General*, Lex Nova Thomson Reuters, 15th edition, Madrid, 2014, p. 62.

28 José Antonio Fernández Amor, "Derecho tributario y cuarta revolución industrial: análisis jurídico sobre aspectos fiscales de la robótica," *cit.*, p. 74.

There is an alarming tendency, "especially in recent years, to clutter the system with special taxes created to deal with purely transitory situations [...] adding an injurious layer of complexity to tax legislation."[29]

Without a harmonized global, or at least European, policy, there can be no effective attempt at taxing robots. As Professor Oberson rightly observed, "Tax issues go [far] beyond the borders of any particular state. They should be analysed globally."[30] Moreover, any national tax will immediately face a variety of problems, from classification to applying double taxation treaties. In order to tax robots fairly and efficiently, the aim should be to achieve international consensus, or at least Europe-wide harmonization. Therefore, the logical course of action is to let the national government establish whatever taxes it sees fit, in line with international proposals, instead of creating fragmentation with separate taxes for each region.

Interestingly, the report of the Committee of Experts for Tax Reform recommended eliminating all regional IDEC taxes, or at least centralizing their regulation and management and using a compensation or conveyance mechanism to pass the revenue on to the regional authorities. According to that report, "Scholarly opinion is conclusive: the tax is detrimental to economic growth and the solidity of our financial system."[31] A robotics tax could have similar effects but on a much larger scale, extending beyond the financial system to every sector of the economy. Many authors believe that creating a robot tax, at this juncture, would undoubtedly be rash[32] and possibly even harmful. For this reason, it would be much better to establish one rather than many taxes.

The aforementioned committee made the two following proposals,[33] which could also apply, *mutatis mutandis*, to a future tax on robots:

> Proposal No. 102: The federal tax on deposits in credit institutions and all equivalent regional taxes should be definitively abolished.

---

29 César García Novoa, "Impuestos atípicos en la era post BEPS" (Chapter 8), in A. Cubero Truyo (dir.), *Tributos asistemáticos del ordenamiento vigente*, Tirant lo Blanch, Valencia, 2018, pp. 223–224.

30 Xavier Oberson, "Taxing robots? From the emergence of an electronic ability to pay to a tax on robots or the use of robots," *cit.*, p. 261.

31 Report of the Committee of Experts for the Reform of the Spanish Tax System, February 2014, pp. 350–351.

32 César García Novoa, "La tributación de los robots y el futurismo fiscal," cit. [Available at https://www.politicafiscal.es/cesar-garcia-novoa/la-tributacion-de-los-robots-y-el-futurismo-fiscal].

33 Report of the Committee of Experts for the Reform of the Spanish Tax System, February 2014, pp. 356–357.

> Proposal No. 103: In any event, and to avoid potentially detrimental consequences that would negatively affect the entire Spanish economy, the IDEC should be considered a non-delegable tax which only the central government is empowered to levy.

It certainly seems like this would also be the best solution in our case, with a single tax regulated and managed solely by the federal government. "An entirely different matter is whether the revenue from that tax is distributed, automatically and in a predetermined manner, between the central and regional governments."[34] This centralized management scheme seems preferable, even if regional authorities are allowed to determine the rate applicable in their territory or are granted certain regulatory powers.

C Possible Solutions

There are several ways in which we could prevent the undesirable proliferation of regional robot taxes: amending the LOFCA, creating a federal tax that could become a ceded tax (regulated entirely by the central government or allowing each region to set the rate within certain parameters), or the stopgap measure of enacting an ordinary harmonization law. In the future, there may come a time when there are multiple robot taxes on the books, each with different characteristics. In that case, the most logical thing would be to adopt several of these solutions, depending on the circumstances.

1 *Creating a Federal Tax*

One possible solution is what the central government did with the IDEC: create a zero-rate federal tax. After a brief overview of the facts in the IDEC case, I will explain how this solution could apply to a robot tax.

The central government reacted to STC 210/2012 of November 14 (TOL2.701.003) by establishing a federal tax on deposits in credit institutions, via Article 19 of Law 16/2012 of December 27, which adopted various tax measures designed to consolidate public finances and stimulate the economy.[35] However, it set the tax rate at zero percent.[36] The obligation to make advance

---

34 *Ibid.*, p. 356. This is what the committee of experts concluded in their report, and I believe it can be extrapolated to taxes on robots.

35 BOE no. 312 of December 28, 2012.

36 First paragraph of Art. 19.8. However, it should be noted that Law 18/2014 of October 15, which approved urgent measures for growth, competitiveness, and efficiency, raised the federal tax rate from zero to 0.03 percent, effective as of January 1, 2014.

payment of 50 percent of the tax rate times the previous year's taxable base is expressly excluded when the rate is zero.[37] Likewise, the obligation to file estimated returns and make the corresponding payments is expressly excluded when the rate is zero.[38]

The preamble expresses "the aim of ensuring a harmonized tax treatment that will allow the financial system to operate more efficiently."[39] However, as Professor García Nova pointed out, "It is hard to accept the existence of a harmonizing intent when we consider that harmonization is a tool intended to reconcile or align different legislations. There can be no aligning intention in a regulation which, faced with the existence of several taxes at different rates, attempts to align them by establishing a zero rate."[40]

This makes it a "fictional or simulated federal tax, in that it imposes no material or formal obligation on the theoretical taxpayers."[41] The question is whether a zero-rate levy can be considered a tax for the purpose of LOFCA Art. 6.2, which forbids imposing regional charges on taxable events already "taxed" by the state. Most scholars would answer this in the negative, as there cannot truly be a "taxed" event if no payment is required.[42]

---

37 Art. 19.10.

38 Sections 9 and 10 *in fine*, Art. 19.

39 In the same vein, the report of the Committee of Experts for Tax Reform, February 2014, p. 355 *in fine*, said, "It must immediately be noted that the action of the government of Spain, in creating a 0% centralized tax on deposits in credit institutions, was taken merely to thwart the collection of regional taxes after losing its appeal to the Constitutional Court. The intention of the central government was not to impose a new tax, but to prevent the disruptive effects of the regional taxes on the national economy and protect credit institutions already in the midst of a serious crisis by taking the place of the regional taxes at a 0% rate."

40 César García Novoa, "El futuro de la fiscalidad autonómica sobre los depósitos bancarios," *Revista Catalana de Dret Públic*, 46, June 2013, pp. 104–134, quote on p. 132.

41 César García Novoa, "El futuro ...," *cit.* p. 129; Ramón Falcón y Tella, "El Impuesto sobre los Depósitos de las Entidades de Crédito: sobre la necesidad de un nuevo modelo para articular la potestad tributaria estatal y autonómica," *Quincena Fiscal*, 1–2, 2013, pp. 11–18, quote on p. 16.

42 In addition to the abovementioned authors, this opinion has been expressed by Ismael Jiménez Compareid, *La imposición propia de las Comunidades Autónomas*, Estudios Jurídicos-Boletín Oficial del Estado, Madrid, 1994, pp. 296 and 297; C. Checa González, "Consideraciones ante la modificación de la LOFCA por la Ley Orgánica 3/2009, de 18 de diciembre," *Quincena Fiscal*, 3, 2010, pp. 49–50, who regrets that the term "taxed" has not been replaced by "effectively taxed," although he argues that it should still be understood in the latter sense; Montserrat Hermosín Álvarez, "Los impuestos ambientales autonómicos: límites derivados del artículo 6 de la LOFCA," *Noticias de la Unión Europea*, 327, 2012, pp. 75–76; and Manuel Lucas Durán, "El panorama actual de la coordinación tributaria entre los distintos entes territoriales: la concurrencia del espacio

In this regard, Professor Lucas Durán has stated that "if an item is not effectively taxed as stipulated in a federal tax (regardless of whether that item is subject to taxation as it falls within the scope of said federal tax), it does not seem logical to limit the regional authorities' power to tax said item, as there will never be an overlap of tax obligations on the same event ... Furthermore, the tentative reservation of a tax space by blocking a taxable item only to not levy any tax, as the state has done recently – albeit only in sporadic cases – could be considered contrary to the principle of financial independence enshrined in Article 156 of the Spanish Constitution and to the principle of institutional loyalty ... in addition to being ineffective from the perspective of LOFCA Article 6.2 for, as stated, said precept only bars regional authorities from occupying a taxable event that is already taxed (meaning effectively taxed) by the federal government."[43]

The central government can limit the taxing power of the regional authorities, forbidding them to levy certain types of taxes, but it must do so in the manner stipulated in Article 157.3 of the Constitution, which requires an organic law to limit the financial powers of the regional governments.[44] In other words, it would have to amend the LOFCA.

The federal government had already used the zero-rate technique to suppress the wealth tax in 2008 and 2009 (although it was later re-established) and prevent certain regions from creating their own version of the tax.[45] This measure was equally questionable and harmless from the perspective of LOFCA Article 6.2, but on that occasion the regional authorities preferred to accept the compensations offered by the state.

---

impositivo estatal, autonómico y local," *Quincena Fiscal*, 5, 2014, pp. 74–76 (BIB 2014\581), source of the quoted material above. For a dissenting opinion, see Carlos María López Espadafor, "Algunas consideraciones sobre recargos y tributos propios en la financiación autonómica," *Revista Valenciana de Hacienda Pública Palau*, 33, 1998, pp. 53 and 54.

43 Manuel Lucas Durán, "El panorama actual de la coordinación tributaria entre los distintos entes territoriales: la concurrencia del espacio impositivo estatal, autonómico y local," *cit.*, pp. 75–76.

44 *Ibid.*, p. 76.

45 Law 4/2007 of December 23 (RCL 2008, 2156 and RCL 2009, 537), which suppressed the wealth tax, generalized the monthly VAT refunds scheme, and introduced other amendments to tax legislation, whose third article discounted 100 percent of the tax rate. Royal Decree-Law 13/2011 of September 16 (RCL 2011, 1690) temporarily reinstated the tax. On this occasion, legislators at least took the precaution of voiding the tax by means of a discount, so that there was still an amount payable (albeit 100% discounted). In any case, while technically there was an effective tax rate, the outcome was the same: no effective taxation.

Valencia decided to create its own tax by enacting Law 5/2013 of December 23 on fiscal, administrative and financial management, and organizational measures of the Regional Government of Valencia, clearly later than the federal law, and the central government responded with Law 18/2014 of October 15, which approved urgent measures for growth, competitiveness, and efficiency and raised the federal tax rate from zero to 0.03 percent to silence complaints about "non-effective taxation."

STC 30/2015 of February 19 (TOL4.765.297 and TOL4.775.455) declared the Valencian IDEC unconstitutional and consequently null and void, thereby ratifying the central government's solution. Even so, in my understanding, one cannot use a zero-rate tax to get around the fact that, according to Article 157.3 of the Constitution, the regional governments' financial powers can only be limited by an organic law. I therefore do not believe this is the best way to prevent the proliferation of regional robot taxes.

Although it is hard to predict the future evolution of our tax system, especially in the wake of the pandemic, tax authorities will probably try to avoid distorting the market and competition. But a "fictional or simulated tax" is not the answer and cannot serve as an ambiguous, generic placeholder. In the case of robotics, we cannot create a zero-rate tax that covers all possible taxable events by means of an exhaustive list or vague wording. The characteristics of that tax are still up for debate.

2 *Amending the Regional Financing Law (LOFCA)*

The central government can prevent the existence of regional taxes, "though not by ordinary law, as it has been doing in recent years, but by an amendment of the LOFCA to this effect, for example, clarifying these terms in Article 6 of said law."[46] In my view, this is not only the most constitutionally consistent solution, but also the most suitable way of restricting the creation of taxes which have not even been defined yet. An amendment of the LOFCA could prevent regional authorities from establishing robot taxes without the need to create a federal robot tax.

Of course, this organic law could channel or redirect regional powers, contemplating a ceded federal tax or the enactment of an ordinary harmonization law, as we will see.

---

46 Manuel Lucas Durán, "El panorama actual de la coordinación tributaria entre los distintos entes territoriales: la concurrencia del espacio impositivo estatal, autonómico y local," *cit.*, p. 76.

3 *The Alternative of a Ceded Federal Tax*

Another alternative is to create a real and effective federal tax that would preclude the establishment of regional taxes on the same taxable event, as long as it is not a purely symbolic encumbrance designed solely to prevent regional taxes. This tax could then be ceded to the regions, in part or in whole; the central government could manage the tax and allow the regional governments to collect it in an agreed manner, or it could cede certain legislative powers to the regional authorities or even allow them to set the tax rate (within certain limits).

LOFCA Article 6.2 should be interpreted to mean that the state is not obligated to compensate for exactly what each region had previously collected in revenues. This is borne out by the fact that the article speaks of "compensation or coordination," which allows us to conclude that compensation is not always necessary, much less exact compensation.

As for the scope of the cession, when taxes are ceded it is also possible to delegate certain managerial faculties[47] and even legislative powers.[48] However, such delegation is not legally required, as "the state is the sole owner of the ceded tax and, therefore, of the power to legislate and manage said tax, unless it chooses to delegate or cede its management in accordance with Article 156.2 or Article 157.1 a) of the Spanish Constitution."[49] Only collection can be ceded, not the tax itself, as we can infer from LOFCA Article 10.1, and that cession does not entail the "transfer of ownership of said tax or of the powers inherent to it."[50]

In the present case, it seems advisable to limit the cession to total or partial collection of the tax revenue. However, from a legal perspective, there is nothing to prevent the delegation of legislative powers to the regional authorities. For instance, they could be given the authority to set tax rates, within the specified maximum and minimum limits. The important thing is to ensure that

47 According to Article 156.2 of the Constitution, management powers can be delegated to the regions in the corresponding acts of cession (LOFCA Article 19.2 and Articles 54–58 of Law 22/2009 of December 18 which regulates the financial system of the autonomous regions). The power to amend applicable acts can also be delegated to the regions via cession laws (LOFCA Art. 20.2 and Art. 59 of Law 22/2009).

48 According to Article 150.1 of the Constitution and Articles 10.3 and 19.2 of the LOFCA, the cession can include legislative powers if this is contemplated in the pertinent cession laws and with the scope determined therein.

49 SSTC 16/2003 of January 30 (TOL239.214) and 31/2010 of June 28 (TOL1.880.189 and TOL6.442.111), regarding the Statute of Catalonia.

50 SSTC 192/2000 of July 13 (TOL81.353), 35/2012 of March 15 (TOL2.502.634), and 161/2012 of September 20 (TOL2.663.055).

criteria are consistent and companies able to compete on equal terms throughout the country.

4 *The Alternative of an Ordinary Harmonization Law*

Finally, I must mention the possibility of passing an ordinary harmonization law, which the central government is empowered to do if it serves the general interest (Art. 150.3 of the Spanish Constitution). However, this is a truly exceptional legislative method.[51] Regional governments may only impose taxes "in accordance with the Constitution and the laws" (Art. 133.2), clearly referring to ordinary federal laws,[52] which would include an ordinary harmonization law. The regional governments could directly levy their own regional robot taxes, in contrast to ceded taxes which are levied by the central government. There are few precedents for harmonization by ordinary law, and the degree of centralization that a robot tax, or several different types of robot taxes, would require makes cession a more feasible option, in my view. Cession goes much farther than harmonization, as it entails a single national tax and strengthens the federal monopoly on legislative and management powers.

D Conclusions

In Spain, the zeal to fill territorial coffers has prompted regional authorities to create taxes for the sole purpose of later seeking compensation from the state. This way of going about things is detrimental to the Spanish economy and the competitiveness of its companies. In the field of robotics, it is essential to curb the enthusiasm of regional legislators for imposing taxes, often before decisions are made by the federal government and without consulting any European authorities. Robot taxation must be negotiated and harmonized at

---

51 On harmonization laws, see Juan Alfonso Santamaría Pastor, *Principios de Derecho Administrativo General, Volumen Primero*, 2nd edition, Iustel, Madrid, 2009, pp. 514ff.

52 Arts. 133.1, 149.1.14, and 157.3 state that the federal government "has the power to regulate not only its own taxes, but also the general framework of the entire tax system and the limits of the regional authorities' financial powers in relation to those of the federal government" (SSTC 192/2000 of July 13, TOL81.353, and 31/2010 of June 28, TOL1.880.189 and TOL6.442.111). Consequently, constitutional case law recognizes the federal government's authority to "coordinate the general interests of each autonomous region .... with the general interests of the nation" (STC 1/1982 of January 28, TOL110.844). The "general coordination of the financial and tax system" is also an exclusive power of the federal government (STC 31/2010 of June 28, TOL1.880.189 and TOL6.442.111).

the international level, or at least the European level, in order to be fair and effective and not have negative repercussions for the Spanish economy.

In my opinion, the best solution would be to establish an effective federal tax. If necessary, part or all of this tax could then be ceded to the regional authorities. However, the scope of this cession should ideally be limited to revenue collection, thereby guaranteeing an even playing field and fair competition for companies in every part of Spain.

CHAPTER 6

Robot Tax

The impact of robotics on contemporary society is one of the newest and most daunting challenges that tax law now faces.[1] Today people are talking about taxing the robots themselves (some have even suggested making them legal persons) or their owners, either by charging them for the use of robotics or by levying a tax on robot-generated income. Others are more concerned with how the revenue from these "new" taxes will be allocated.[2] In my view, the primary focus should not be on allocation but on perfecting existing and future taxes to achieve a more harmonious, streamlined tax system.

There are several possible solutions to the problems that the intensive and extensive development of robots may pose: adapting existing taxes, creating specific taxes, or a combination of both.

In some cases, robot taxation could be limited to paying a simple fee[3] for bureaucratic processes, such as obtaining a registration or license plate or passing a mandatory inspection as motor vehicles are required to do.[4] But this fee could also be accompanied by other taxes, with a view to helping our system adjust to the new robotic reality.

The potential combinations are too numerous and unpredictable at this moment to list them all. They will depend on the political will of legislators,

1 As evidenced by the steady stream of scholarly publications on this subject in recent years. Among others: María Amparo Grau Ruiz, "La adaptación de la fiscalidad ante los retos jurídicos, económicos, éticos y sociales planteados por la robótica," *cit.*, pp. 35–61. Alberto Gabriel Ayala Sanhueza, "Incentivos fiscales a la innovación en robótica: Una necesaria reformulación," *cit.*, pp. 207–260. José María Quílez Moreno and Lucía Aparicio Chofrégil, "Robots e inteligencia artificial: ¿Debería exigirse algún tipo de cotización?," *Diario La Ley*, Editorial Wolters Kluwer, 5, March 14, 2017.

2 "There are several suggestions of ways in which robotics could help to sustain public expenditure. The majority are less concerned with the structure of robot taxes than with their allocation. The important thing is not deciding how robots will be taxed, but ensuring that the resulting revenue is earmarked for specific purposes," César García Novoa, "Impuestos atípicos en la era post BEPS" (Chapter 8), in Antonio Cubero Truyo (dir.), *Tributos asistemáticos del ordenamiento vigente*, Tirant lo Blanch, Valencia, 2018, p. 221.

3 Xavier Oberson, *Taxing Robots*, *op. cit.*, pp. 130–131.

4 María Amparo Grau Ruiz, "Taxing Autonomous Vehicles: The Californian Case," in José L. Pons (ed.), *Inclusive Robotics for a Better Society, Selected Papers from INBOTS Conference 2018, 16–18 October, 2018, Pisa, Italy*, Springer, Cham, Switzerland, 2019.

 | DOI:10.1163/9789004538511_007

the guidance received from European institutions, and the evolution of robotics itself.

It should be noted that most of these options are not incompatible; in fact, a single measure may not be sufficient to address this new challenge, requiring us to use a combination of measures with varying scopes. Establishing a single, all-encompassing robot tax does not seem feasible or even likely to be effective. We must therefore be open to assembling a package of complementary measures which together offer a unified, coherent response.

The following sections are dedicated to what I see as the main points of interest in this area.

A The New Robot Tax

As we have seen in previous chapters, experts from several different fields have mooted the idea of creating a tax on robots in recent years. The exact details – the taxable event, taxpayer, taxable base, etc. – of the tax vary widely from one proposal to the next. In fact, it would be safe to say that most of these proposals are not detailed plans but general recommendations, invitations to consider the possibility of creating a tax in the future.

Always bearing in mind that these are speculations on the future of a field whose full impact has yet to be determined, in the following pages I will analyze some of the legal characteristics of a possible robot tax, paying special attention to type and structure. My analysis will focus on a robot usage tax rather than a tax on robots themselves;[5] in other words, it is based on the premise that robots are the object, rather than the subject, of taxation, The third section of this part takes a closer look at the issue.

1 *Different Types of Taxes*

In order to impose a new tax on robots, first we must decide what type of tax we want to create. Taxes can be classified in many different ways and according to a variety of criteria, several of which are not relevant to robotics (periodic and one-off taxes, for example, which will not be discussed here). However, the three classifications which do have bearing on a potential robot tax are described below.

5 Xavier Oberson, *Taxing Robots*, *op. cit.*, p. 113.

a Direct and Indirect Taxes

"Direct taxes are those levied on a direct indicator of financial capacity,"[6] such as income or wealth, while "indirect taxes are based on an indirect indicator"[7] like consumption. Most robot taxation proposals call for direct taxes, based on the real or imputed income generated by robots. It seems clear that, if a tax on robots (as taxpayers) or on their use is created someday, it will most likely be a direct tax.

Nevertheless, we should not forget that robots are already subject to indirect taxes such as VAT, like any other item that can be bought and sold. Even software sales can be considered a service for VAT purposes if they meet certain requirements. Nor can we overlook the special indirect taxes that already exist, such as the digital services tax, which I will come back to later.

b Subjective and Objective Taxes

Subjective taxes "take into account the personal circumstances of each taxpayer and adjust the burden to those circumstances,"[8] whereas objective taxes are levied without regard for the taxpayer's personal situation.[9] If a robot tax is established, in most cases it would probably be a subjective tax, taking into account the situation of the robot's owner or the characteristics of the robot itself, if it acquires robotic personhood and taxpayer status.

Even so, robots are ideal candidates for a hypothetical object tax,[10] similar in design to property tax. A tax of this type has drawbacks, in terms of social justice and equity, which mean it would bring in relatively little revenue, but the first attempts to tax robots will probably be object taxes because they are easy to apply, implement, and revise.

Again, we must remember that VAT is an object tax which already applies to robots, and would still apply even if they were robotic persons acting in the legal and economic world.

---

6 Fernando Pérez Royo, *Derecho Financiero y Tributario. Parte General, op. cit.*, p. 55. See also Ramón Falcón y Tella, *Derecho Financiero y Tributario (Parte General), op. cit.*, p. 62; and Juan Martín Queralt, Carmelo Lozano Serrano, José M. Tejerizo López and Gabriel Casado Ollero, *Curso de Derecho Financiero y Tributario, op. cit.*, pp. 74–75. Similarly, see Alejandro Menéndez Moreno (dir.), *Derecho Financiero y Tributario. Parte General, op. cit.*, pp. 150–151.

7 *Ibid.*

8 Fernando Pérez Royo, *Derecho Financiero y Tributario. Parte General, op. cit.*, p. 56. See also Ramón Falcón y Tella, *Derecho Financiero y Tributario (Parte General), op. cit.*, p. 62; and Juan Martín Queralt, Carmelo Lozano Serrano, José M. Tejerizo López and Gabriel Casado Ollero, *Curso de Derecho Financiero y Tributario, op. cit.*, p. 73.

9 *Ibid.*

10 Xavier Oberson, *Taxing Robots, op. cit.*, pp. 129–130.

c Personal and Real Taxes

"This distinction is based on a widely accepted doctrine (Sainz de Bujanda) that says: personal taxes are those whose taxable base can only be conceived in relation to certain persons; all other taxes are considered real."[11]

In the field of robotics, most taxes will probably be personal as the majority of proposals focus on income. However, it would be possible to levy a real tax on robots, similar to the existing property tax or municipal motor vehicles tax. Such a tax sounds reasonably straightforward, except for the difficulty of defining a robot, and may be easy to implement, at least on certain types of robots (for example, driverless cars, drones, or domestic service robots).

2 *Structure of the Robot Tax*

Given the fact that there is no robot tax in Spain at present, or even a specific draft bill proposing its creation, a detailed analysis of its structure is impossible. The options for designing a robot tax are as varied as the range of potential new taxable items. However, we can look at some general elements of the structure of future robot taxes.

a Subjective Element

The subjective element is "the *de facto* or *de jure* relationship between the material component of the tax and the person obligated to pay it."[12] There are two possible situations in robotics: the robot as taxpayer, or the robot as part of the material component. Of course, "the subjective element must not be confused with the taxpayer;" the subjective element is a relationship, whereas the taxpayer is the instigator of the taxable event or that person's proxy.[13]

As explained in Chapter 2, robots could only be taxpayers if they had a specific personality. If they were recognized as persons, in the case of income tax, for example, the robot would be the taxpayer earning that income. On the other hand, in the case of an income tax on robot usage, the robot would be

---

11 Fernando Pérez Royo, *Derecho Financiero y Tributario. Parte General, op. cit.*, p. 56. See also Ramón Falcón y Tella, *Derecho Financiero y Tributario (Parte General), op. cit.*, p. 63; and Juan Martín Queralt, Carmelo Lozano Serrano, José M. Tejerizo López and Gabriel Casado Ollero, *Curso de Derecho Financiero y Tributario, op. cit.*, p. 73. Also Luis María Cazorla Prieto, *Derecho Financiero y Tributario, op. cit.*, pp. 201–202.

12 Fernando Pérez Royo, *Derecho Financiero y Tributario. Parte General, op. cit.*, p. 151. See also Ramón Falcón y Tella, *Derecho Financiero y Tributario (Parte General), op. cit.*, p. 165. Similarly, see Juan Martín Queralt, Carmelo Lozano Serrano, José M. Tejerizo López and Gabriel Casado Ollero, *Curso de Derecho Financiero y Tributario, op. cit.*, p. 228.

13 Ramón Falcón y Tella, *Derecho Financiero y Tributario (Parte General), op. cit.*, pp. 165–166.

part of the objective element necessary for the income earned by the robot's owner or user to be considered a subjective element.

b Objective Element

The objective element or premise comprises the material, spatial, and temporal aspects of the taxable event,[14] and the material element "is the wealth or manifestation of financial capacity incorporated"[15] in the taxable event. Given the absence of specificities related to the nature of robotics, in general, it seems that the objective elements of the taxable event would be the same, or at least similar enough, to those of other analogous taxes.

3 *The Concept of Theoretical Imputed Income*

One of the biggest problems when designing a tax on the use of robots is how to calculate the value of their usage. We are not talking about a tax on robots as taxpayers with legal personhood, in which case it would be relatively easy to determine the income they generate, but a tax levied on the income generated by using them.

If robots replace workers, those workers no longer pay income tax on their salaries, which are not replaced by a taxable income for robots. "The solution to compensate the disappearing labor tax base is to bring it back into the system."[16] To make up for this loss of revenue with a robot usage tax, some authors recommend introducing a hypothetical "imputed salary."[17] This would achieve a neutral tax treatment of human and robot workers, as business owners would have to pay tax on workers' salaries as well as on the imputed salary of robots.[18]

A similar situation already exists in Spain, where taxpayers must declare imputed rent on their personal income tax returns. If the potential rent of property owners is taxed, we could also tax the business owner's potential savings on the salaries of the replaced human workers, i.e., the robots' imputed salaries.

Of course, there are serious practical impediments to such a solution. It is practically impossible to accurately determine the amount of that imputed income. Robots may be only partial replacements for human workers or take

14 *Ibid.*, pp. 162–163.

15 Fernando Pérez Royo, *Derecho Financiero y Tributario. Parte General, op. cit.*, p. 150. Similarly, see Juan Martín Queralt, Carmelo Lozano Serrano, José M. Tejerizo López and Gabriel Casado Ollero, *Curso de Derecho Financiero y Tributario, op. cit.*, pp. 227–229.

16 Xavier Oberson, *Taxing Robots, op. cit.*, p. 114.

17 *Ibid.*

18 *Ibid.*

over tasks from multiple workers.[19] The company might need to hire new people to work alongside the robots. They could replace workers with different skills and salary levels. Or they might not replace any worker, performing tasks that were previously impossible.

Conducting in-depth functional analysis, as in transfer pricing methodology, might be one way to determine a fair and accurate taxable income.[20]

Another possible solution is to use *ratios*, such as the *ratio* of workers' salaries to company revenues, as Abbott and Bogenschneider have suggested.[21] But there are technical difficulties with this solution, too – namely, deciding which *ratio* to use and how to calculate it,[22] and gauging the impact on various industries depending on their level of automation.[23]

B International Perspective

The impact of robotics is a global phenomenon. The effects of the robotization process cannot be confined to a single country and have no respect for political borders. Robot regulations, in tax law or any other field, cannot be designed by ignoring the international scope of this technology. Many of the issues in need of regulation cannot be adequately addressed without international cooperation and, in Spain's case, especially not without the consensus of fellow EU member-states. The conflicts that arise from robotics require a legislative response coordinated among multiple countries to avoid inequalities or differences that might place users and other people in a vulnerable position. Unilateral measures attempt to remedy the lack or belated introduction of international proposals, but they end up exacerbating a problem which the OECD is trying to solve by harmonizing and standardizing standards and measures.[24]

Harmonization is very necessary in tax law, for taxes or tax incentives are only as effective as their scope of application. Without a consensus that transcends borders, it is impossible to prevent citizens and enterprises from

19 *Ibid.*, p. 115.

20 *Ibid.*

21 *Ibid.*, p. 121.

22 Depending on the type of *ratio* used, not all companies would be fairly taxed on the hypothetical income generated by replacing workers with robots, as there is not a direct exchange of human workers for robots in companies with a certain level of automation.

23 Xavier Oberson, *Taxing Robots*, *op. cit.*, pp. 120–121.

24 *Ibid.*, pp. 70–71.

relocating to countries where the tax burden is low or non-existent. Changes in international law and tax policy will require well-balanced and coordinated solutions; "it seems therefore necessary to define an international level playing field for the design of appropriate treaty rules."[25]

1 *Impact on DTTs*

Robotics will undoubtedly have an impact on the application of the OECD Model Tax Convention. In fact, it already has affected the definition of permanent establishment, as we will see in the next section. However, if new taxes on the use of robots or on robots as such are introduced, "specific and new treaty issues would come into play."[26]

As explained in Part A of this chapter, robot taxes could be introduced in several different ways, and their effects on double taxation treaties will vary depending on the adopted solution.

One of the first things to consider is that indirect taxes do not fall within the scope of international agreements, as per Article 2 of the model convention, and therefore would not be affected by DTTs. However, the same is not true of direct taxes, i.e. taxes on income and capital.

The next question is whether robots can be considered persons for the purposes of tax treaties. We must consider two scenarios: one where robots have legal personhood in one of the countries party to the agreement, and another where they do not, as a legal personality is not synonymous with a person for the purposes of enforcing the DTT. The next section contains a more detailed analysis of this question, but for now I will simply point out that, if robots were considered persons for the purposes of the DTT and received real taxable income, they would clearly fall within the scope of the agreement and be protected from double taxation.

The third possibility to consider is if the robots' users or owners are liable to pay the tax. Again, it would have to be a direct income tax – for instance, on the robots' hypothetical imputed salary and chargeable to their owner or user – rather than an indirect tax.

We must then ask ourselves if this "fictitious income" can be considered taxable revenue or increased benefits – in other words, if it qualifies as income for the purposes of the tax treaty[27] – and if calculating a theoretical imputed income might affect the tax's classification. As an example of this, Oberson mentioned the imputed theoretical rent for homeowners, which is considered

25 *Ibid.*, p. 158.
26 *Ibid.*, p. 144.
27 *Ibid.*, p. 146.

taxable income by several countries, including Spain.[28] I believe that such rent/income should fall under the scope of tax treaties.

As for computing a robot's hypothetical imputed salary, I think any calculation method based on an increase of the company's financial capacity in the country where it is based would keep that income within the scope of the treaty. It makes no difference whether this imputed salary is based on what the human workers replaced by robots would have earned, or on robot-to-worker *ratios*,[29] for in both cases the tax targets economic capacity.

The fourth issue is the allocation of the income and wealth taxes that fall under the scope of a treaty. In my opinion, as a general rule, taxable income should be classified according to the nature of the taxable person, always seeking analogies with existing taxes and their classification methods.

If robots had legal personhood, it would make sense for the revenue attributable to them – either as corporate profits or salary – to be governed by Articles 7 and 15 of the OECD Model Convention, depending on what specific type of legal personality they were granted.[30] Eventually this income might even be classified as royalty payments, such as those received by artists or athletes; however, from a technological, social, and legal standpoint, we still have a long way to go before we can even begin to consider the possibility of smart robots owning intellectual property or collecting pensions – if we ever do get that far.[31]

If robots are not legal persons, their income (including imputed salary in this case) would have to be taxed in the place where their users or owners are based and therefore be governed by Article 7 on corporate profits.[32] Even if the imputed salary is based on "lost" human wages, it makes no sense to argue that it should be treated as income from employment, governed by Article 15, because the tax is levied on the financial capacity of the owners rather than the "salary-generating" robots. Ultimately, the aim is to tax the economic advantage they obtained by using automation instead of human workers.

2 *Robots as Permanent Establishments*

Professor Oberson wrote that, as part of enterprises or as independent legal persons, "robots would contribute to the realization of taxable profits."[33] Given

28 *Ibid.*, pp. 146–147.

29 "It follows that these automation taxes, to the extent that they are levied on profits of companies, could also fall under the scope of the DTT," in *ibid.*, pp. 147–148.

30 *Ibid.*, pp. 154–155.

31 *Ibid.*

32 *Ibid.*, pp. 148–149.

33 *Ibid.*, p. 49.

the natural of today's global, digitalized economy, those profits could well be transnational. Cross-border profits arising from automation should be taxed in the enterprise's (or robot's) country of residence. However, they could also be attributed to a foreign permanent establishment (PE) and taxed at that level.

Robots may represent nothing new with regard to permanent establishments, because their inclusion in internal organizations and structures which are already considered PEs would not alter the nature of an PE. However, robots could also force us to rethink the permanent establishment concept, analyze its definition, and update it if necessary.

a Application of the Traditional Concept of Permanent Establishment

Article 5 of the OECD Model Convention regulates permanent establishment. In general terms, a PE can mean one of two things: a fixed place of business where an enterprise conducts all or part of its operations; or, for the purposes of the convention, a person who acts on behalf of an enterprise (not as an independent agent) in a contracting state and possesses and regularly exercises the authority to enter into contracts in the company's name.

It is worth analyzing whether robots could be considered PEs, channeling the income generated in certain countries to those where the corporate owners have their place of business, and consequently subject to taxation.

As we saw in Chapter 3, robots could be granted legal personhood at some point. We must therefore consider two scenarios: one where a robot is a PE without legal personality, and another where a robot is granted legal personhood as a permanent establishment.

If a robot acted on a company's behalf and had the authority to enter into contracts, it would be considered an agent, in which case there are two alternatives. One would be a state granting robots a special type of legal personhood that would allow them to enter into contracts, which in turn would make robots eligible to be considered persons for the purposes of the OECD Model Convention. If this happened, robots might well act like any other person and be dependent agents of an enterprise. Although this may seem like a remote possibility today, we cannot entirely rule it out, as the conversation on potential robotic personalities is only getting started.

The first possibility we need to examine is that of a robot as a PE, in the sense of a fixed place of business. Unlike the notion of PE as agent, this is undoubtedly a real possibility in the present moment. According to the interpretation of Article 5 of the OECD Model Convention, "A permanent establishment may exist if the business of the enterprise is carried on mainly through automatic equipment, the activities of the personnel being restricted to setting up, operating, controlling and maintaining such equipment."[34] As Oberson observed, the same logic should "apply to any automated operation, including robots' activities, carried out by equipment sited in the relevant state."[35] And I agree that "a permanent establishment may exist [...] if the enterprise which sets up the machines also operates and maintains them"[36] on its own account, even without human personnel, if the machines in question are smart robots. Of course, in order for these robots to be considered PEs, they must meet the conditions of being a fixed place of business where company operations are carried out and where these are not limited to preparatory or auxiliary activities. These requirements would not have to be adapted or tailored to fit robots; application would be identical to other cases of permanent establishment.

Robots could also be recognized as agents if the interpretation of "person" in Article 1 of the OECD Model Convention is changed. Obviously, if robots are considered persons for the purposes of the convention, even without legal personhood, they could act as agents and constitute permanent establishments. There is precedent for such a change, as the OECD Model Convention has recognized some entities, like trusts, as persons, even if they are not considered legal persons according to the laws of many countries.[37]

As with the special tax capacity of robots and the possibility of them being considered taxpayers without personhood discussed in Chapter 3, this does not strike me as a suitable solution. There are always persons behind these supposedly "person-less" entities, and the possibility of treating them as taxpayers is simply a legislative (and perhaps not entirely appropriate) solution to the problem of identifying multiple persons or an indeterminate person. This is not the case of robots, which is why I do not think they should be agents, i.e., considered persons for the purpose of the OECD Model Convention, but with no legal personality.

However, if robotic personalities begin to pop up chaotically and at different times in various OECD countries, considering robots persons for the purpose of the convention might be a practical means of unifying different interpretations of these concepts. In any case, technological advances will have to be made in robotic autonomy in order to even consider the possibility of a smart robot agent as PE.

---

34 Model Tax Convention on Income and on Capital: Commentary on Article 5, Paragraph 1, 41.

35 Xavier Oberson, *Taxing Robots*, *op. cit.*, p. 52.

36 Model Tax Convention on Income and on Capital: Commentary on Article 5, Paragraph 1, 41.

37 Xavier Oberson, *Taxing Robots*, *op. cit.*, pp. 53–54.

b The New Concept of Digital Permanent Establishment

Our increasingly digitalized economy has given rise to a new type of permanent establishment, the digital PE. This approach introduces other, non-physical criteria for a PE, such as significant digital presence, attempting to determine the existence of a digital nexus that evidences a purposeful and sustained interaction with the economy of the country in question.[38] This new concept can be found in the OECD Interim Report on Action 1 of the BEPS Project (2018).

The European Union has also moved toward this idea by proposing a directive[39] under which a PE will be present if a company has a significant digital and economic presence, for which it must meet one of the following conditions:

- Total revenues in excess of 7 million euros
- More than 100,000 users
- Over 3,000 contracts[40]

The United States seems to be headed in the same general direction,[41] even though there is no VAT or federal sales tax in this country. However, each state has the authority to levy sales tax, a single-stage tax on sales collected at the retail stage.

"In theory, in order to apply sales tax, the retailer must have a 'significant physical presence' or connection, known as the 'nexus,' to the place where the sale is made. The 'nexus' is a concept similar to permanent establishment, used particularly to tax the income of non-residents."[42]

The US Supreme Court's decision in the matter of *South Dakota v. Wayfair*[43] overturned the conventional criteria established in *Quill v. North Dakota*.[44] This decision stated that the physical presence rule, which had become a legal tax haven, was incorrect and not a requirement of the Commerce Clause.[45]

---

38 *Ibid.*, p. 71.

39 Proposal for a Council Directive laying down rules relating to the corporate taxation of a significant digital presence, COM/2018/0147 final – 2018/072 (CNS).

40 Xavier Oberson, *Taxing Robots*, *op. cit.*, pp. 65–66.

41 *Ibid.*, pp. 74–75.

42 Ramón Falcón y Tella, "El 'nexus' en la doctrina del Tribunal Supremo de Estados Unidos: el asunto Dakota del Sur v. Wayfair," *Quincena Fiscal*, 18, 2018, pp. 9–14.

43 South Dakota v. Wayfair, Inc. 585 US ___, 138 S. Ct. 2080; 201 L. Ed. 2d 403 (2018).

44 Quill Corp. v. North Dakota, 504 US 298, 112 S. Ct. 1904, 119 L. Ed. 2d 91 (1992).

45 "Despite this precedent, on June 21, 2009, the Supreme Court rejected an appeal by Capital One Bank against a ruling of the Massachusetts Supreme Court which determined that issuing cards with the Capital One logo to state residents constituted a substantial 'nexus' that justified the tax (economic presence being sufficient even without a physical presence). But this decision involved a tax based on revenues, making it highly unlikely that it could also apply to sales tax," in Ramón Falcón y Tella, "El 'nexus' en la doctrina del Tribunal Supremo de Estados Unidos: el asunto Dakota del Sur v. Wayfair," *cit.*, pp. 9–14.

"Moving past the physical presence requirement, the nexus is now defined as a virtual, economic, not necessarily physical presence. To establish a nexus, it is enough that the taxpayer 'avails itself of the substantial privilege of carrying on business' in that jurisdiction."[46]

In Europe, this problem does not affect VAT, but "when it comes to direct taxes, it is safe to say that the concept of permanent establishment as a fixed place of business or dependent agent has become a tax haven, one specifically created by the OECD Model Convention and double taxation treaties, insofar as income obtained without involving the permanent establishment can only be taxed in the place of residence, not at the source."[47]

"Contrary to the traditional approach," the digital permanent establishment is a concept "aimed at diluting the requirement for permanence and physical presence at a specific geographical place to establish a nexus for net-basis taxation."[48] As yet, there is no consensus among OECD members on the scope of the new digital permanent establishment, the qualifying threshold, or the attribution of profits to that PE.[49]

Given the lack of significant progress on BEPS Action 1, "the European Commission has presented a legislative initiative to define the existence of a 'taxable digital presence' – in other words, to broaden the concept of permanent establishment to include the 'virtual permanent establishment,'"[50] which would depend on the existence of objective elements such as number of customers, revenues, or activity measured in the number of contracts or transactions. "That new nexus would allow authorities to tax profits obtained via digital channels not connected to a permanent establishment in the traditional sense."[51]

Attempts to adapt these norms to the digital economy have real consequences for an economy based on AI and robots.[52] The digital economy uses data and software (or algorithms) to make automated decisions, which is the basis of robotics and AI. As technology evolves, companies will find it increasingly easy to operate without human workers who are physically present in a fixed place of business.[53] When that happens, we will have two options: reduce

46 *Ibid.*, pp. 9–14.

47 *Ibid.*

48 Xavier Oberson, *Taxing Robots*, *op. cit.*, p. 76.

49 *Ibid.*

50 Ramón Falcón y Tella, "El 'nexus' en la doctrina del Tribunal Supremo de Estados Unidos: el asunto Dakota del Sur v. Wayfair," *cit.*, pp. 9–14.

51 *Ibid.*

52 Xavier Oberson, *Taxing Robots*, *op. cit.*, pp. 80–81.

53 *Ibid.*, p. 82.

or entirely eliminate the physical presence requirement for such personnel, as in e-commerce and other activities (the extraction of natural resources, for instance) where the equipment operates on its own;[54] or expand the definition of personnel to include AI and smart robots with a certain degree of autonomy.[55]

The solutions proposed for the digital economy are at least partially applicable to robotics. As many of these have yet to be implemented and are still under debate, we should keep an eye on new developments and challenges in robotics and try to design solutions that cover both the digital economy and automation processes.

C Other Ways of Taxing Robots: Taxes and Fees

1 *Creating New Taxes*

Creating a tax on the income earned by robots, treating them as persons under the law, or on the income earned by their owners or users is not the only possible solution to the problem. There are many different ways in which we could tax robots, from adjusting existing taxes to inventing new ones or a combination of both.

Robot taxation could be limited to paying a simple fee[56] for bureaucratic processes, such as obtaining a registration or license plate or passing a mandatory inspection as motor vehicles are required to do. Such a fee could be complemented by a new income tax or an updated version of existing income taxes that reflects the new automated reality.

At this point in time, the possibilities and combinations are too numerous and unpredictable to list them all. They will depend on the political will of legislators and European institutions, and on the evolution of robotics itself. For now, I will simply point out that most of these possibilities are not incompatible; in fact, a single measure may not be sufficient to address this new challenge. The most likely solution will entail not one grand proposal but a package of measures that vary in scope and size.

---

54 Model Tax Convention on Income and on Capital: Commentary on Article 5, e-commerce, 42.6.

55 Xavier Oberson, *Taxing Robots*, *op. cit.*, p. 82.

56 Xavier Oberson, *Taxing Robots*, *op. cit.*, pp. 130–131.

2 *Adjusting Existing Taxes*

We ought to consider whether existing taxes can be adjusted to meet the needs of this new reality before creating new ones. It should not be too difficult to adapt taxes levied on the activities of natural or legal persons to the robots which have taken over those activities. Let us examine this possibility in relation to the taxes that are most relevant in terms of total revenue or their connection to robotics.

a Personal, Corporate, and Non-Resident Income Tax

There are currently three types of income tax levied in Spain, the application of which varies depending on the type of person (although non-resident income tax is based on other factors, which I will not get into here, as would also be the case of robots). Robots can hardly be expected to pay these taxes if they are not persons under the law, much less assigned a special tax capacity that does not even exist. If, at some point in the future, they are given a special robotic personality, perhaps one of these income taxes could be adapted to extend to robots. Ultimately, the consideration of robots as taxpayers will depend on what type of personhood, if any, they are granted.

Other measures could be used to adjust these taxes without altering the existing system of tax liability. For example, we could change the way robot-generated income is measured and add it to the base of an income tax which would still be paid by natural or legal persons. However, this could pose a double taxation risk, if we add a new way of measuring robot-generated income without taking into account that it is already taxed at the level of the subject. It is also vital to consider the new characteristics of the economy and labor market, in order to make a fair and true assessment.

One particularly interesting option is increasing corporate income tax to offset the loss of revenue from personal income tax.[57] The reasoning is that this would compensate for the fact that the revenue obtained from other taxes is decreasing, despite the boost in productivity facilitated by robots, because human workers and robots are not treated equally. It could take the form of a general hike in the corporate income tax rate,[58] or the elimination

57 *Ibid.*, p. 139.

58 A measure of this type overlooks the fact that not all companies have the same level of automation, which means some would be paying higher taxes but reaping none of the benefits. It also fails to consider that not all companies with some level of automation have replaced human workers with robots; some robots perform tasks that human beings could never do, thereby opening up new areas of production and operation which result in net job creation.

or reorientation of tax advantages to achieve a more neutral tax treatment between human and robot workers. In either form, I believe this would be a serious mistake. Creating an *ad hoc* tax seems to be a better option for the purposes of transparency and simplicity in tax regulations.

b VAT

Value Added Tax was introduced in France in 1954 at the initiative of Maurice Lauré, director of the French Tax Administration at the time.[59] VAT became quite a success and was adopted by the European Economic Community, forerunner of the European Union.[60] As we know, VAT is an indirect, real, objective, proportional, one-off,[61] multi-stage consumption tax based on the principles of generality and neutrality.[62]

There are three main issues to explore with regard to VAT and robots. The first is the application of VAT to robots when they are bought or sold. The second has to do with the activities of robots which, for tax purposes, are part of the business assets of an enterprise (legal person) or individual (natural person), and which undoubtedly fall within the scope of this tax.[63] The third is the possibility that smart robots may one day be considered business owners for VAT purposes, with all that this entails.

When robots are bought or sold, VAT is paid on the transactions. In theory, a robot sale should be considered a supply of goods, although it could also be regarded as an electronic service in some cases.[64] The former would apply if the robot is physically delivered to the customer; if, on the other hand, we are dealing with software or the predominance of the transaction consists in the robot's ability to help, interact, and learn with the new owner, a characterization as a service should prevail.[65] As Oberson correctly observed, "Existing principles seem to solve most of the classical issues [affecting robotics], such

59 Xavier Oberson, *Taxing Robots*, *op. cit.*, p. 87; and Antonio Cubero Truyo, "El Impuesto sobre el Valor Añadido (I)," Chapter XI, in Fernando Pérez Royo (dir.), *Curso de Derecho Tributario. Parte Especial*, 11th edition, Tecnos, Madrid, 2017, p. 712.

60 *Ibid.*

61 Antonio Cubero Truyo, "El Impuesto sobre el Valor Añadido (I)," Chapter XI, *cit.*, p. 712; and José Almudí Cid, "Impuesto sobre el Valor Añadido," Chapter VIII, in Ramón Falcón y Tella, Gaspar de la Peña and Miguel Ángel Martínez Lago (coords.), *Sistema Fiscal Español (Impuestos Estatales, Autonómicos y Locales)*, 8th edition, Iustel, Madrid, 2018, pp. 276–277.

62 Among others, Xavier Oberson, *Taxing Robots*, *op. cit.*, p. 89.

63 "It is not disputable that such activities, to the extent they are effectuated by enterprises in exchange of a consideration, would fall under the scope of the VAT," *Ibid.*, p. 88.

64 Xavier Oberson, *Taxing Robots*, *op. cit.*, p. 92.

65 *Ibid.*, p. 93.

as the character of the transaction (supply of goods or services) and the corresponding place of supply."[66]

Like all other goods or services, robots with this consideration are subject to VAT at the enterprise level. While this may sound obvious, I feel it is worth recalling because many people appear to forget this when they talk about robots paying taxes, giving the impression that those robots exist outside the tax system and are "free" of obligations.

The same is true of companies subject to VAT which use robots to provide services or supply goods. Today, there are many ways in which robots participate in the production or commercial operations of enterprises, for example in the automotive industry.

Finally, we must consider "whether robots as such could in the future become required to charge VAT on their activities. This conclusion would require either that robots, under some conditions, would be recognized as legal entities, and therefore subject to tax or, even without a legal personality, would qualify as sufficiently autonomous and independent to become VAT taxpayers."[67]

VAT taxpayers are business owners and self-employed professionals, as defined in Article 5, 1 a) of the Spanish VAT Law: "Persons or entities engaged in business or professional activities." This could mean that, at some point, smart robots might be considered taxpayers without being recognized as legal entities,[68] provided they are able to act autonomously and be organizationally independent.[69] However, although smart robots could perhaps be considered taxable persons for VAT purposes, there would still be the obstacle of special tax capacity. It makes no sense to impose an obligation to pay tax on an entity that cannot own assets.

Perhaps smart robots could be considered business owners or freelance professionals, and consequently VAT taxpayers, if they were granted a robotic "capacity of representation." Of course, in this case, as in the case of robots acquiring a specific legal personality, they could also be considered consumers for VAT purposes and therefore be charged input VAT.

c Others

This section examines special taxes and others of particular relevance to the field of robotics. In my analysis, I will distinguish between robots as subjects and objects of taxation.

---

66 *Ibid.*, p. 110.

67 *Ibid.*, p. 111.

68 *Ibid.*, pp. 90 and 135.

69 *Ibid.*, p. 90.

If robots acquire a specific legal personality, they will be subject to the same obligations as legal and natural persons (within the scope and capabilities stipulated for their personality). Therefore, robots with personhood would be liable to pay special taxes, just like any other taxpayer. This would not pose a different problem for each tax but a general one related to personality, and could therefore be solved by addressing the capacity of robots according to their legal personhood rather than by adjusting each tax separately.

However, viewing robots as objects rather than subjects, there are three taxes that seem particularly suitable for reflecting the reality of robots.

i *Special Tax on Certain Modes of Transportation*

This tax, known by its Spanish acronym IEDMT, is a perfect candidate for adaptation to robots. It is reasonable to think that driverless cars would automatically enter the same categories as cars with human drivers, but they might also be joined by other robots that can move around on their own and even some that are not modes of transportation *per se*. Adapting the IEDMT, or creating a similar tax solely for robots, is a method of control and revenue collection that would be simple and easy to introduce in our system, where the structure and logic of such a tax already exists in the IEDMT.

We could extend the scope of the IEDMT to include only driverless vehicles, excluding robots which can move but are not vehicles, or creating a separate tax for the latter. The possibilities are varied, but the justification would be similar to that of the existing tax.

The IEDMT is levied not only in consideration of the ability to pay manifested by ownership of the vehicle in question, but also of "the additional implications of its use for incurring specific social costs in the fields of healthcare, infrastructure, or the environment."[70] These or similar reasons can be used to impose a tax burden on robots in the same way as other taxes do on certain modes of transportation.

Of course, such a tax would not solve the revenue problem, but it could be one of various measures to help our tax system adjust to a changing economic world where digitalization, robotization, and artificial intelligence are introducing increasingly complex, advanced, autonomous forms.

70 Preamble to Law 38/1992 of December 28 on special taxes.

ii Special Electricity Tax

The electricity tax was a special manufacturing tax enacted by Law 66/1997 of December 30 on fiscal, administrative, and social order measures. However, in 2014 it was eliminated and replaced by a special electricity tax.

This new tax "was no longer a tax on manufacturing but a tax on the supply of electricity for consumption or self-consumption by producers of that electricity [...] the goal of this modification being to cut administrative costs for the different agents on the electricity market as well as for the government, adapting Spanish legislation to the stipulations of the European Union directive."[71] Consequently, it became a tax on the consumption or self-consumption of electrical energy.

Robots are electricity consumers because they need it to function, even if they generate their own energy (with solar panels, for instance), as the tax is also levied on self-consumption. If they had a specific robotic personality, they would clearly be considered taxpayers. If not, their owners would be consuming more electrical power, thereby increasing revenue obtained from this tax.

One way to limit the sensational growth spurt of robotics is to tax its "fuel": electricity. If this tax rate goes up, so does the cost of using robots, thus reducing their use. Even so, it would be unwise to propose an increase of this tax without considering how it will affect society as a whole. Tax exemptions could be used to promote the use of robots or of renewable energy sources, for example by making the self-consumption of electricity generated by environmentally sustainable methods exempt.

There are many possibilities, including but not limited to tax exemptions, different tax rates depending on where the electricity is consumed, or the introduction of a scale. Correctly adapting this tax to the new reality has the potential to be a highly effective measure, as robots are entirely dependent on electricity consumption.

---

71 Preamble to Law 28/2014 of November 27, which amended Law 37/1992 of December 28 on the value added tax, Law 20/1991 of June 7, amending fiscal aspects of the Tax and Economic Regime of the Canary Islands, Law 38/1992 of December 28 on special taxes, and Law 16/2013 of October 29, which established certain measures in environmental taxation and adopted other financial and tax measures. The old electricity tax was a special manufacturing tax, enacted by Law 66/1997 of December 30 on fiscal, administrative, and social order measures. However, in 2014 it was eliminated and replaced by a special electricity tax.

iii *Public Radio-Electric Spectrum Reservation Rate*

The public radio-electric spectrum reservation rate is regulated in Annex I of General Telecommunications Law 9/2014 of May 9, which is further developed in the law on federal budgets.

In addition to electricity, robots must use frequencies on the public radio-electric spectrum to process the data required to perform their assigned tasks. While not all robots will need that spectrum, or use it to the same degree, it seems likely that they will make a relatively intense use of the same, like any other new technology.

The need for new frequencies, already apparent today, will become even more pressing if robots continue their exponential growth and their dependence on the public radio-electric spectrum increases as it is expected to do.

Thus, as in the case of electricity, there is a direct correlation between an increase of this tax and an increase in the cost of using robots, which could reduce their usage. Imposing a suitable tax on the other essential "fuel" of robots, data – indirectly, in this case, via the public radio-electric frequencies used to transmit those data – is another way to limit the impact of robotics.

D Social Security Contributions

In light of the imminent automation of the labor market and its economic and budgetary consequences, many are wondering if robots should pay Social Security tax.[72] The "potential job loss due to robots replacing human capital" forces us to at least consider "the possibility that those new robots contribute in some way to the Social Security coffers."[73] It seems appropriate, from the perspective of economic and social policy, that robots should help finance Social Security, which would then help unemployed workers who lost their jobs due to automation.[74]

---

72 "Assuming a progressive increase of the robotic presence in the workplace, the next logical question is to ask if they, by taking a job, will have the obligation to pay like any other worker, thereby helping to finance public social security systems." Esther Puente Pérez, "Los robots en el Derecho del Trabajo," Chapter VI, in Moisés Barrio Andrés (dir.), *Derecho de los robots, op. cit.*, p. 159.

73 José María Quílez Moreno and Lucía Aparicio Chofrégil, "Robots e inteligencia artificial: ¿Debería exigirse algún tipo de cotización?," *cit.*

74 Xavier Oberson, *Taxing Robots, op. cit.*, p. 137.

1 *Concept and Nature of Contributions*

In order to determine if robots should contribute to Social Security,[75] we must first understand the concept of contribution. According to Article 41 of the Spanish Constitution, the federal government is required to maintain a public Social Security regime, and contributions are contemplated as one of the means of financing this system in Article 109.1 b) of the General Social Security Act. These contributions are mandatory payments made by employees and employers which, in a proportional manner,[76] help finance the Social Security administration.[77]

That proportionality and other features of its design are precisely what allow contributions to be used for pursuing other economic policy goals[78] and not just for funding.

From one angle, these contributions can be considered para-fiscal charges similar to taxes.[79] They are compulsory public charges or, to put it another way, a para-fiscal tax.[80] However, this does not help us determine whether robots

75 "On the controversial topic of whether or not robots should contribute, after analyzing the matter from a technical-legal perspective, one can conclude that robots have no obligation to contribute to social security, and they neither are nor will be subjects obligated to contribute." Carolina Serrano Falcón, "A propósito de una controversia: ¿tienen que cotizar los robots a la Seguridad Social?," in Cristina García-Herrera Blanco (dir.), *VI Encuentro de Derecho Financiero y Tributario "Tendencias y retos del Derecho Financiero y Tributario" (1.ª parte), Documentos de trabajo del IEF*, 10, 2018, p. 73.

76 Miguel de Haro Izquierdo, "La sustitución de trabajadores por robots: impacto en las contribuciones a la Seguridad Social y su posible financiación por tributos" (Chapter 4), in Fernando Serrano Antón (dir.), *Fiscalidad e Inteligencia Artificial: Administración Tributaria y contribuyentes en la Era Digital, op. cit.*, p. 122.

77 "In consonance with the Toledo Pact, ratified on April 6, 1995, the separate sources of funding principle was enshrined in Law 24/1997 of July 15, which consolidated and streamlined the social security system. Contributory benefits are essentially financed by social security contributions, and non-contributory benefits are covered by transfers from the state," in María Amparo Grau Ruiz, "Empleo y robótica: La legitimidad de adoptar medidas extrafiscales para la urgente capacitación tecnológica funcional" (forthcoming).

78 "For no one can deny their effects on the economy in general and on employment in particular." Begoña Pérez Bernabeu, "La naturaleza tributaria de las cotizaciones sociales en el actual contexto de separación de fuentes de financiación de la Seguridad Social" (Chapter 21), in Antonio Cubero Truyo (dir.), *Tributos asistemáticos del ordenamiento vigente*, Tirant lo Blanch, Valencia, 2018, p. 469.

79 "Para-fiscal charges include, among others, social security contributions" and "Social contributions, for example, are comparable to a tax." Ramón Falcón y Tella, *Derecho Financiero y Tributario (Parte General), op. cit.*, p. 66.

80 Juan Martín Queralt, Carmelo Lozano Serrano, José M. Tejerizo López and Gabriel Casado Ollero, *Curso de Derecho Financiero y Tributario, op. cit.*, p. 49.

should or can contribute. To do so, we must turn to the specific regulations that govern the Social Security system and contributions.

2 *Adapting the Concept of Contributions to a Potential Social Security Tax on Robots*

In order to thoroughly examine the possibility of levying a Social Security tax on robots, we must first determine the identity and legal capacity of the taxpayer.[81] Several scenarios must be analyzed before we can answer the question of whether or not robots should contribute to Social Security. These scenarios are the different possibilities arising from two variable factors: the robot's role in the employment relationship (worker or employer); and the robot's legal personality (specific robotic personhood or none), as "the feasibility of contributing to Social Security must be considered in relation to the principle of legal capacity of the robots."[82]

The combination of these factors gives rise to three different scenarios: a robot-worker with no legal personality, a robot-worker with legal personality, and a robot-employer. I will examine these scenarios in the following paragraphs, seeking solutions to the specific problems each one poses and discussing how they would affect the possibility of levying a Social Security tax on robots.

In the case of the robot-worker, the first stumbling block is found in Article 7.2 of Royal Decree 2064/1995 of December 22, which approved the general regulation on contributions and settlements of other Social Security rights, "for the obligation to contribute can only be imposed on natural or legal persons, neither of which currently fits or applies to a robot."[83] As mentioned in the third chapter of this book, on the personhood of robots, at present robots are legally considered mere things, although this could change in the future. To overcome this difficulty, "one solution might be to create a new legal concept of robotic personhood."[84] However, any attempt to give robots a personality would entail changes in legislation and legal interpretation. It therefore seems clear that "for now robots, no matter how intelligent or autonomous, cannot be subject to the obligation to contribute."[85]

---

81 Miguel de Haro Izquierdo, "La sustitución de trabajadores por robots: impacto en las contribuciones a la Seguridad Social y su posible financiación por tributos," *cit.*, p. 125.

82 *Ibid.*

83 José María Quílez Moreno and Lucía Aparicio Chofrégil, "Robots e inteligencia artificial: ¿Debería exigirse algún tipo de cotización?," *cit.*

84 *Ibid.*

85 *Ibid.*

Even though this problem could be overcome by creating a special robotic personality, it is not the only obstacle to charging Social Security tax on robots. "If we require robots to contribute to Social Security, we will have to establish parameters for determining the exact amount each robot should contribute or be charged, which would undoubtedly be a process fraught with problems and conflicts."[86]

Perhaps the biggest problem is actually the very nature of the Social Security regime and contributions. "If we consider a robot's legal personality in light of the benefits to which that legal person could be entitled as a contributor to Social Security, we may find that, just as that robot contributes (as certain sectors have proposed), so it would also have a right to claim the benefits of that contribution. Failure to claim said benefits would result in a manifest imbalance, and the original meaning and purpose of Social Security contributions would be distorted."[87] If robots had the obligation to contribute, they would also have to benefit from the protective action of the Social Security system, even though we know that "robots have no real use for some of the benefits of the Social Security system's current protective action."[88]

This problem could only be solved by "creating a specific set of benefits, a special protective scheme for these robotic employees,"[89] perhaps rights or benefits similar to those afforded to human workers but tailored to the robotic needs of these new contributors. However, this scenario is predicated on situations and advances in robotic technology and science that have yet to materialize and probably will not in the near future. Devising a robotic Social Security scheme with robot-specific contributions is an overly futuristic and, for now, unrealistic option. Moreover, it would not address the root of the problem: people want robots to contribute because the Social Security administration needs

---

86 María Amparo Grau Ruiz and María Yolanda Sánchez-Urán Azaña, "Plataformas Digitales y Robótica. Su proyección en el Sistema de Seguridad Social," E-print, UCM, 2021, p. 26. [Available online at https://eprints.ucm.es/64676/].

87 Miguel de Haro Izquierdo, "La sustitución de trabajadores por robots: impacto en las contribuciones a la Seguridad Social y su posible financiación por tributos," *cit.*, p. 128.

88 José María Quílez Moreno and Lucía Aparicio Chofrégil, "Robots e inteligencia artificial: ¿Debería exigirse algún tipo de cotización?," *cit.* A similar opinion is expressed in Miguel de Haro Izquierdo, "La sustitución de trabajadores por robots: impacto en las contribuciones a la seguridad social y su posible financiación por tributos," *cit.*, p. 132. "We understand, a priori, that it is not possible for a robot to claim such benefits as if it were a legal person with rights and obligations."

89 José María Quílez Moreno and Lucía Aparicio Chofrégil, "Robots e inteligencia artificial: ¿Debería exigirse algún tipo de cotización?," *cit.*

more revenue to cover its growing expenses, but if the proposed solution adds to those expenses, it would do little good.

If we require robots to contribute, "there would be an entire class of workers that contributes solely and exclusively to cover the needs of others, with no prospect of ever receiving the same rights and benefits while shouldering a heavy burden of obligations."[90] We can only conclude that, in this scenario, "it makes no sense to demand a contribution, as this concept is currently designed."[91]

This does not mean that robots cannot help to finance the Social Security system, only that obligatory contributions are not the way to go, as it would make no sense to redefine the nature and characteristics of such contributions. The problem, as we have seen throughout this book, is essentially a lack of sufficient financial resources, a situation of decreasing revenues and rising costs. "The potential shortage of revenue due to the destruction of human jobs, which in turn will increase the number of people needing benefits"[92] tells us that this is basically a financial issue that cannot be solved by "devious formulas hiding under the umbrella of contributions."[93] If robots are to help sustain public expenditure, particularly Social Security, the taxes levied on them could be allocated to guarantee that the revenue obtained is used for that specific purpose.[94] However, as I have already mentioned elsewhere, allocating newly created taxes or existing taxes amended to reflect the new robotic reality is not the way to go, in my opinion. I believe that revenue allocation distorts the essence of the tax and, moreover, represents an attempt on the legislator's part to control future budgetary decisions.

---

90 *Ibid.*

91 *Ibid.* A similar analysis can be found in Miguel de Haro Izquierdo, "La sustitución de trabajadores por robots: impacto en las contribuciones a la Seguridad Social y su posible financiación por tributos," *cit.*, p. 132: "Forcing robots to pay social security contributions as such is implausible, as this would distort the very essence of the concept of such contributions, which are benefits and measures implemented by the social security administration to provide for, mitigate, or overcome certain situations of misfortune or necessity that tend to result in a loss of income or extra expenses for those who experience them."

92 José María Quílez Moreno and Lucía Aparicio Chofrégil, "Robots e inteligencia artificial: ¿Debería exigirse algún tipo de cotización?," *cit.*

93 *Ibid.*

94 "There are several suggestions of ways in which robotics could help to sustain public expenditure. The majority are less concerned with the structure of robot taxes than with their allocation. The important thing is not deciding how robots will be taxed, but ensuring that the resulting revenue is earmarked for specific purposes." César García Novoa, "Impuestos atípicos en la era post BEPS" (Chapter 8), in Antonio Cubero Truyo (dir.), *Tributos asistemáticos del ordenamiento vigente, op. cit.*, p. 221.

The other possibility we must consider is that of robot-employers paying Social Security contributions on behalf of their employees. In this case, as long as they have a specific legal personality allowing them to hire workers, it seems reasonable that robots should have the same obligations as other employers. This scenario does not pose the same difficulties as the previous one. All employers, whether legal or natural persons, are required to pay a percentage of their workers' Social Security contributions, and this seems to be the only situation in which robots could justifiably be obligated to pay Social Security tax: not only would it be fair, as otherwise the new robotic personality would have a competitive edge over human employers, but it would also be necessary for the sake of the employees, as they deserve to have the same protection as any other worker employed by a legal or natural person.

In conclusion, I am convinced that "requiring robots to pay Social Security contributions as such is not the best option,[95] as it distorts the very essence of the concept of contribution,"[96] even if robots had a specific legal personality which allowed them to operate in the legal and economic world and be employed as workers.

There are better solutions[97] to the budgetary problems of the Social Security system, such as levying new taxes or adapting old ones, as we have already seen. Of the various scenarios reviewed above, only one seems viable: provided they have specific legal personhood, robots could pay Social Security contributions on behalf of their employees, who would always be natural persons, just as other employers, whether natural or legal persons, are required to do. Even so, I do not view this as a solution but as a logical adaptation to the appearance of a specific legal personality which would allow robots to hire employees.

95 Miguel de Haro Izquierdo, "La sustitución de trabajadores por robots: impacto en las contribuciones a la Seguridad Social y su posible financiación por tributos," *cit.*, p. 128.

96 "If business owners are forced to pay contributions for their robots, they would not be paying to protect those employees against contingencies; instead, it would seem like they were being charged a tax to cover social security benefits and remedy the system's financing problems," in María Amparo Grau Ruiz and María Yolanda Sánchez-Urán Azaña, "Plataformas Digitales y Robótica. Su proyección en el Sistema de Seguridad Social," E-print, UCM, 2021, p. 25. [Available online at https://eprints.ucm.es/64676/].

97 One is the possibility of offering employers tax incentives on their social security contributions if they invest in employee training, with the aim of offsetting the negative impact of automation on workers and, by extension, on social security expenditure. María Amparo Grau Ruiz and Alfredo Díaz Peña, "Social Security and Robotization: Possible Ways to Finance Human Reskilling and Promote Employment," *Paladyn Journal of Behavioural Robotics*, 2020.

E Other Solutions

Robots are already being taxed today, just not in the way that some social and economic agents would wish. As we have seen, the IEDMT can be levied on robots (cars with varying degrees of autonomy) to the extent that they are vehicles, while personal, corporate, and non-resident income taxes can be levied on the income generated by robots in the owners' place of business. These taxes place an "accidental" burden on robotics, as they are not designed for or specifically focused on robots.

Nevertheless, these are technically the first taxes on robot activities, and they may even be the key to solving the problem before us. "Robots should not be the target of taxation."[98] In other words, the aim should not be to reduce the number of robots but to mitigate their possible negative impact. If taxation pursues this non-fiscal purpose, then tax should be levied on the activities of robots responsible for that impact. The ultimate goal is to internalize negative externalities, the social, labor, and economic costs of automation.

Focusing on the effects of robots that we perceive as negative and imposing taxes to mitigate or prevent them could be an effective solution, at least until it becomes necessary to tax robots with personhood. Furthermore, these taxes are already designed, perhaps not with robots in mind, but they do address their potentially harmful consequences, from the social cost of net job loss to a shortage of revenue due to untaxed sources with the ability to pay.

In the face of public fears that the wide-scale implementation of robotics will bring fiscal difficulties, several other tentative solutions have been suggested, involving indirect taxation of the activities of robots[99] (rather than direct taxation of robots themselves) or the tax system as a whole.

1 *Tobin Tax or Financial Transaction Tax*

The Tobin tax[100] on financial transactions is named after James Tobin (1981 Nobel Laureate in Economics) and can be considered one of the earliest fiscal attempts to mitigate the impact of automation and digitalization. While the "type of financial transaction tax defined by the European Union (directive proposal 2011/0261) was designed to neutralize speculative risks,"[101] it can be

98 Tulio Rosembuj, *Inteligencia Artificial e Impuesto*, 2nd ed., elFisco, Barcelona, 2019, p. 175.

99 Xavier Oberson, *Taxing Robots*, *op. cit.*, p. 113.

100 On this subject, see Ramón Falcón y Tella, "La llamada Tasa Tobin o impuesto sobre las transacciones financieras especulativas," *Quincena Fiscal*, 9, 2001.

101 Tulio Rosembuj, *Inteligencia Artificial e Impuesto, op. cit.*, pp. 94–95.

argued that those very risks[102] were created by the increasing use of digitalization, robotization, and automation in banking and finance. Such risks are, in a sense, the product of robotics.

In fact, the stock market runs on "algorithms that rely on supercomputers to issue high-speed buy or sell orders."[103] Robots have at least partially replaced humans in the financial market. "High-frequency trading on Wall Street is a classic example, where the number of milliseconds of network latency can determine whether an offer is accepted or rejected."[104] And only robots can do this, operating at speeds no person could hope to match.

In this context, we could say that the Tobin tax "accidentally" applies to robots (at least a very specific part of automated transactions). It can be construed as a cost or charge on financial robots, in the same sense that a fuel tax can be viewed as a charge on cars. What it actually taxes is not the robots that carry out financial transactions, but an activity which only they can do.

Perhaps introducing this tax in the EU "could have done away with predatory algorithms"[105] and become an effective tool for mitigating the effects of robotization while simultaneously eliminating aggressive speculation, which still seems to be thriving. Apparently, the "contemporary version of the Tobin tax is the best way to throw sand in the wheels of *algo-trading* while also collecting revenue for public resources,"[106] if implemented uniformly throughout the EU.

It is hard to measure the effectiveness of these taxes, especially when creating them in certain member-states may serve to promote fiscal planning while also combating speculation and the negative consequences of automation.

France has already implemented a Tobin tax,[107] beginning at 0.1% and gradually raising it to the current rate of 0.3%, three times higher than that recommended by Europe. French authorities have even gone one step further and introduced a tax on high-frequency trading.[108]

Spain introduced its own Tobin tax at a rate of 0.2%, regulated by Law 5/2020 of October 15 on the financial transaction tax. It was supposed to take effect at the beginning of 2021, but the process was complicated by a lack of

102 Proposal for a Council Directive on a common system of financial transaction tax and amending Directive 2008/7/EC, COM/2011/0594 final – 2011/0261 (CNS) */.

103 Tulio Rosembuj, *Inteligencia Artificial e Impuesto, op. cit.*, p. 91.

104 John Jordan, *Robots, op. cit.*, p. 83.

105 Tulio Rosembuj, *Inteligencia Artificial e Impuesto, op. cit.*, pp. 94–95.

106 *Ibid.*

107 French General Tax Code, tax on financial transactions (Article 235 ter ZD).

108 French General Tax Code, tax on high-frequency trading (Article 235 ter ZD bis).

enabling regulations,[109] and consequently the first payment in February (for the month of January) had to be pushed back to April. Moreover, it has only brought in a fraction of what the administration hoped to collect.

2 *Google Tax or Digital Services Tax*

Given the global scope of the tax problems posed by certain digital business models, the international community appears to agree that a common solution is needed. One of the EU's star initiatives for rising to the challenges of the digital economy is the digital services tax which,[110] like the digital permanent establishment, aims to better address the taxation of multinational digital giants and the role of users.[111] The initial proposal was informed by OECD works and was intended as an interim measure while waiting for a more comprehensive solution,[112] but the states were unable to reach the consensus needed to act on it.

Given the delay in adopting and implementing internationally agreed measures, especially in the OECD, several countries have begun to take unilateral measures.[113] Even the European Union has decided to forge ahead in this area. The EU wants to implement a digital services tax, among other measures, to address the challenges arising from the digital economy.[114] "This proposal[115] takes note of the current works at the OECD level on the BEPS project. However, as we have seen, no clear consensus has been found among states so far. It appears that the EU wants to go further and pioneer rules on the digital economy."[116]

The European proposal consisted in an "indirect" tax on revenues from the provision of certain digital services and was intended as an interim measure while waiting for a more comprehensive solution,[117] but the states were unable to reach the necessary consensus.

---

109 The necessary regulation was finally ratified with retroactive effect in Royal Decree 366/2021 of May 25, which established the procedure for reporting and paying the tax on financial transactions and amended other tax regulations.

110 Proposal for a Council Directive on the common system of a digital services tax on revenues resulting from the provision of certain digital services, COM/2018/0148 final – 2018/073 (CNS).

111 Xavier Oberson, *Taxing Robots, op. cit.,* p. 61.

112 *Ibid.*, p. 68.

113 *Ibid.*, p. 71.

114 Proposal for a Council Directive on the common system of a digital services tax on revenues resulting from the provision of certain digital services, COM/2018/0148 final – 2018/073 (CNS).

115 Xavier Oberson, *Taxing Robots, op. cit.,* p. 61.

116 *Ibid.*, p. 67.

117 *Ibid.*, p. 68.

The indirect nature of this tax makes it controversial.[118] One could argue that this digital services tax is actually a direct tax, but disguised as indirect because otherwise it would not be allowed under the terms of existing double taxation treaties. The fact that the taxable base is calculated in a manner similar to income taxes also belies its supposedly indirect nature.

Spain beat the EU to the punch with Law 4/2020 of October 15 regarding the tax on certain digital services,[119] which introduced this provisional charge[120] on the grounds of "fiscal fairness and sustainability of the tax system."[121] The first payment period was the first quarter of 2021, but collection was postponed until July and was significantly lower than the administration had expected. Furthermore, it seems likely that this tax will be short-lived since Spain has signed a multilateral agreement with the United States, France, Italy, the United Kingdom, and Austria, committing to withdraw their unilateral Google taxes before December 31, 2023, provided the US terminates the trade actions announced after they took effect.

This tax can be understood as a levy on data, the "fuel" on which robots run, as it applies to the provision of digital services, a highly automated activity. We can therefore say that it has a specific economic effect on robotics and can be considered a forerunner to a genuine robot tax.

In the long term, "The data tax will be appropriate if it adopts the structure and function of a Tobin tax or bit tax. In both cases, an infinitesimally small charge on agents in the financial or ICT systems could raise huge revenues or reduce negative externalities."[122] To achieve this the tax will need to

118 "The legal nature of this tax is controversial. As such, it does not look like an income tax. It is levied at a fixed rate on specific digital supplies, which seems more like an excise. This proposal has received mixed reactions," in *ibid.*, p. 71.

119 María Amparo Grau Ruiz, "El gravamen 'provisional' de los servicios digitales y la dudosa justificación de reacciones unilaterales," *Revista Técnica Tributaria*, 128, 2020, pp. 7–13.

120 "Therefore, as indicated in the OECD reports on the digital economy, the establishment of unilateral measures is transitory. This new tax is only meant to endure until the new legislation designed to incorporate the internationally agreed solution is enacted." Preamble to Law 4/2020 of October 15 regarding the tax on certain digital services.

121 "Given the long time that has passed since international discussions of this matter began, with no practical solutions having been adopted to date, as well as for reasons of social pressure, fiscal fairness, and the sustainability of the tax system, it has become necessary to adopt, following in the footsteps of other countries, a unilateral solution which will allow Spain to immediately exercise the right to impose taxes in its own territory that correspond to it under law, as the place of origin of the data and contributions of users that generate value for the company." Preamble to Law 4/2020 of October 15 regarding the tax on certain digital services.

122 Tulio Rosembuj, *Inteligencia Artificial e Impuesto*, *op. cit.*, p. 163.

be redefined, particularly its taxable base and the parameters used to identify taxpayers. We should try to find a way for it to be a truly indirect tax, applied on an international or at least a European scale and focused on taxing data and mitigating the negative externalities of the automation and digitalization of the economy, rather than a way to tax income that escapes to other countries for the sole purpose of increasing revenue.

3 *Related Solutions that Affect Robots*

Several international initiatives that are not specifically geared toward the challenges arising from robotics and even predate the AI era can have an enormous effect on the tax system and, consequently, on the changes required to adapt robot taxation.

The BEPS Action 1 Final Report (OECD/20)[123] on the tax challenges of the digital economy concluded that while this economy does not generate unique BEPS[124] issues, it can exacerbate existing risks,[125] and the same is generally true of robotics.

a CCTB and CCCTB

On the subject of robot taxation, we must also recall the European plans to establish a common consolidated corporate tax base in the EU. Although the latest developments in robotics were not even on the horizon when these initiatives were first drafted, today they may offer a solution to the problems arising from automation and digitalization for the entire European Union, standardizing the method of calculating the base of corporate income tax to combat aggressive tax planning.

Two proposals have been made: a proposal for a Council directive on a Common Corporate Tax Base (CCTB);[126] and a proposal for a Council directive on a Common Consolidated Corporate Tax Base (CCCTB),[127] a single set of

---

123 OECD Publishing: *Addressing the Tax Challenges of the Digital Economy, Action 1 2015 Final Report*, OECD/G20 Base Erosion and Profit Shifting Project, October 2015, Paris.

124 "Base erosion and profit shifting (BEPS) refers to tax planning strategies that exploit gaps and mismatches in tax rules to artificially shift profits to low or no-tax locations where there is little or no economic activity or to erode tax bases through deductible payments such as interest or royalties." Available at https://www.oecd.org/tax/beps/.

125 The BEPS Action 1 Final Report specifically mentions Action 7 on PE status, which was discussed in part B of this chapter.

126 Proposal for a Council Directive on a Common Corporate Tax Base, COM/2016/0685 final – 2016/0337 (CNS).

127 Proposal for a Council Directive on a Common Consolidated Corporate Tax Base, COM/2016/0683 final – 2016/0336 (CNS).

rules to calculate consolidated profits and consolidated taxable income in all member-states.[128]

"It is interesting to note that, according to the EU Commission, the proposal for a Common Consolidated Corporate Tax Base (CCCTB) would be the optimal solution to ensure a fair corporate taxation in the EU,"[129] even though it is not tailored to the digital economy or robots. Without getting into the details of these proposals, I will simply point out that they need to be adjusted to reflect the impact of robotics and the changes to the tax system it may entail; at the very least, we must consider that if these proposals are implemented, they will have a tremendous impact on taxation and revenue, and the new distribution of corporate profits might make it unnecessary to tax robots.

F Conclusions

The Spanish tax system, like most tax systems around the world, is based primarily on the taxation of labor income. Over-dependence on such income in this technological transition period of lightning-fast changes must be corrected by reducing its importance in our system and focusing on other types of income, although it is hard to see this happening in the short or medium term.

As things stand today, robots are only "accidentally" taxed. Certain taxes, in the purposes they aim to fulfill, also indirectly point the way to future robot taxation.

In my view, the primary goal of tax legislation should not be to reduce the number of robots in circulation but to mitigate their possible negative effects on the economy and, by extension, on society. With this extra-fiscal aim in mind, taxes should only be levied on activities that generate negative externalities (thereby minimizing or eliminating them), and at the same time tax incentives can be used to promote the positive effects of robotics.

The wisest approach to robot taxation, at least for the near future, would be to focus on activities carried out predominantly or exclusively by robots and their effects. This gives us an effective interim tax solution until such time as it becomes necessary to tax robots as legal persons.

As we have seen throughout this chapter, there are two radically different possibilities on the table. The first – and least likely in the short-to-medium term – entails robots having a "specific legal personality" which gives them

128 https://www.consilium.europa.eu/es/policies/ccctb/#. Accessed April 25, 2021.

129 Xavier Oberson, *Taxing Robots*, *op. cit.*, p. 67.

taxpayer status. The second, which we are already beginning to see in some legislative initiatives and proposals today, is to consider robots "objects," taxable items used to calculate the taxpayer's financial capacity.

This is the more viable option in the short term, especially when creating new taxes. As mentioned, there are several real, objective taxes that could easily be levied on robots, such as a version of the municipal motor vehicles tax specifically designed for robots with a physical support. Within this possibility, we could also apply the concept of a robot-worker's theoretical "imputed salary," although I do not think this is the right road to take. Attempting to assign hypothetical salaries to robots based on the job they do (taking it away from human workers) may sound like a good way to minimize the negative impact of automation and fairly tax the profits that robots generate, at least in theory. But in practice, we would run into countless problems when figuring out how to calculate those hypothetical earnings.

Conclusions

This study was begun with the aim of addressing the challenges that robot taxation poses and looking at possible solutions.

1. Throughout this book, we have examined a series of legal problems that arise in the process of establishing a robot tax. The first step in this process is to arrive at a suitable *definition* of robot and, more specifically, of *smart robot*. The need for a clear definition of what exactly constitutes a "smart robot" is made patent in the opening lines of the European Parliament resolution of February 16, 2017, with recommendations to the Commission on Civil Law Rules on Robotics. That definition is the basis for developing any type of robot regulation, especially with regard to taxation.

At present, both the law and the field of robotics have gaps in their definition of robot. The majority of scholarly literature agrees that a robot must have certain characteristics but does not share one exact, definitive definition of the term. For this reason, the meaning of the word is still hotly *debated* among legal scholars as well as robotic scientists. Looking to comparative law, we find that South Korea is the only country with a legal definition of intelligent robots.

As we have seen, there are different types of smart robots depending on their features and uses. The differences between these *types* may have legal relevance when establishing a specific definition for each one. For instance, the obvious distinctions that exist between autonomous vehicles and surgical robots will naturally give rise to different regulation needs.

Most definitions put forward in scholarly literature agree that a robot must be able to sense, decide, and act. They also include self-learning as a feature that separates robots (simple objects) from smart robots (a possible new category).

After reviewing the legal literature on this subject, I would like to propose the following general definition, informed by a tax law perspective:

> A smart robot is "*an autonomous self-learning program, with or without physical support, which, by means of sensors, processors, and actuators, makes an impact by altering and interacting with its environment.*"

In my view, *corporeality* is not a requirement, but there must be *interaction with and alteration of the environment*. The impact of smart robots should matter more than their physical form or lack thereof. Furthermore, when measuring their impact, it is not enough to merely consider the *physical* effects (of an

 | DOI:10.1163/9789004538511_008

autonomous vehicle using the roads, for instance); it is also necessary to gauge *economic impact* (say, of computer programs conducting high-frequency trading) and consequences in other areas.

Tax law could adopt this definition for its own use by passing legislation on robot taxation, although the *generalizing* intent may make it too broad and ambiguous. However, this general definition can be customized, creating specific definitions for certain subgroups of smart robots on which taxes are to be levied. For example, if we create a kind of motor vehicle tax specifically for drones, that tax would require an exact definition of "smart drone"; and another definition would be needed if we decide to pass a law recognizing the legal personhood of robots. These two definitions would have little in common other than the same general foundation. Therefore, what I propose is merely a preliminary definition, intended to guide and direct the various robot-related concepts that our legal system will need to define.

2. Just as a specific legal status was granted to *slaves* under Roman law, so the proposal of granting a specific legal personality to robots takes into account their "autonomous" abilities as well as their steadily growing impact on social and economic life.

The regulation of slavery in ancient Rome can serve as a basis for constructing a legal regime that grants robots a "capacity of representation" (for conducting certain legal business) while continuing to recognize these artificial agents as *goods*. This solution would *shatter the traditional dichotomy between persons and things.*

3. Robots are not comparable to *natural* persons and cannot be granted personhood in those terms. Robotic personhood would need to be either an adaptation of *traditional legal* personhood or a *new* type of legal personality, which is theoretically possible as juridical personhood is a legal "fiction." Moreover, we would have to make sure that they can effectively operate in the legal world, which would probably require a *supplement* to their *capacity to act.*
4. If robots do acquire personhood, they could become *taxable persons* and therefore liable to pay taxes levied on them. Without a legal personality they cannot be treated as taxpayers, as there is no *special* tax capacity in this case. If legislators refer to them as taxpayers in a legal text, this should be understood as an abbreviated allusion to a *person*, not to the robots themselves.

Under Spanish tax law, robots are production assets that *contribute to the turnover and profits* of corporations and enterprises. Consequently, the activities of robots are already subject to taxation, but only at the level of the enterprises that *own, control, or use* them.

5. Another important consideration is the comparative *tax treatment of robots and human workers*. The tax system is not neutral when it comes to choosing robots or people to perform production tasks, and in fact *favors automation* over hired workers. Enterprises that use robots instead of workers enjoy several *tax advantages*, such as free *depreciation* and tax incentives for research, development, and innovation (*R&D + i*). They also have fewer expenses, given the reduced burden of indirect taxes and the fact that they do not have to pay Social Security contributions for robotic workers.

The tax system has not yet caught up with the new reality and is encouraging the replacement of conventional human personnel with robots.

6. Perhaps one of the first steps toward taxing robots should be to reduce these tax advantages or adjust them to pursue labor and social policy goals, although they could coexist with newly created taxes.
7. In Spain, the zeal to fill territorial coffers has prompted *regional authorities* to create taxes for the sole purpose of later seeking compensation from the state. This way of going about things is detrimental to the Spanish economy and the competitiveness of its companies. In the field of robotics, it is essential to *curb* the enthusiasm of regional legislators for imposing taxes, often before the federal government has made a decision and without consulting any European authorities.

Robot taxation must be negotiated and *harmonized at the international level*, or at least the European level, in order to be fair and effective and not have negative repercussions for the Spanish economy.

In my opinion, the best solution would be to establish an *effective federal tax*. If necessary, part or all of this tax could then be *ceded* to the regional authorities. However, the scope of this cession should ideally be limited to *revenue collection*, thereby guaranteeing an even playing field and fair competition for companies in every part of Spain.

The allocation of tax revenue is a political-economic issue rather than a legal matter, which is why I do not argue in favor of either federal or the regional authorities.

8. The Spanish tax system, like most tax systems around the world, is based primarily on the *taxation of labor income*. Over-dependence on such *income* in this technological transition period of lightning-fast changes must be corrected by reducing its importance in our system and focusing on other types of income, although this is unlikely to happen in the short or medium term.

As things stand today, robots are only "*accidentally*" taxed. Certain taxes, in the purposes they aim to fulfill, also *indirectly* point the way to future robot taxation.

9. In my view, the primary *goal* of tax legislation should not be to reduce the number of robots in circulation but to mitigate their possible *negative effects* on the economy and, by extension, on society. With this *extra-fiscal* aim in mind, taxes should only be levied on activities that generate *negative* externalities (thereby minimizing or try eliminating them), and at the same time tax *incentives* can be used to promote the *positive* effects of robotics.

The wisest approach to robot taxation, at least for the near future, would be to focus on activities carried out *predominantly or exclusively* by robots and on their *effects*. This gives us an effective interim tax solution until such time as it becomes necessary to tax robots as *legal persons*.

10. As we have seen throughout this book, and especially in the final chapters, there are two radically different *possibilities* on the table. The first – and least likely in the short-to-medium term – entails robots having a *specific legal personality*, which would give them *taxpayer* status. The second, which we are already beginning to see reflected in some legislative initiatives and proposals today, is to treat robots as *objects, taxable items* used to calculate the taxpayer's financial capacity.

This may be the more viable option in the short term, especially when creating *new taxes*. As I have pointed out, there are several real, objective taxes that could easily be levied on robots, such as a version of the *municipal motor vehicles tax* specifically designed for robots with a physical support. Within this second possibility, we could also explore the concept of a *theoretical imputed salary*, the income that robots would "earn" as workers, although I do not think this is the best way to go.

In *theory*, assigning hypothetical salaries to robots based on the job they do (taking it away from human workers) may sound like a good way to minimize the negative impact of automation and fairly tax the profits that robots generate. But in *practice* we would run into countless problems when figuring out how to calculate those hypothetical earnings.

In summary, *we are still long way from establishing a tax on robot income or profits. It is even too early to consider robotic legal personhood as a real alternative, at least in the short term. However, in light of the unstoppable progress and consequences of robotization, the legal and tax system undeniably needs to be updated and adjusted to this new reality.*

Bibliography

Abbott, Ryan Benjamin; and Bogenschneider, Bret, "Should Robots Pay Taxes? Tax Policy in the Age of Automation," *Harvard Law & Policy Review*, Vol. 12–1, 2018.

Abbott, Ryan Benjamin; and Bogenschneider, Bret, "Why we should start taxing the robots that are taking human jobs," *The Conversation*, February 28, 2018.

Adapt, Fim-Cisl, *Libro Bianco su Lavoro e Competenze in Impresa 4.0*, September 25, 2017.

Albaladejo, Manuel, *Derecho Civil I*, 17th edition, Edisofer, Madrid, 2006.

Allen, Tom; and Widdison, Robin, "Can computers make contracts?," *Harvard Journal of Law & Technology*, 9, 1, 1996, pp. 26–52.

Almudí Cid, José Manuel, "Impuesto sobre el Valor Añadido," in Ramón Falcón y Tella; Gaspar de la Peña; and Miguel Ángel Martínez Lago (coords.), *Sistema Fiscal Español (Impuestos Estatales, Autonómicos y Locales)*, 8th edition, Iustel, Madrid, 2018, Chapter VIII, pp. 271–360.

Alonso Murillo, Felipe, *Fiscalidad de la I + D + i. Tratamiento de los gastos en el Impuesto sobre Sociedades*, Netbiblo, La Coruña, 2010.

Álvarez Martínez, Joaquín, *La Responsabilidad de los Administradores de las Personas Jurídicas en la nueva Ley General Tributaria*, Thomson Aranzadi, Cizur Menor, Navarra, 2004.

Andonian, Sero; *et al.*, "Device failures associated with patient injuries during robot-assisted laparoscopic surgeries: A comprehensive review of FDA Maude database," *The Canadian Journal of Urology*, 15, 1, 2008, pp. 3.912–3.916.

Anguiano, José María, "Las personas electrónicas," *Diario La Ley*, Wolters Kluwer, Section "Ciberderecho," 14, January 18, 2018.

Antón Antón, Álvaro; and Bilbao Estrada, Iñaki, *Retos y oportunidades de la Administración en la era digital*, Thomson Reuters, 2019.

Aramburo y Machado, Mariano, *La capacidad civil: estudio de las causas que la determinan, modifican y extinguen, según la filosofía del derecho, la historia de la legislación y el derecho vigente en España*, Reus, Madrid, 1931.

Arntz, Melanie; Gregory, Terry; and Zierahn, Ulrich, *The Risk of Automation for Jobs in OECD Countries: A Comparative Analysis*, OECD Social, Employment and Migration Working Papers, 189, OECD Publishing, Paris, 2016. Available at http://dx.doi.org/10.1787/5jlz9h56dvq7-en.

Asaro, Peter M., "Robots and Responsibility from a Legal Perspective," *Proceedings of the IEEE, 2007 International Conference of Robotics and Automation*, Workshop on Robot Ethics, April 14, 2007, Rome. Available at http://www.peterasaro.org/writing/ASARO%20Legal%Pespective.pdf.

Asaro, Peter M., "A body to kick, but still no soul to dams: Legal perspectives on robotics," in Patrick Lin; Keith Abney; and George A. Bekey (coords.), *Robot ethics: the ethical and social implications of robotics*, MIT Press, Cambridge, Massachusetts, 2012.

Asimov, Isaac, *Robot*, Gnome Press, New York, 1950.

Asociación de Profesores de Derecho Civil, *Asociaciones y Fundaciones. Jornadas de Alicante, 11 a. 2004*, Servicio de Publicaciones, Universidad de Murcia, Murcia, 2005.

Autor, David, "Why Are There Still So Many Jobs? The History and Future of Workplace Automation," *Journal of Economic Perspectives*, Volume 29, Issue 3, 2015, pp. 3–30.

Ayala Sanhueza, Alberto Gabriel, "Incentivos fiscales a la innovación en robótica: Una necesaria reformulación," *Revista General de Legislación y Jurisprudencia*, 2, 2019, pp. 207–260.

Ayllón Santiago, Héctor S.; and Fernández González, Carlos Manuel, *El uso legal de los drones (RPA): ámbito policial y uso privado*, Reus, Madrid, 2018.

Balkin, Jack, "The path of robotics law," *California Law Review Circuit*, 6, 2015, pp. 45–60.

Barona Vilar, Silvia, *Algoritmización del Derecho y de la justicia: de la Inteligencia Artificial a la Smart Justice*, Tirant lo Blanch, Valencia, 2021.

Barrientos, Antonio, *Fundamentos de robótica*, McGraw-Hill, Interamericana de España, Madrid, 2007.

Barrio, Fernando, "Autonomous robots and the law," *Society for Computers and Law*, 2008. Available at htttp://www.scl.org/site.aspx?ibox.

Barrio Andrés, Moisés (dir.), *Derecho de los robots*, La Ley, Wolter Kluwer, Madrid, 2018.

Barrio Andrés, Moisés, *Derecho de los drones*, La Ley, Wolter Kluwer, Madrid, 2018.

Barrio Andrés, Moisés, *Fundamentos del Derecho de Internet*, Centro de Estudios Políticos y Constitucionales, Madrid, 2017.

Barrio Andrés, Moisés, *Internet de las cosas*, Reus, Madrid, 2018.

Barrio Andrés, Moisés, "Hacia una personalidad electrónica para los robots," *Revista de Derecho Privado*, 102, 3, March-April, 2018, pp. 89–107.

Barrio Andrés, Moisés, "Del Derecho de Internet al Derecho de los robots," in *Derecho de los robots*, Wolters Kluwer, Madrid, 2018, pp. 61–86. And in *Diario La Ley*, 16, Section "Ciberderecho," Wolters Kluwer, March 13, 2018.

Barrio Andrés, Moisés, "Robótica, Inteligencia Artificial y Derecho," *Análisis del Real Instituto Elcano*, Real Instituto Elcano, ARI, 103, September 7, 2018.

Barrio Andrés, Moisés, "Drones. Concepto. Clases e historia. Usos actuales. El Derecho de los drones," in Barrio Andrés, Moisés (dir.), *Derecho de los drones*, La ley, Wolter Kluwer, Madrid, 2018.

Barrio Andrés, Moisés, "El Derecho de los robots, una disciplina jurídica naciente," in *Estudios de Derecho Público en Homenaje a Luciano Parejo Alfonso*, Vol. 1, Tirant lo Blanch, Valencia, 2018, pp. 1.119–1.143.

Barrio Andrés, Moisés, "Los principios generales del Derecho de los robots," *Derecho Digital e Innovación*, 1, January-March, 2019.

Bello Janeiro, Domingo, *Nuevas tecnologías y responsabilidad civil*, Reus, Madrid, 2020.

Bensoussan, Alain; and Bensoussan, Jeremy, *Droit des robots*, Larcier, Brussels, 2016.

Berliri, Antonio, *Principi*, vol. I, Giuffrè, Milan, 1952.

Berliri, Antonio, *Il testo unico delle imposte dirette*, Giuffrè, Milan, 1960.

Berliri, Luigi Vittorio, "Note alla Decisione della Commissione centrale per le imposte dirette," (November 22, 1939), Issue 19.471, *Giurisprudenza delle Imposte Dirette*, 1940.

Berliri, Luigi Vittorio, "¿Capacità giuridica tributaria o concurso di debitori d'imposta?," *Rivista Italiana di Diritto Finanziario*, 1940.

Berthoud, Gérald, "Los saberes hoy: desafíos y apuestas," *Andamios*, Vol. 7, Issue 14, 2010, pp. 349–375.

Blázquez Lidoy, Alejandro; and Martín Dégano, Isidoro, *Manual tributario de entidades no lucrativas (asociaciones y fundaciones)*, CEF D.L., Madrid, 2012.

Borrego Moro, Cristóbal J., *El reparto de la materia imponible entre la Hacienda Autonómica y Local*, Tirant lo Blanch, Valencia, 2008.

Bottone, Germana, "A tax on robots? Some food for thought," *Dipartamento delle Finanze Working Papers*, 3, September 2019.

Bournakis, Joannis; Vecchi, Michela; and Venturini, Francesco, "Off-shoring, Specialization and R&D," *Review of Income and Wealth*, Vol. 64, Issue 1, March 2018, pp. 26–51.

Braña Pino, Francisco Javier, *Cuarta revolución industrial, automatización y digitalización: una visión desde la periferia de la Unión Europea en tiempos de pandemia*, Instituto Complutense de Estudios Internacionales (ICEI), 2020.

Bria, Francesca, "Ingreso básico y precariedad laboral en la economía de los robots," *Nueva Sociedad*, 279, January-February 2019, pp. 114–121.

Caballero Trenado, Laura, *Review* to Barrio Andrés, Moisés (dir.), *Derecho de los robots, Revista de Derecho Privado*, 37, 2019, pp. 367–371.

Calo, Ryan, "Robots and Privacy," in Patrick Lin; Keith Abney; and George A. Bekey (coords.), *Robot ethics: the ethical and social implications of robotics*, MIT Press, Cambridge, Massachusetts, 2012.

Calo, Ryan, "Robotics and the Lessons of Cyberlaw," *California Law Review*, Vol. 103, Issue 3, 2015, pp. 513–563.

Calo, Ryan, "Robots as legal metaphors," *Harvard Journal of Law and Technology*, Vol. 30, Issue 1, 2016, pp. 209–237.

Calo, Ryan, "Robots in American Law," *University of Washington School of Law Research Paper*, Issue 4, 2016.

Calo, Ryan; Froomkin, A. Michael; and Kerr, Ian (eds.), *Robot Law*, Edward Elgar, Cheltenham, UK, 2016.

Cano Martínez de Velasco, José Ignacio, *La decadencia del contrato: El Derecho robot*, Bosch Civil, Barcelona, 2011.

Čapek, Karel, *R.U.R. Rossum's Universal Robots*, Penguin Random House, Penguin Classics, London, 2004.

Capilla Roncero, Francisco, *La persona jurídica: funciones y disfunciones*, Tecnos, Madrid, 1984.

Carrasco Perera, Ángel; and González Carrasco, María del Carmen, *Introducción al Derecho y fundamentos de Derecho Privado*, 2nd edition, Difusora Larousse – Tecnos, Madrid, 2018. Ebook.

Casado Raigón, Rafael; and Gallego Domínguez, Ignacio (coords.), *Personalidad y capacidad jurídicas. 74 contribuciones con motivo del XXV Aniversario de la Facultad de Derecho de Córdoba, Tomo I*, 1rst edition, Servicio de Publicaciones, Universidad de Córdoba, Córdoba, 2005.

Casado Raigón, Rafael; and Gallego Domínguez, Ignacio, *Personalidad y capacidad jurídicas. 74 contribuciones con motivo del XXV Aniversario de la Facultad de Derecho de Córdoba, Tomo II*, 1rst edition, Servicio de Publicaciones, Universidad de Córdoba, Córdoba, 2005.

Casarrubios Sánchez, Luis, *Responsabilidad social corporativa en el ámbito fiscal*, Madrid, 2018.

Castro, M., "La acción autónoma del robot," *Legal Today*, April 4, 2018, Aranzadi. Available at http://www.legaltoday.com/opinion/articulos-de-opinion/la-accion-autonoma-del-robot.

Cazorla Prieto, Luis María, *Derecho Financiero y Tributario*, 18th edition, Thomson Reuters – Aranzadi, Cizur Menor, Navarra, 2018.

Ceballos Rosero, Franco Alirio, "Otros sujetos de Derecho o personas (?)," *Revista de Estudios Socio-Jurídicos*, Vol. 22, Issue 1, 2020, pp. 321–351.

Cerrillo i Martínez, Agustí; and Peguera Poch, Miguel (coords.), *Retos jurídicos de la inteligencia artificial*, Thomson Reuters – Aranzadi, Cizur Menor, Navarra, 2020, with the following contributions: "Cómo la inteligencia artificial está impactando en las sociedades," by Lorena Jaume-Palasí, pp. 27–39; "En búsqueda de un marco normativo para la inteligencia artificial," by Miguel Peguera Poch, pp. 41–56; "Retos de la inteligencia artificial y adaptabilidad del Derecho de daños," by Antoni Rubí Puig, pp. 57–71; "El impacto de la inteligencia artificial en las Administraciones Públicas: estado de la cuestión y una agenda," by Agustí Cerrillo i Martínez, pp. 75–92; "Automatización, inteligencia artificial y empleados públicos," by Ramón Galindo Caldés, pp. 93–109; "Automatización y obsolescencia humana," by Ignasi Beltrán de Heredia Ruiz, pp. 113–124; "La inteligencia artificial, su uso en la gestión de recursos humanos y los riesgos para los trabajadores," by Antonio Fernández García, pp. 125–141; "Luces y sombras del uso de la inteligencia artificial en el sistema de justicia penal," by Marc Balcells, pp. 145–159; and "Inteligencia artificial y acceso a la justicia: retos y prospectiva," by Aura Esther Vilalta Nicuesa, pp. 161–178.

Cevasco, L.; Corvalán, J. G; and Le Fevre Cervini, E. M., *Artificial Intelligence and Work, Building a New Employment Paradigm*, Astrea, CABA, 2019.

Ciccotti, Ettore, *La esclavitud en Grecia, Roma y el mundo cristiano: apogeo y ocaso de un sistema atroz*, Círculo Latino, San Andrés de la Barca, 2006.

Coca Vila, Ivó, "Self-driving Cars in Dilemmatic Situations: An Approach Based on the Theory of Justification in Criminal Law," *Criminal Law and Philosophy: An International Journal for Philosophy of Crime, Criminal Law and Punishment*, Vol. 12, Issue 1, 2018, pp. 59–82.

Comanducci, Paolo, "Le tre leggi della robotica e l'insegnamento della filosofia del diritto," *Materiali per una Storia della Cultura Giuridica*, Vol. 36, Issue 1, 1986, pp. 191–197.

Comisión de expertos para la reforma del sistema tributario español, *Informe*, Madrid, February 2014.

Conde Canaviri, Martha M., "Generaciones de La Robótica," *RITS [online]*, 2008, 1, pp. 129–131.

Consejo Económico y Social de España, *Informe sobre la digitalización de la economía*, Sesión ordinaria del Pleno, October 25, 2017.

Corrales, Marcelo; Fenwick, Mark; and Forgó, Nikolaus (eds.), *Robotics, AI and the Future of Law*, in the Series "Perspectives in Law, Business and Innovation," Springer, Singapore, 2018.

Court of Auditors, "Informe de Fiscalización de las actuaciones de la Agencia Estatal de Administración Tributaria en relación con los beneficios fiscales, ejercicio 2015."

Cubero Truyo, Antonio (dir.), *Tributos asistemáticos del ordenamiento vigente*, Tirant lo Blanch, Valencia, 2018.

Cubero Truyo, Antonio, "El Impuesto sobre el Valor Añadido (I)," in Pérez Royo, Fernando (dir.), *Curso de Derecho Tributario. Parte Especial*, 11th edition, Tecnos, Madrid, 2017, Chapter XI, pp. 711–870.

Cubiles Sánchez-Pobre, Pilar, "La tributación de la economía digital a la espera de una solución global," *Quincena Fiscal*, 8, 2019, pp. 17–40.

Checa González, Clemente, "Consideraciones ante la modificación de la LOFCA por la Ley Orgánica 3/2009, de 18 de diciembre," *Quincena Fiscal*, 3, 2010, pp. 43–58.

Chopra, Samir; and White, Laurence F., *A legal theory for autonomous artificial agents*, The University of Michigan Press, Ann Arbor, 2011.

Daubanis, J.; and Yanni, Y. P., "La imposición óptima de los robots," *La tributación de los robots*, IEB Report 2/2019.

Dautenhahn, Kerstin, "Socially intelligent robots: Dimensions of human-robot interaction," *Philosophical Transactions of the Royal Society B: Biological Sciences*, 362, 1480, 2007, pp. 679–704.

De Asís Roig, Rafael, *Una mirada a la robótica desde los derechos humanos*, Dykinson, Madrid, 2015.

De Bruyne, Jan; and Vanleenhove, Cedric (eds.), *Artificial Intelligence and the law*, Intersentia Ltd., Cambridge, 2021.

De Haro Izquierdo, Miguel, "La sustitución de trabajadores por robots: impacto en las contribuciones a la Seguridad Social y su posible financiación por tributos," in Serrano Antón, Fernando (dir.), *Fiscalidad e Inteligencia Artificial: Administración Tributaria y contribuyentes en la Era Digital*, Thomson Reuters – Aranzadi, Cizur Menor, Navarra, 2020, Chapter 4, pp. 113–133.

Delanay, Kevin J., "The robot that takes your job should pay taxes, says Bill Gates," February 17, 2017, *Quartz* (*qz.com*) [Available at https://qz.com/911968/bill-gates-the-robot-that-takes-your-job-should-pay-taxes/] (last access, May 2019).

De Verda y Beamonte, José Ramón; and Alventosa del Río, Josefina, *Derecho civil I: (Derecho de la persona)*, Tirant lo Blanch, Valencia, 2016.

Díaz Alabart, Silvia, *Robots y responsabilidad civil*, Reus, Madrid, 2018.

Díaz Alabart, Silvia, "Robots y Responsabilidad Civil," in Rogel Vide, Carlos (coord.), *Los robots y el Derecho*, Reus, Madrid, 2018, pp. 99–114.

Díez-Picazo, Luis, *Experiencias jurídicas y Teoría del Derecho*, Ariel, Barcelona, 1973.

Díez-Picazo, Luis; and Gullón Ballesteros, Antonio, *Sistema de Derecho Civil. Volumen I*, 11th edition, Tecnos, Madrid, 2005.

Durán Cabré, José María, "Hola, soy un robot: ¿tengo que pagar impuestos?," *La Tributación de los Robots*, IEB Report 2/2019.

Ellram, Lisa M., "Offshoring, Reshoring and the Manufacturing Location Decision," *Journal of Supply Chain Management*, Vol. 49, Issue 2, April 2013, pp. 3–5.

Ercilla García, Javier, *Normas de Derecho Civil y Robótica: Robots Inteligentes, Personalidad Jurídica, Responsabilidad Civil y Regulación*, Thomson Reuters – Aranzadi, Cizur Menor, Navarra, 2018.

Erdoğdu, M. Mustafa; and Karaca, Coşkun, "The Fourth Industrial Revolution and a Possible Robot Tax," in Berksoy, Irem; Dane, Kutlu; and Popovic, Milenko (eds.), *Institutions & Economic Policies: Effects on Social Justice, Employment, Environmental Protection & Growth*, IJOPEC Publication, London, 2017, Chapter 5, pp. 103–122.

European Commission, *Employment and Social Developments in Europe, Annual Review 2016*, Publications Office of the European Union, December 2016.

European Commission, *Robots at work, A report on automatable and non-automatable employment shares in Europe*, Publications Office of the European Union, January 2018.

European Commission, *Comunicación de la Comisión al Parlamento Europeo, al Consejo Europeo, al Consejo, al Comité Económico y Social Europeo y al Comité de las Regiones, Inteligencia artificial para Europa*, {*SWD (2018) 137 final*}, April 25, 2018.

European Commission, *Ethics Guidelines for Trustworthy AI*, High-Level Expert Group on Artificial Intelligence, April 2019.

European Commission, *Comunicación de la Comisión al Parlamento Europeo, al Consejo Europeo, al Consejo, al Comité Económico y Social Europeo y al Comité de las Regiones, Generar confianza en la inteligencia artificial centrada en el ser humano*, April 8, 2019.

European Commission, *Comunicación de la Comisión al Parlamento Europeo, Informe anual sobre las actividades de investigación y desarrollo tecnológico de la UE y seguimiento de Horizonte 2020 en 2018*, July 3, 2019.

European Commission, *Liability for Artificial Intelligence and other emerging digital technologies*, 2019.

European Commission, *Comunicación de la Comisión al Parlamento Europeo, al Consejo Europeo, al Consejo, al Comité Económico y Social Europeo y al Comité de las Regiones, Una Estrategia Europea de Datos*, February 19, 2020.

European Commission, *Report From The Commission To The European Parliament, The Council And The European Economic And Social Committee, Report on the safety and liability implications of Artificial Intelligence, the Internet of Things and robotics*, Publications Office of the European Union, February 19, 2020.

European Commission, *Shaping Europe's Digital Future*, Publications Office of the European Union, February 2020.

European Commission, *On Artificial Intelligence – A European approach to excellence and trust*, Publications Office of the European Union, February 2020.

European Economic and Social Committee, *Dictamen del Comité Económico y Social Europeo sobre la «Inteligencia artificial: las consecuencias de la inteligencia artificial para el mercado único (digital), la producción, el consumo, el empleo y la sociedad» (Dictamen de iniciativa)*, Diario Oficial de la Unión Europea, C 288/1, August 31, 2017.

European Economic and Social Committee, *Impact of digitalisation and the on-demand economy on labor markets and the consequences for employment and industrial relations, Final Study*, 2017.

European Parliament, *Report with recommendations to the Commission on Civil Law Rules on Robotics (2015/2103(INL))*, session document A8-005/2017, January 27, 2017.

European Parliament, *Informe sobre una política industrial global europea en materia de inteligencia artificial y robótica (2018/2088(INI))*, Documento de sesión, A8-0019/2019, January 30, 2019.

Eurostat, "Employment and activity by sex and age – annual data," updated on April 23, 2018.

Executive Office of the President National Science and Technology Council, *Preparing for the future of Artificial Intelligence*, October 2016.

Fabra Valls, Modesto J.; and Falchi, Paolo, "Los incentivos fiscales para el fomento de la innovación empresarial en España e Italia," *Quincena Fiscal*, Aranzadi, 9, 2017, pp. 59–110.

Falcón Pulido, Álvaro, "Taxing Robots: Clarifications on Legal and Economic Capacity, Capacity to Act and Representation," in Pons, José L. (ed.), *Inclusive Robotics for a*

Better Society, Selected Papers from INBOTS Conference 2018, 16–18 October, 2018, Pisa, Italy, Springer International Publishing, Cham, Switzerland, 2019, pp. 40–44.

Falcón Pulido, Álvaro, "Taxes on the Use of Robots," in *Interactive Robotics: Legal, Ethical, Social and Economic Aspects. Selected Contributions to the INBOTS Conference 2021, 18–20 May, 2021*, Springer International Publishing, Cham, Switzerland, 2021, pp. 106–110.

Falcón Pulido, Álvaro, "Aproximación a la tributación de los robots," in *Revista Técnica Tributaria*. Transferencia, 132, January-March 2021, pp. 239–251.

Falcón Pulido, Álvaro, *Fiscalidad y robótica*, Tirant lo Blanch, Valencia, 2022.

Falcón Pulido, Álvaro, *Tax and Robotics*, Brill-Nijhoff, Leiden-Boston, 2023.

Falcón y Tella, Ramón, *Análisis de la trasparencia tributaria*, Instituto de Estudios Fiscales, Madrid, 1984.

Falcón y Tella, Ramón, "Los entes de hecho como sujetos pasivos de la obligación tributaria," *Civitas. Revista española de derecho financiero*, 88, 1995, pp. 657–670.

Falcón y Tella, Ramón, "La llamada Tasa Tobin o impuesto sobre las transacciones financieras especulativas," *Quincena Fiscal*, 9, 2001.

Falcón y Tella, Ramón, "Los entes sin personalidad como sujetos pasivos en la Ley 58/2003, General Tributaria," in Casado Raigón, Rafael and Gallego Domínguez, Ignacio (coords.), *Personalidad y capacidad jurídicas. 74 contribuciones con motivo del XXV Aniversario de la Facultad de Derecho de Córdoba, Tomo I*, 1rst edition, Servicio de Publicaciones, Universidad de Córdoba, Córdoba, 2005, pp. 449–470.

Falcón y Tella, Ramón, "El Impuesto sobre los Depósitos de las Entidades de Crédito: sobre la necesidad de un nuevo modelo para articular la potestad tributaria estatal y autonómica," *Quincena Fiscal*, 1, 2013, pp. 11–18.

Falcón y Tella, Ramón, "El «nexus» en la doctrina del Tribunal Supremo de Estados Unidos: el asunto Dakota del Sur v. Wayfair," *Quincena Fiscal*, 18, 2018, pp. 9–14.

Falcón y Tella, Ramón, In Muñoz Machado, Santiago (ed.), *Comentario mínimo a la Constitución española*, Crítica, Barcelona, 2018.

Falcón y Tella, Ramón, *Derecho Financiero y Tributario* (*Parte General*), 8th edition, Servicio de Publicaciones, Facultad de Derecho, Universidad Complutense de Madrid, 2019.

Falcón y Tella, Ramón; De la Peña, Gaspar; and Martínez Lago, Miguel Ángel (coords.), *Sistema Fiscal Español* (*Impuestos Estatales, Autonómicos y Locales*), 8th edition, Iustel, Madrid, 2018.

Falcón y Tella, Ramón; and Pulido Guerra, Elvira, *Derecho Fiscal Internacional*, 3rd edition, Marcial Pons, Madrid, 2018.

Fenwick, Mark; Vermeulen, Erik P. M.; and Corrales, Marcelo, "Business and Regulatory Responses to Artificial Intelligence: Dynamic Regulation, Innovation Ecosystems and the Strategic Management of Disruptive Technology," in Corrales, Marcelo;

Fenwick, Mark; and Forgó, Nikolaus (eds.), *Robotics, AI and the Future of Law*, in the Series "Perspectives in Law, Business and Innovation," Springer, 2018, pp. 81–103.

Fernández Amor, José Antonio, "Derecho Tributario y cuarta revolución industrial: análisis jurídico sobre aspectos fiscales de la robótica," *Nueva fiscalidad*, 1, 2018, pp. 47–96.

Fernández de Buján, Antonio, *Derecho Privado Romano*, 5th edition, Iustel, Madrid, 2012.

Fernández Macías, Enrique; Klenert, David; and Antón, José Ignacio, "Not so disruptive yet? Characteristics, distribution and determinants of robots in Europe," *Structural Change and Dynamics*, 58, 2021, pp. 76–89.

Fernández Sarasola, Ignacio; and Sánchez Álvarez, Eduardo, *Manual de Fundamentos de Derecho Público y Privado*, Tecnos, Madrid, 2017.

Ferrara, Francesco, *Teoría de las personas jurídicas*, translation from the 2nd Italian revised edition by Eduardo Ovejero y Maury, Reus, Madrid, 1929.

Finley, Moses I.; and Moya, Antonio Prometeo, *Esclavitud antigua e ideología moderna*, Crítica, Barcelona, 1982.

Fosch Villaronga, Eduard, "Legal and Regulatory Challenges for Physical Assistant Robots," *eChallenges e-2015 Conference*, Proceedings of the IEEE, Vilnius, Lithuania, 2015.

Fosch Villaronga, Eduard, "What do roboticists need to know about the future of robot law?," 2016.

Fosch Villaronga, Eduard, "ISO 13482:2014 and Its Confusing Categories. Building a Bridge Between Law and Robotics," in Wenger, Philippe; Chevallereau, Christine; Pisla, Doina; Bleuler, Hannes; and Rodić, Aleksandar (eds.), *New Trends in Medical and Service Robots*, Springer, Cham, Switzerland 2016, pp. 31–44.

Fosch Villaronga, Eduard, *Towards a Legal and Ethical Framework for Personal Care Robots: Analysis of person Carrier, physical assistant and mobile servant robots*, Bellaterra, 2017.

Fosch Villaronga, Eduard, "Legal frame of Non-social Robots," in Husty, Manfred; and Hofbaur, Michael (eds.), *New Trends in Medical and Service Robots*, MESROB 2016: International Workshop on Medical and Service Robots, Mechanism and Machine Science, Vol. 48, Springer, Cham, Switzerland, 2018, pp. 229–242.

Fosch Villaronga, Eduard; and Albo-Canals, Jordi, ""I'll take care of you" said the robot. Reflecting upon the legal and ethical aspects of the use and development of social robots for therapy," *Paladyn, Journal of Behavioural Robotics*, Vol. 10, Issue 1, 2019, pp. 77–93.

Fosch Villaronga, Eduard; and Golia, Angelo Jr., "Robots, standards and the law: Rivalries between private standards and public policymaking for robot governance," *Computer Law & Security Review*, Vol. 35, Issue 2, 2019, pp. 129–144.

Fosch Villaronga, Eduard; and Grau Ruiz, María Amparo, "Expert Considerations for the Regulation of Assistive Robotics. A European Robotics Forum Echo," in Toboso

Martín, Mario; Aparicio Payá, Manuel; and López Castro, Daniel, *Ética, robótica y tecnologías asistenciales*, DILEMATA, *Revista Internacional de Éticas Aplicadas*, 30, 2019, pp. 149–169.

Fosch Villaronga, Eduard; and Heldeweg, Michel, "'Regulation, I presume?' said the robot. Towards an interactive regulatory process for robot governance," *Computer Law & Security Review*, Vol. 34, Issue 6, 2018, pp. 1.258–1.277.

Freitas Jr., Robert A., "The legal rights of robotics," *Student Lawyer*, 13, 1985, pp. 54–56.

Frey, Carl Benedikt; and Osborne, Michael A., "The future of employment: How susceptible are jobs to computerization?," *Technological Forecasting and Social Change*, 114, January 1, 2017. And in *Oxford Martin*, 114, 2013.

Fundación para el Diálogo Social, *Economía Digital: su impacto sobre las condiciones de Trabajo y Empleo, Estudio de caso sobre dos empresas de base tecnológica*, December 2017.

García Armada, Elena, *Robots*, Catarata, Madrid, 2015.

García Canclini, Néstor, "How to research the communicational era of capitalism," *Desacatos*, 56, 2018, pp. 90–105.

García Garrido, Manuel Jesús, *Derecho Privado Romano*, 16th edition, Ediciones Académicas, Madrid, 2008.

García Luis, Tomás, *Fiscalidad de fundaciones y asociaciones*, Lex Nova, Valladolid, 1995.

García Mexía, Pablo, "Lex robótica y derecho digital," *Revista de Privacidad y Derecho Digital*, 2, 2016.

García Mexía, Pablo, "Entes Capaces No Personales. ¿Hacia una personalidad para los robots," [Available at https://www.automatas.tech/pablo-garcia-mexia-colaboracion.html].

García Novoa, César, "El futuro de la fiscalidad autonómica sobre los depósitos bancarios," *Revista Catalana de Dret Públic*, 46, June 2013, pp. 104–134.

García Novoa, César, "La tributación de los robots y el futurismo fiscal," *Taxlandia*, April 17, 2018. [Available at https://www.politicafiscal.es/cesar-garcia-novoa/la-tributacion-de-los-robots-y-el-futurismo-fiscal].

García Novoa, César, "Impuestos atípicos en la era post BEPS," in Cubero Truyo, Antonio (dir.), *Tributos asistemáticos del ordenamiento vigente*, Tirant lo Blanch, Valencia, 2018, Chapter 8.

García Novoa, César, "Herramientas fiscales innovadoras y tributación de los robots," in Grau Ruiz, María Amparo; and Sánchez-Urán Azaña, María Yolanda, *Nuevas tecnologías y Derecho*, Juruá, Porto, 2019.

García Novoa, César, *La tributación en el contexto de la pandemia del COVID-19*, Thomson Reuters – Aranzadi, Cizur Menor, Navarra, 2020.

García Novoa, César (dir.), *4ª Revolución Industrial: la fiscalidad de la sociedad digital y tecnológica en España y Latinoamérica*, Thomson Reuters – Aranzadi, Cizur Menor, Navarra, 2019. With the following contributions: "Los grandes retos fiscales de la economía digital desde la perspectiva europea," by César García Novoa, pp. 25–67; "Alternativas para la tributación de la economía digital: el establecimiento permanente virtual," by Saturnina Moreno González, pp. 69–105; "El impuesto sobre determinados servicios digitales como opción para gravar la nueva economía digitalizada," by Cristina García-Herrera Blanco, pp. 107–130; "Soluciones unilaterales para la fiscalidad de la economía digital. Especial referencia al 'equalization tax'," by Soraya Rodríguez Losada, pp. 131–154; "La búsqueda de alternativas para la tributación de los robots: la tasa californiana aplicable a los vehículos autónomos," by María Amparo Grau Ruiz, pp. 155–174; and "Retos fiscales de la digitalización. Perspectiva desde Chile," by Christian Blanche, pp. 303–318.

García Novoa, César; Santiago Iglesias, Diana (dirs.); Torres Carlos, Marcos R.; Garrido Juncal, Andrea; and Miranda Boto, José María (coords.), *4ª Revolución industrial: impacto de la automatización y la inteligencia artificial en la sociedad y la economía digital*, Thomson Reuters – Aranzadi, Cizur Menor, Navarra, 2018.

García Portero, Roberto, "Los robots en la sanidad," in Barrio Andrés, Moisés (dir.), *Derecho de los Robots*, La Ley, Wolter Kluwer, 2018.

García-Prieto Cuesta, Juan, "¿Qué es un Robot?," in Barrio Andrés, Moisés (dir.), *Derecho de los Robots*, La Ley, Wolter Kluwer, 2018.

Garrigues, Joaquín, *Hacia un nuevo Derecho Mercantil*, Tecnos, Madrid, 1971.

Garrigues, Joaquín, *Curso de Derecho Mercantil. Tomo I*, 7th edition, JG, Madrid, 1979.

Garrigues, Joaquín, *Curso de Derecho Mercantil. Tomo II*, 7th edition, JG, Madrid, 1980.

Geraldes da Cunha Lopes, Teresa María, "Impuestos, Robots y Financiación del Estado del Bienestar," October 2017.

Gete-Alonso y Calera, María del Carmen, *La nueva normativa en materia de capacidad de obrar de la persona,* Civitas, Madrid, 1985. 2nd edition 1992.

Gigglberger, Juan, "Breves apuntes sobre la evolución de la sociedad comercial," *Revista Jurídica* (*Universidad de Ciencias Empresariales y Sociales, UCES*), 14, 2010.

Gil del Campo, Miguel, *Fiscalidad de fundaciones, asociaciones y del mecenazgo*, 2nd edition, Ciss, Valencia, 2005.

Gil García, Elizabeth, *Los incentivos fiscales a la I + D + i*, Tirant lo Blanch, Valencia, 2017.

Gil García, Elizabeth, "La seguridad en la aplicación de los incentivos a la I + D + i," *Quincena fiscal*, 17, 2018, pp. 37–64.

Gómez Salado, Miguel Ángel, "Robótica, empleo y Seguridad Social. La cotización de los robots para el actual Estado de Bienestar," *Revista Internacional y Comparada de Relaciones Laborales y Derecho del Empleo*, Adapt University Press, Vol. 6, Issue 3, July-September 2018.

Gómez Salado, Miguel Ángel; and Vila Tierno, Francisco (eds.), *Cuarta revolución industrial y su impacto sobre la productividad, el empleo y las relaciones jurídico-laborales: desafíos tecnológicos del siglo XXI*, Aranzadi, Cizur Menor, Navarra, 2021.

González Botija, Fernando, *Los drones y el Derecho de la Unión Europea: Reglamento (UE) nº 2018/1139 y propuestas de EASA*, Atelier, Barcelona, 2019.

Graetz, G.; and Michaels, G., "Robots at work," *The Review of Economics and Statistics*, 100, 5, 2018.

Grau Ruiz, María Amparo, "La adaptación de la fiscalidad ante los retos jurídicos, económicos, éticos y sociales planteados por la robótica," *Nueva fiscalidad*, 4, 2017, pp. 35–61.

Grau Ruiz, María Amparo, "Responsabilidad social de la empresa: impacto financiero y tributario," in Merino Jara, Isaac (dir.), *Entidades con valor social: nuevas perspectivas tributarias*, Introduction by Rafael Calvo Ortega, Ministerio de Hacienda y Función Pública, Instituto de Estudios Fiscales, Madrid, 2017, pp. 693–713.

Grau Ruiz, María Amparo, *Sostenibilidad global y actividad financiera. Los incentivos a la participación privada y su control*, foreword by Jacques Malherbe, Thomson Reuters – Aranzadi, Cizur Menor, Navarra, 2019.

Grau Ruiz, María Amparo, "Some Lessons Learnt from Environmental Labelling Information Schemes: Could Certification Of Inclusive Robotics Follow A Similar Path?," E-print UCM, 2019. [In: https://eprints.ucm.es/50680/].

Grau Ruiz, María Amparo, "La búsqueda de alternativas para la tributación de los robots: la tasa californiana aplicable a los vehículos autónomos," in García Novoa, César (dir.), *4ª Revolución industrial: la fiscalidad de la sociedad digital y tecnológica en España y Latinoamérica*, Thomson Reuters – Aranzadi, Cizur Menor, Navarra, 2019.

Grau Ruiz, María Amparo, "Tributación y robótica responsables para una economía digital sostenible," Scientific conference document: *Derecho Financiero, servicios digitales y robótica*, May 17, 2019, Málaga. In Braccia, M. F. (dir.), *Tributación de la economía digital*, Thomson Reuters La Ley, Buenos Aires, 2019, pp. 655–668.

Grau Ruiz, María Amparo, "Taxing Autonomous Vehicles: The Californian Case," in Pons, José L. (ed.), *Inclusive Robotics for a Better Society, Selected Papers from INBOTS Conference 2018, 16–18 October, 2018, Pisa, Italy*, Springer, Cham, Switzerland, 2019.

Grau Ruiz, María Amparo, "El gravamen «provisional» de los servicios digitales y la dudosa justificación de reacciones unilaterales," *Revista Técnica Tributaria*, 128, 2020, pp. 7–13.

Grau Ruiz, María Amparo, "El Derecho artificial y la artificiosidad de los derechos," in Falcón y Tella, María José; and Martínez Muñoz, Juan Antonio (dirs.), *Estudios Jurídicos Multidisciplinares. José Iturmendi Morales, Maestro Complutense. Homenaje*, Tirant lo Blanch, Valencia, 2020, pp. 839–857. There is an English translation, "Artificial law and 'artificious' rights," in Falcón y Tella, María José; and Martínez Muñoz, Juan Antonio (eds.), *Challenges to Legal Theory. Essays in Honour of Professor José Iturmendi Morales*, Brill Nijhoff, Leiden-Boston, 2021, pp. 227–242.

Grau Ruiz, María Amparo, "Empleo y robótica: la legitimidad de adoptar medidas extrafiscales para la urgente capacitación tecnológica funcional," in Molina, C., *La transformación digital de la economía y del trabajo y su impacto en los sistemas de protección social: Retos de futuro inmediato* (forthcoming).

Grau Ruiz, María Amparo; Aymerich Franch, Laura; Fosch Villaronga, Eduard; Chaves Chaparro, Juliana; Ancos Franco, Helena; Falcón Pulido, Álvaro; and Adi, Mohamad Nadim, *Self-coaching tools for conducting responsible research and innovation (RRI) with social robots (International Workshop at ICSR, Madrid 2019)*. In Self-coaching tools for conducting responsible research and innovation (RRI) with social robots, November 26, 2019, Eleventh International Conference on Social Robotics (ICSR2019). E-print UCM, 2019. [Available at https://eprints.ucm.es/ 59171/].

Grau Ruiz, María Amparo; and Díaz Peña, Alfredo Luis, "Social Security and Robotization: Possible Ways to Finance Human Reskilling and Promote Employment," *Paladyn Journal of Behavioural Robotics*, 2020.

Grau Ruiz, María Amparo; *et al*, *Ethics, Tools for Inclusive Robotics: RRI, Taxation & Social Dialogue*, European Robotics Forum – WP2 INBOTS Workshop, March 5, 2020. Eprint UCM Open Access https://eprints.ucm.es/59990/.

Grau Ruiz, María Amparo; and Sánchez-Urán Azaña, María Yolanda, "Robotics and Work: Labor and Tax regulatory Framework," in *International Congress Technological Innovation and Future of Work*, April 5–6, 2018, Santiago de Compostela. E-print, UCM, 2018. [Available at https://eprints.ucm.es/47718/].

Grau Ruiz, María Amparo; and Sánchez-Urán Azaña, María Yolanda, "El impacto de la robótica, en especial la robótica inclusiva, en el trabajo: aspectos jurídico-laborales y fiscales," *Revista Aranzadi de Derecho y Nuevas Tecnologías*, 50, 2019; also as E-print UCM, 2018. [available at https://eprints.ucm.es/47523/].

Grau Ruiz, María Amparo; and Sánchez-Urán Azaña, María Yolanda, "Plataformas Digitales y Robótica. Su proyección en el Sistema de Seguridad Social," E-print, UCM, 2021. [available at https://eprints.ucm.es/64676/].

Guerreiro, J.; Rebelo, S.; and Teles, P., "Should robots be taxed?," *Northwestern University mimeo*.

Hannaford, Blake (dir.), *Surgical robotics: systems applications and visions*, Springer, New York, 2011.

Hemel, Daniel J., "Does the Tax Code Favor Robots?," *Ohio State Technology Law Journal*, Vol. 16, Issue 1, Ohio State University, Moritz College of Law, 2020, pp. 219–243.

Hermosín Álvarez, Montserrat, "Los impuestos ambientales autonómicos: límites derivados del artículo 6 de la LOFCA," *Noticias de la Unión Europea*, 327, 2012, pp. 67–78.

Hinojosa Torralvo, Juan José; Cruz Padial, Ignacio (dirs.); and Sánchez-Archidona Hidalgo, Guillermo (coord.), *Tributos, servicios digitales y robótica*, Thomson Reuters – Aranzadi, Cizur Menor, Navarra, 2020. With the following contributions: "De la economía digital a la robótica: algunas cuestiones tributarias," by Ignacio Cruz Padial, pp. 203–232; "Inteligencia artificial, robótica y Derecho Tributario. Los presupuestos del cambio de paradigma," by Pedro Ángel Colao Marín, pp. 233–259; "¿Sueñan los androides con impuestos finalistas?," by Norberto Miras Marín, pp. 261–288; "El impuesto sobre los robots: revisión de sus perfiles y encaje jurídico," by José Antonio Fernández Amor, pp. 289–311; "La tributación de los robots en el marco de la búsqueda de nuevas formas de gravamen," by César García Novoa, pp. 313–325; "El actual dilema fiscal por el impacto de la robótica: ¿innovación o empleo?," by María Amparo Grau Ruiz, pp. 327–346; and "Avances tecnológicos versus mercado laboral y pensiones públicas," by Miguel Gutiérrez Bengoechea, pp. 347–373.

House of Commons Science and Technology Committee, *Robotics and artificial intelligence*, Fifth Report of Session 2016–17, October 12, 2016.

IBA, International Bar Association; and Global Employment Institute: *Artificial Intelligence and Robotics and Their Impact on the Workplace*, April 2017.

IFR, International Federation of Robotics, *The Impact of Robots on Productivity, Employment and Jobs: A positioning paper by the International Federation of Robotics*, April 2017.

IFR, International Federation of Robotics, *World Robotics R&D Programs, Information paper*, Frankfurt, May 2020.

IFR, International Federation of Robotics, *Executive Summary World Robotics 2020: Industrial Robots.*

IFR, International Federation of Robotics, *Executive Summary World Robotics 2020: Service Robots.*

Iglesias Cabero, Manuel, *Robótica y Responsabilidad: Aspectos legales en las diferentes áreas del Derecho*, Colex, La Coruña, 2017.

ILO, International Labour Organisation (Nübler, Irmgard), *New technologies: A jobless future or golden age of job creation?*, Research Department Working Paper N.º 13, Geneva, November 2016.

ILO, International Labour Organization, *Inception Report for the Global Commission on the Future of Work*, International Labour Office, Geneva, 2017.

ILO, International Labour Organization, *Trabajar para un futuro más prometedor*, Comisión Mundial sobre el Futuro del Trabajo, Oficina Internacional del Trabajo, Geneva, 2017.

ILO, International Labour Organization, *Robots worldwide: The impact of automation on employment and trade*, International Labour Office, Research Department Working Paper N. º 36, October 2018.

Instituto Cuatrecasas de Estrategia Legal en RRHH, *Robótica y su impacto en los Recursos Humanos y en el Marco Regulatorio de las Relaciones Laborales*, La Ley, Madrid, 2018.

Jiménez Compareid, Ismael, "La imposición propia de las Comunidades Autónomas," *Estudios Jurídicos-Boletín Oficial del Estado*, Madrid, 1994.

Jonas, Hans, *The Imperative or Responsibility: In Search of an Ethics for the Technological Age,* Chicago University Press, Chicago, 1984. *El principio de responsabilidad. Ensayo de una ética para la civilización tecnológica*, translation into Spanish by Javier María Fernández Arteaga, Herder, Barcelona, 1995.

Jordan, John, *Robots*, MIT Press, Cambridge, Massachusetts, 2016.

Joubioux, Claire; and Vanpoucke, Evelyne, "Towards right-shoring: a framework for off- and re-shoring decision making," *Operations Management Research: Advancing Practice through Theory*, Vol. 9, Issues 3–4, 2016, pp. 117–132.

Joyanes Aguilar, Luis, *Industria 4.0 La cuarta revolución industrial*, Marcombo, 2020. Ebook.

Keynes, John Maynard, "Economic Possibilities for our Grandchildren (1930)," in *Essays in Persuasion*, W.W.Norton & Co., New York, 1963, pp. 358–373.

Klenert, David; Fernández Macías, Enrique; and Antón, José Ignacio, *Do robots really destroy jobs? Evidence from Europe*, Seville, European Commission, 2020, JRC118393.

Kofler, Georg; Pantazatou, Katerina; and Rust, Alexander (eds.), *Tax and the digital economy: challenges and proposals for reform*, Kluwer Law International, Netherlands, 2019.

Kovacev, Robert, "A Taxing Dilemma: Robot Taxes and the Challenges of Effective Taxation of AI, Automation and Robotics in the Fourth Industrial Revolution," *Ohio State Technology Law Journal*, Vol. 16, Issue 1, Ohio State University, Moritz College of Law, 2020, pp. 182–217.

Kurki, Visa A. J.; and Pietrzykowski, Tomasz (eds.), *Legal Personhood: Animals, Artificial Intelligence and the Unborn*, Law and Philosophy Library 119, Springer, Cham, Switzerland, 2017.

Lacruz Mantecón, Miguel L., "Potencialidades de los robots y capacidades de las personas," in Rogel Vide, Carlos (coord.), *Los robots y el Derecho*, Reus, Madrid, 2018.

Lacruz Mantecón, Miguel L., "Cibernética y Derecho Europeo: ¿Una inteligencia robótica?," *Diario La Ley*, Issue 9.376, 2019.

Lacruz Mantecón, Miguel L., *Robots y personas: una aproximación jurídica a la subjetividad cibernética,* Reus, Madrid, 2020.

Lago Peñas, Santiago; and Vaquero García, Alberto, *Descentralización y Sistema Tributario: Lecciones de la experiencia comparada*, Fundación Impuestos y Competitividad, Madrid, 2016.

Lambea Rueda, Ana, "Entorno digital, robótica y menores de edad," *Revista de Derecho Civil*, Vol. 5, Issue 4, October-December 2018, pp. 183–232.

Lampreave Márquez, Patricia, *La Competencia Fiscal Desleal en los Estados Miembros de la Unión Europea*, Thomson Reuters – Aranzadi, Cizur Menor, Navarra, 2010.

Lau, Pin Lean, "The extension of legal personhood in Artificial Intelligence," *Revista de Bioética y Derecho*, Vol. 46, pp. 447–466.

Laukyte, Migle, "Social Robots: Boundaries, Potential, Challenges: Marco Norskov (ed.) (Ashgate, Dorchester, 2016)," *NanoEthics: Studies of New and Emerging Technologies*, Vol. 11, Issue 3, pp. 273–275.

Lavan, Myles, *Slaves to Rome: paradigms of empire in Roman culture*, Cambridge University Press, Cambridge, 2013.

Lin, Patrick; Abney, Keith; and Bekey, George A. (coords.), *Robot ethics: the ethical and social implications of robotics*, MIT Press, Cambridge, Massachusetts, 2012.

López Calvo, José (coord.), *El nuevo marco regulatorio derivado del Reglamento Europeo de Protección de Datos*, Bosch, Madrid, 2018.

López Espadafor, Carlos María, "Algunas consideraciones sobre recargos y tributos propios en la financiación autonómica," *Revista Valenciana de Hacienda Pública*, 33, 1998, pp. 37–54.

Lucas Durán, Manuel, "El panorama actual de la coordinación tributaria entre los distintos entes territoriales: la concurrencia del espacio impositivo estatal, autonómico y local," *Quincena Fiscal*, 5, 2014, pp. 39–89.

Maia Alexandre, Filipe, *The Legal Status of Artificially Intelligent Robots: Personhood, Taxation and Control*, Tilburg, 2017.

Mallada Fernández, Covadonga, *Nuevos retos de la ciberseguridad en un contexto cambiante*, Aranzadi, Cizur Menor, Navarra, 2019.

Malvárez Pascual, Luis ; Martínez Gálvez, J. Pablo; Ramírez Gómez, Salvador; and Sánchez Pino, Antonio José, *Régimen Fiscal de la Empresa*, Tecnos, Madrid, 2016.

Marín López, Juan José, *Asociaciones, fundaciones y cooperativas*, Consejo General del Poder Judicial, Madrid, 1996.

Martín Bernal, José Manuel, *Asociaciones y Fundaciones*, Civitas, Madrid, 2005.

Martín Jiménez, Adolfo J., "BEPS, the Digital(ized) Economy and the Taxation of Services and Royalties," *Intertax*, Vol. 46, Issues 8–9, 2018, pp. 620–638.

Martín Moreno, José Luis, "Constitucionalidad del impuesto sobre depósitos de las entidades de crédito: STC 210/2012, de 14 de noviembre," *Aletheia Cuadernos Críticos de Derecho*, 2, 2012.

Martín Queralt, Juan; Lozano Serrano, Carmelo; Tejerizo López, José M.; and Casado Ollero, Gabriel, *Curso de Derecho Financiero y Tributario*, 22nd edition, Tecnos, Madrid, 2011.

Martínez-Carrasco Pignatelli, José Miguel, *Las notificaciones electrónicas obligatorias en materia tributaria*, foreword by Gabriel Casado Ollero, Thomson Reuters – Aranzadi, Cizur Menor, Navarra, 2020.

Marwala, Tshilidzi, "On Robot Revolution and Taxation," Eprint, 2018. [Available at CoRR arXiv:1808.01666 [cs.CY]].

Mazur, Orly, "Taxing the Robots," *Pepperdine Law Review*, Vol. 46, Issue 2, 2019, pp. 277–330.

Melo, Verónica E., "El derecho ante la inteligencia artificial y la robótica," *El Derecho. Diario de Doctrina y Jurisprudencia*, Vol. 14.343, Year LVI, February 6, 2018, pp. 1–3.

Menéndez Moreno, Alejandro (dir.), *Derecho Financiero y Tributario. Parte General*, 15th edition, Lex Nova Thomson Reuters, Madrid, 2014.

Mercader Uguina, Jesús R., *El futuro del trabajo en la era de la digitalización y la robótica*, Tirant lo Blanch, Valencia, 2017.

Mercader Uguina, Jesús R., "El impacto de la robótica y el futuro del trabajo," *Revista de la Facultad de Derecho de México*, Mexico, UNAM, Vol. LXVII, Issue 269, September-December 2017.

Merino Jara, Isaac (dir.), *Entidades con valor social: nuevas perspectivas tributarias*, foreword by Rafael Calvo Ortega, Ministerio de Hacienda y Función Pública, Instituto de Estudios Fiscales, Madrid, 2017.

Metropolitan Policy Program, Brookings, *Automation and artificial intelligence, How machines are affecting people and places*, January 2017.

MGI, McKinsey Global Institute, *A future that works: Automation, Employment, and Productivity*, January 2017.

MGI, McKinsey Global Institute, *Jobs lost, jobs gained: Workforce transitions in a time of Automation*, December 2017.

MGI, McKinsey Global Institute, *Skill shift: Automation and the future of the workforce*, May 2018.

Michalczak, Rafal, "Chapter 6: Animals' Race against the Machines," in Kurki, Visa A. J.; and Pietrzykowski, Tomasz (eds.), *Legal Personhood: Animals, Artificial Intelligence and the Unborn*, Law and Philosophy Library 119, Springer, Cham, Switzerland, 2017, pp. 91–101.

Microsoft, *The Future Computed, Artificial Intelligence and its role in society*, 2018.

Mir Jordano, Rafael, "Capacidad. Conjugación de palabras, ideas y conceptos," in Casado Raigón, Rafael; and Gallego Domínguez, Ignacio (coords.), *Personalidad y capacidad jurídicas, 74 contribuciones con motivo del XXV Aniversario de la Facultad de Derecho de Córdoba, tomo II*, Servicio de Publicaciones, Universidad de Córdoba, Córdoba, 2005, pp. 881–891.

Miró Llinares, Fernando, "Inteligencia artificial y justicia penal: más allá de los resultados lesivos causados por robots," *Revista de Derecho Penal y Criminología*, 20, 2020, pp. 87–130.

MIT, *The Work of the future: Shaping Technology and Institutions*, MIT work of the Future, Fall Report, 2019.

Moliner Navarro, Rosa (coord. and author); and Reyes López, María José (coord.), *La persona jurídica /Cuaderno IV*, Dykinson, Madrid, 2010.

Moravec, Hans, *Robot: Mere machine to transcendent mind*, Oxford University Press, London, 1999.

Moreno, L., "Robotization, Europanization and minimum income (EuVisions)," *Research Gate*, January 18, 2019.

Mozo Seoane, Antonio, "La revolución tecnológica y sus retos: medios de control, fallos de sistemas y ciberdelincuencia," in Rogel Vide, Carlos (coord.), *Los robots y el Derecho*, Reus, Madrid, 2018.

Muñoz Machado, Santiago (ed.), *Comentario mínimo a la Constitución española*, Crítica, Barcelona, 2018.

Navas Navarro, Susana (dir.), *Nuevos desafíos para el Derecho de autor: Robótica, Inteligencia Artificial, Tecnología*, Reus, Madrid, 2019.

Nevejans, N., "Les robots: tentative de definition," in Besaumon, *Les robots, objets scientifiques, objets de droit,* Collection de Presses Universitaires de Sceaux, 2016.

Nevejans, N., "Comment proteger l'homme face aux robots?," *Archives de Philosophie du Droit,* 59, 2016, pp. 131–163.

Núñez Zorrilla, María del Carmen, "Los nuevos retos de la Unión Europea en la regulación de la responsabilidad civil por los daños causados por la inteligencia artificial," *Revista Española de Derecho Europeo*, 66, April-June 2018, pp. 9–53.

Núñez Zorrilla, María del Carmen, *Inteligencia artificial y responsabilidad civil: régimen jurídico de los daños causados por robots autónomos con inteligencia artificial*, Reus, Madrid, 2019.

Oberson, Xavier, "Taxing robots? From the emergence of an electronic ability to pay to a tax on robots or the use of robots," *Aktuelle Juristische Praxis* (*AJP*) / *Pratique Juridique Actuelle* (*PJA*), 2, 2017, pp. 232–239.

Oberson, Xavier, "Taxer les robots? L'émergence d'une capacité contributive électronique," *World Tax Journal: WTJ,* Vol. 9, Issue 2, 2017, pp. 249–261. Translated into Spanish by Antón Beiras, in *Taxlandia*, May 16 and 22, 2018.

Oberson, Xavier, *Taxing Robots*, Edward Elgar, Cheltenham, UK, 2019.

Observatorio Económico BBVA, *¿Cuán vulnerable es el empleo en España a la revolución digital?*, Observatorio Económico, March 19, 2018. In English: BBVA Research, "How vulnerable is Spanish employment to the digital revolution?", working paper.

OECD Publishing, *Addressing the Tax Challenges of the Digital Economy, Action 1 2015 Final Report*, OECD/G20 Base Erosion and Profit Shifting Project, Paris, October 2015.

OECD Publishing, *R&D Tax Incentives: France 2017,* Directorate for Science, Technology and Innovation, April 2018.

OECD Publishing, *R&D Tax Incentives: United Kingdom, 2017*, Directorate for Science, Technology and Innovation, April 2018.

OECD Publishing, *Compendium of R&D tax incentive schemes: OECD countries and selected economies*, 2018. Available at http://www.oecd.org/sti/rd-tax-stats.htm.

OECD Publishing, *Estudios Económicos de la OCDE: Chile, 2018,* February 2018. Available at www.oecd.org/eco/surveys/economic-survey-chile.htm.

OECD Publishing, *Programme of Work to Develop a Consensus Solution to the Tax Challenges Arising from the Digitalisation of the Economy*, OECD/G20 Inclusive Framework on BEPS, OECD, Paris, 2019. Available at www.oecd.org/tax/beps/programme-of-work-to-develop-aconsensus-solution-to-the-tax-challenges-arising-from-the-digitalisation-of-the-economy.htm.

Orena Domínguez, Aitor, "Fundaciones: cuestiones sobre su fiscalidad," in Merino Jara, Isaac (dir.), *Entidades con valor social: nuevas perspectivas tributarias*, foreword by Rafael Calvo Ortega, Ministerio de Hacienda y Función Pública, Instituto de Estudios Fiscales, Madrid, 2017, pp. 557–586.

Ortega Klein, Andrés, *La imparable marcha de los robots*, Alianza, Madrid, 2016.

Pagallo, Ugo, "Robotrust and legal responsibility," *Knowledge, Technology & Policy*, 23, 2010, pp. 367–379.

Pagallo, Ugo, "The human master with a modern slave? Some remarks on robotics, ethics, and the law," in Arias-Oliva, M.; Bynum, T. W.; Rogerson, S.; and Torres Corona, T., *Backwards, forwards and sideways*, Universitat Rovira I Virgili, Tarragona, 2010.

Pagallo, Ugo, *The Laws of Robots. Crimes, Contracts, and Torts*, in "Law, Governance and Technology Series 10," Springer, Dordrecht – Heidelberg – New York – London, 2013.

Pagallo, Ugo; Corrales, Marcelo; Fenwick, Mark; and Forgó, Nikolaus, "The Rise of Robotics & AI: Technological Advances & Normative Dilemmas," in Corrales, Marcelo; Fenwick, Mark; and Forgó, Nikolaus (eds.), *Robotics, AI and the Future of Law*, in the Series "Perspectives in Law, Business and Innovation," Springer, 2018, pp. 1–13.

Palmerini, Erica, "Liability and risk management in robotics," *Digital Revolution: Challenges for Contract Law in Practice Nomos*, Vol. 1, Issue 1, 2016.

Palmerini, Erica, "Robótica y Derecho: sugerencias, confluencias, evoluciones en el marco de una investigación europea," *Revista de Derecho Privado*, 32, January-June 2017, pp. 53–97.

Pascual, David Álvaro, *Inteligencia artificial: un panorama de algunos de sus desafíos éticos y jurídicos*, PhD dissertation, Girona University, Spain, 2017.

Pastor del Pino, María del Carmen, *El incentivo fiscal a la inversión en actividades empresariales de innovación en el Impuesto sobre Sociedades*, La Ley, Madrid, 2009.

Pérez Bernabeu, Begoña, "La naturaleza tributaria de las cotizaciones sociales en el actual contexto de separación de fuentes de financiación de la Seguridad Social," in Cubero Truyo, Antonio (dir.), *Tributos asistemáticos del ordenamiento vigente*, Tirant lo Blanch, Valencia, 2018, Chapter 21.

Pérez Bes, Francisco (coord.), *El Derecho de Internet*, Atelier, Barcelona, 2016.

Pérez Royo, Fernando, *Derecho Financiero y Tributario. Parte General*, 25th edition, Civitas Thomson Reuters, Cizur Menor, Navarra, 2015.

Pérez Royo, Fernando (dir.), *Curso de Derecho Tributario. Parte Especial*, 11th edition, Tecnos, Madrid, 2017.

Pfeifer, Rolf; and Sheier, Christian, *Understanding Intelligence*, MIT Press, Cambridge, Massachusetts, 1999.

Pietrzykowski, Tomasz, "Chapter 4: The Idea of Non-personal Subjects of Law" in Kurki, Visa A. J.; and Pietrzykowski, Tomasz (eds.), *Legal Personhood: Animals, Artificial Intelligence and the Unborn*, Springer, Cham, Switzerland, 2017, pp. 49–67.

Pons, José L. (ed.), *Inclusive Robotics for a Better Society, Selected Papers from INBOTS Conference 2018, 16–18 October, 2018, Pisa, Italy*, Springer, Cham, Switzerland, 2019.

Puente Pérez, Esther, "Los robots en el Derecho del Trabajo," in Barrio Andrés, Moisés (dir.), *Derecho de los robots*, La Ley, Wolter Kluwer, Madrid, 2018, Chapter VI.

PWC, *Will robots really steal our jobs? An international analysis of the potential long term impact of automation*, 2018.

Quílez Moreno, José María; and Aparicio Chofrégil, Lucía, "Robots e inteligencia artificial: ¿Debería exigirse algún tipo de cotización?," *Diario La Ley*, Wolters Kluwer, 5, March 14, 2017.

Quintero Olivares, Gonzalo, "La robótica ante el Derecho Penal: el vacío de respuesta jurídica a las desviaciones incontroladas," *Revista Electrónica de Estudios Penales y de la Seguridad*, Editorial Jurídica Continental, Costa Rica, 1, 2017.

Rebollo Álvarez-Amandi, Alejandro, *La nueva Ley de fundaciones*, Centro de Estudios Financieros, Madrid, 1994.

Reese, Byron, *The Fourth Age: Smart Robots, Conscious Computers, and the Future of Humanity*, Atria Books, New York, 2018.

Reuters, "Fears of evictions as Bangladesh gives rivers legal rights," [Available at https://www.reuters.com/article/us-bangladesh-landrights-rivers/fears-of-evictions-as-bangladesh-gives-rivers-legal-rights-idUSKCN1TZ1ZR].

Rifkin, Jeremy, *El fin del trabajo. Nuevas tecnologías contra puestos de trabajo: el nacimiento de una nueva era*, Booket, Madrid, 2014.

Rodríguez, J. M. D., "El Derecho del Trabajo ante el futuro (presente) tecnológico y económico: Robots, Plataformas digitales, nuevos trabajos y viejos tiranos," *Trabajo y Derecho*, 40, 2018.

Rodríguez Bajón, Santiago, "La era Asimov. Análisis de la propuesta del PE en materia de robótica," *Diario La Ley*, Wolters Kluwer, Section Ciberderecho, 4, February 13, 2017.

Rodríguez Fernández, María Luz, *Humanos y robots: Empleo y condiciones de trabajo en la era tecnológica*, Bomarzo, Albacete, 2020.

Rogel Vide, Carlos (dir.), *Los robots y el Derecho*, Reus, Madrid, 2018. With the following contributions: "Robots y personas," by Carlos Rogel Vide; "Potencialidades de los robots y capacidades de las personas," by Miguel L. Lacruz Mantecón; "La revolución tecnológica y sus retos: medios de control, fallos de los sistemas y ciberdelincuencia," by Antonio Mozo Seoane; and "Robots y respondabilidad civil," by Silvia Díaz Alabart.

Rosembuj, Tulio, *Inteligencia Artificial e Impuesto*, 2nd edition, elFisco, Barcelona, 2019.

Roth, Bernard, "Introducción," in Siciliano, Bruno; and Khatib, Oussuma (eds.), *Springer Handbook of robotics*, viii, Berlin, 2008.

Rubio Guerrero, Juan José, "Incentivos fiscales a la inversión empresarial en el Impuesto de Sociedades," *Clm. economía Revista económica de Castilla – La Mancha*, 16, 2010, pp. 257–280.

Ruibal Pereira, Luz, *La Tributación de las Rentas Obtenidas por las Entidades en Atribución de Rentas*, Thomson Aranzadi, Cizur Menor, Navarra, 2003.

Russell, Stuart J.; and Norvig, Peter, *Artificial Intelligence: A Modern Approach*, Pearson Prentice Hall, 2nd edition, 2003.

Sánchez Archidona Hidalgo, Guillermo, "La tributación de la robótica y la inteligencia artificial como límites del Derecho Financiero y Tributario," *Quincena Fiscal*, 12, June 2019, pp. 69–96.

Sánchez del Campo Redonet, Alejandro, *Reflexiones de un replicante legal: Los retos jurídicos de la robótica y las tecnologías*, Preface by Juan Pablo Nieto Mengotti, Thomson Reuters – Aranzadi, Cizur Menor, 2016.

Sánchez del Campo Redonet, Alejandro, "Cuestiones jurídicas que plantean los robots," *Revista de Privacidad y Derecho Digital*, 2, 2016.

Sánchez del Campo Redonet, Alejandro, "Europa quiere regular a los robots," *Diario La Ley*, Wolters Kluwer, 4, February 28, 2017.

Sánchez-Urán Azaña, María Yolanda; and Grau Ruiz, María Amparo (dirs.); Lorencini, Bruno César; and Francisco, José Carlos (coords.), *Nuevas tecnologías y Derecho. Retos y oportunidades planteados por la Inteligencia Artificial y la Robótica*, Juruá, Porto, 2019. With the following contributions: "Robótica y Derecho: primera aproximación," by Carlos Rogel Vide, pp. 13–30; "Internet de las Cosas: Desafíos jurídicos en un mundo de la conectividad total," by Moisés Barrio Andrés, pp. 31–47; "Internet das coisas e os aspectos economicos de cibersegurança ante a criaçao no Brasil de criaçao da autoridade nacional de proteçao de dados," by Thiago Lopes Matsushita, pp. 49–69; "Herramientas fiscales innovadoras y tributación de los robots," by César García Novoa, pp. 73–88; "Una Seguridad Social para el futuro, con un apunte sobre automatización, robots y Seguridad Social," by Alberto Llorente Álvarez, pp. 127–147; and "Epílogo – Nuevas Tecnologías y Derecho. Retos y oportunidades planteados por la Inteligencia Artificial y la Robótica: Balance y prospectiva," by María Yolanda Sánchez-Urán Azaña; and María Amparo Grau Ruiz, pp. 263–274.

Sánchez-Urán Azaña, María Yolanda; and Grau Ruiz, María Amparo (creators), *El impacto de la robótica, en especial la robótica inclusiva, en el trabajo: aspectos jurídico-laborales y fiscales*. Archive footage.

Sánchez-Urán Azaña, María Yolanda; and Grau Ruiz, María Amparo, (creators), *Robotics and Work: Labor and Tax regulatory Framework*, Routledge, 2028-05.

Santamaría Pastor, Juan Alfonso, *Principios de Derecho Administrativo General, Volumen Primero*, 2nd edition, Iustel, Madrid, 2009.

Santos González, María José, "Regulación Legal de la Robótica y la Inteligencia Artificial: Retos de Futuro," *Revista Jurídica de la Universidad de León*, 4, 2017, pp. 25–50.

Santos Morón, María José, *Lecciones de Derecho Civil Patrimonial*, 2nd edition, Difusora Larousse – Editorial Tecnos, Madrid, 2018. Ebook.

Schwab, Klaus, *La cuarta revolución industrial*, Debate, Barcelona, 2016.

Searle, John, *Minds, Brains and Science*, Harvard University Press, Cambridge, Massachusetts, 1984.

Segura Alastrue, Mario, "Los robots en el Derecho Financiero y Tributario," in Barrio Andrés, Moisés (dir.), *Derecho de los robots*, La Ley, Wolter Kluwer, Madrid, 2018, pp. 167–188.

Serrano Antón, Fernando (dir.), *Fiscalidad e inteligencia artificial: administración tributaria y contribuyentes en la era digital*, Thomson Reuters – Aranzadi, Cizur Menor, Navarra, 2020. With the following contributions: – Chapter 1. "Fiscalidad y Robótica: funcionalidades disruptivas en el Derecho tributario," by Fernando Serrano Antón. – Chapter 2. "Robot y persona: Reflexiones sobre la capacidad económica atribuible a robots inteligentes," by Israel Santos Flores. – Chapter 3. "Soluciones fiscales a los problemas derivados de la robotización: especial referencia a España," by Jesús Rodríguez Márquez. – Chapter 4. "La sustitución de trabajadores por robots: impacto en las contribuciones a la Seguridad Social y su posible financiación por tributos," by Miguel de Haro Izquierdo. – Chapter 5. "Inteligencia Artificial y Administración tributaria," by Ubaldo González de Frutos. – Chapter 6. "Big Data y la gestión tributaria," by Javier Hurtado Puerta. – Chapter 7. "Algunas aplicaciones de la inteligencia artificial en la Administración tributaria," by Santiago Segarra. – Chapter 8. "El uso de la inteligencia artificial y el análisis de información en la Agencia Tributaria," by José Borja Tomé. – Chapter 9. "Derechos y garantías de los contribuyentes en la cuarta revolución industrial: Aproximación desde las transformaciones de la relación jurídica tributaria en la era de la inteligencia artificial," by Adolfo A. Iriarte Yanicelli. – Chapter 10. "El uso del big data y la inteligencia artificial por las Administraciones tributarias en la lucha contra el fraude fiscal. Particular referencia a los principios que han de regirla y a los derechos de los contribuyentes," by Cristina García-Herrera Blanco. – Chapter 11. "Operaciones en red, impacto del blockchain y los smartcontract: Oportunidades de negocio, uso de las plataformas en red, en la era de las aplicaciones, y la tecnología 5G," by Ramón Bonell Colmenero.

Serrano Falcón, Carolina, "A propósito de una controversia: ¿tienen que cotizar los robots a la Seguridad Social?," in García-Herrera Blanco, Cristina (dir.), *VI Encuentro de Derecho Financiero y Tributario "Tendencias y retos del Derecho Financiero y Tributario" (1.ª parte), Documentos de trabajo del* IEF, No. 10/2018, p. 73.

Serrat Romaní, Marina, *Los derechos y garantías de los contribuyentes en la era digital*, Aranzadi, Cizur Menor, Navarra, 2018.

Sierra, S., "Inteligencia artificial y justicia administrativa: Una aproximación desde la teoría del control de la Administración Pública," *Revista General de Derecho Administrativo*, 53, 2020.

Singer, Paul, *Wired for War: the robotics revolution and conflict in the 21st century*, Penguin Press, New York, 2009.

Solaiman, S. M., *Legal personality of robots, corporations, idols and chimpanzees: a quest for legitimacy*, University of Wollongong, 2017.

Soler Cantalapiedra, María Teresa (ed.), *Asociaciones y Fundaciones*, 5th edition, Thomson Civitas, Cizur Menor, Navarra, 2007.

Soler Roch, María Teresa, "El principio de capacidad económica y la tributación medioambiental," *Tratado de Tributación Medioambiental*, Vol. 1, Thomson Aranzadi Iberdrola, Cizur Menor, 2008.

Stiglitz, Joseph E., "The coming great transformation," *Journal of Policy Modelling*, 39, 2017, pp. 625–638.

Storr, Pam; and Storr, Christine, "The Rise and Regulation of Drones: Are We Embracing Minority Report or WALL-E?," in Corrales, Marcelo; Fenwick, Mark; and Forgó, Nikolaus (eds.), *Robotics, AI and the Future of Law*, in the Series "Perspectives in Law, Business and Innovation," Springer, 2018, pp. 105–122.

Suárez Blázquez, Guillermo, *Derecho de empresas en la Roma clásica*, Dykinson, Madrid, 2014.

Suberbiola Garbizu, Irune, "Beneficios fiscales en las sociedades laborales en la Ley 44/2015, de 14 de octubre, de sociedades laborales y participadas," *Lex Social*, Vol. 7, Issue 2, July-December 2017, pp. 103–129.

Sullins, John P., "Introduction: Open questions in roboethics," *Philosophy and Technology*, Vol. 24, Issue 3, 2011, pp. 233–238.

Thuemmel, U., "Optimal Taxation of Robots," *CEifo Working Paper*, April 3, 2018, pp. 31 and 32.

Thuemmel, U., "¿Tiene sentido que los robots tributen?," *La Tributación de los Robots*, IEB Report, 2, 2019.

Tirado Robles, Carmen (creator), "What is a robot? Comparative legal analysis of the Japanese and European proposals," in Mirai, *Estudios japoneses*, Vol. 4, 2020: *Monográfico: Japón en un mundo global: Iniciativas y posicionamientos*, Ediciones Complutenses, 2020, pp. 35–48.

Turing, Alan Mathison, "Computing Machinery and Intelligence," *Mind*, 49, 1950, pp. 433–460.

Turner, Jacob, *Robot Rules: Regulating Artificial Intelligence*, Palgrave Macmillan, Cham, Switzerland, 2018.

UniCredit, *The rise of the machines: Economic and social consequences of robotization*, Economics & FI/FX Research Global Themes Series, N. ° 36, August 31, 2016.

United Nations Conference on Trade and Development, *Trade and Development Report 2017, Beyond Austerity: Towards a Global New Deal, Chapter III: Robots, Industrialization and Inclusive Growth*, United Nations, New York – Geneva, 2017.

Uría, Rodrigo, *Derecho Mercantil*, 18th edition, Marcial Pons, Madrid, 1991.

Van den Hoven van Genderen, Robert, "Do We Need New Legal Personhood in the Age or Robots and AI?," in Corrales, Marcelo; Fenwick, Mark; and Forgó, Nikolaus (eds.), *Robotics, AI and the Future of Law*, in the Series "Perspectives in Law, Business and Innovation," Springer, 2018, pp. 15–55.

Vázquez García, Ramón José, "Protección de datos, privacidad y seguridad jurídica en la contratación electrónica," in Casado Raigón, Rafael; and Gallego Domínguez, Ignacio (coords.), *Personalidad y capacidad jurídicas, 74 contribuciones con motivo del XXV Aniversario de la Facultad de Derecho de Córdoba*, tomo II, Servicio de Publicaciones, Universidad de Córdoba, Córdoba, 2005, pp. 1.305–1.323.

Vegas Lozano, Esteban; and Reverter Comer, Ferrán (authors); Monleón, Antonio (dir.): *Big Data: Hacia la cuarta revolución industrial*, Universitat de Barcelona, Barcelona, 2017.

Vicent Chuliá, Francisco, *Derecho Mercantil. Tomo I. Vol. I*, 3rd edition, José M.ª Bosch, Madrid, 1991.

Vicent Chuliá, Francisco, *Derecho Mercantil. Tomo I. Vol. II*, 3rd edition, José M.ª Bosch, Madrid, 1991.

Vilalta Nicuesa, Aura Esther, *Smart legal contracts y blockchain. La contratación inteligente a través de la tecnología blockchain*, Wolters Kluwer, Madrid, 2019.

WEF, World Economic Forum, *Impact of the Fourth Industrial Revolution on Supply Chains*, October 2017.

Westermann, W. L., *The slave system of Greek and Roman antiquity*, American Philosophical Society, Philadelphia, 1955.

Zurita Martín, Isabel María, *La responsabilidad civil por los daños causados por los robots inteligentes como productos defectuosos*, Reus, Madrid, 2020.

Press Articles

Anonymous, "Podrían imponer impuestos a robots," *NOTIMEX*, September 16, 2017.

Calzada, Gabriel, "Los robots nos van a chupar la sangre," *Actualidad Económica*, July 1, 2017, p. 10.

Jiménez, Marimar, "¿Y habrá impuesto a robots que no sustituyan a humanos?," *Cinco Días*, February 21, 2017.

Portillo, Juande, "¿Deben pagar impuestos los robots?," *Cinco Días*, September 7, 2019.

"Esclavicemos a los robots y liberemos a los pobres," *El Comercio*, February 16, 2014.

"¿Cómo funciona Sofía?, la primera robot ciudadana del mundo," *El País*, October 27, 2017.

"Según Bill Gates, los robots deberían pagar impuestos," CE *Noticias Financieras*, February 22, 2017.

"Proponen que robots paguen impuestos para financiar pensiones," *El Universal*, October 8, 2018.

"¿Deben los robots pagar impuestos?," CE *Noticias Financieras*, September 27, 2019.

"El robot que pague," *El País*, June 5, 2019.

"Robot-lución: el gran reto de gobernar y convivir con las máquinas," *El País*, August 24, 2019.

"¿Llegará el día en que los robots sean sujetos de Derecho?," *Infobae*, December 26, 2020.

"Ways for robots to pay taxes," CE *Noticias Financieras*, January 31, 2021.

Index

www.ingramcontent.com/pod-product-compliance
Lightning Source LLC
Chambersburg PA
CBHW031325230926
51848CB00001B/96

* 9 7 8 9 0 0 4 5 3 8 5 0 4 *